Alternative countrysides

MANCHESTER
1824

Manchester University Press

Alternative countrysides

Anthropological approaches to rural Western Europe today

EDITED BY JEREMY MACCLANCY

Manchester University Press

Published by Manchester University Press
Altrincham Street, Manchester M1 7JA
www.manchesteruniversitypress.co.uk

British Library Cataloguing-in-Publication Data
A catalogue record for this book is available from the British Library

Library of Congress Cataloging-in-Publication Data applied for

ISBN 978 07190 9684 6 hardback

First published 2015

Typeset by Out of House Publishing
Printed in Great Britain by
CPI Group (UK) Ltd, Croydon, CR0 4YY

Contents

Figures

List of contributors

Paul Collinson is an honorary research associate and former lecturer in the Department of Anthropology, Oxford Brookes University. His research interests are in the anthropologies of development, conflict and food, focused largely on the Republic of Ireland. His latest publications include *Food in Zones of Conflict* (Berghahn 2014), co-edited with Helen Macbeth. He is currently the UK Chair of the International Commission on the Anthropology of Food and Nutrition.

Chantal Crenn Lecturer in Social Anthropology at the University of Bordeaux mountain, researcher at CNRS research laboratory UMI ESS 3189 Dakar and LAM / IEP UMR 5115 Bordeaux, specialises in international migration, ethnic relations, and practices and representations related to food. She conducts her fieldwork in France, Senegal and Madagascar. Recent publications include *Mobility and Migration: contemporary figures and challenges* (L'Harmattan, Coll Presses Universitaires de Sceaux, 2014), co-edited with Gérard Azoulay, Véronique Ancey, Daniel Dormoy, André and André Mangu Thomashausen, and 'Migration and rural Worlds', *Hommes et migrations*, Working Paper No. 1301, January/February/March 2013, co-edited with Simona Tersigni. She is a member of the editorial board of *Anthropology of food* (aof.revues.org).

Kepa Fernández de Larrinoa (PhD, London School of Economics; MA, University of Western Ontario) is a Basque anthropologist dedicated to the study of cultural models in specific ecological systems undergoing processes of social change. As an ethnographer, he is largely engaged in arts-informed lines of inquiry, such as rural theatre and performance, folk literary genres, and indigenous new media, especially radio stations and video production. He conducts fieldwork among European agropastoralists in the Pyrenees Mountains, and hunter-gatherer peoples in the Amazonian rainforest of Ecuador.

Elena Freire Paz Associate Professor in Social Anthropology, University of Santiago de Compostela, specialises in heritage processes (crafts and food). Her most recent publications include 'Modelando la tradición. El papel de las mujeres en la artesanía del barro' in *Interculturalidad, género y derechos humanos: dilemas sobre* *la cultura subsahariana*, (Editorial AXAC, 2014), edited by Xaquín Rodríguez Campos; and, with Ana Cabana Iglesia, 'Vendedoras de barro. Mujeres rurales y los límites de "lo doméstico" a mediados del siglo XX' Teresa Mª Ortega López (ed.), Sociedad Española de Hª Agraria-Monografías de Historia Rural.

Jeremy MacClancy Professor of Anthropology, and Director of the Anthropological Centre for Conservation, the Environment and Development, Oxford Brookes University, specialises in the anthropologies of Europe, art, sport, food, and nationalism, as well as writing on research methods and the history of anthropology, both academic and popular. His latest books are *Anthropology in the public arena. Historical and contemporary contexts* (Wiley, 2013), and *Ethics in the field: Contemporary Challenges* (Berghahn, 2013), co-edited with Agustín Fuentes.

Josetxu Martínez Montoya was Lecturer in Social and Cultural Anthropology at the University of Deusto, Bilbao, in the Basque Country, from 1995 to 2011. Now retired from academia, he continues his research in the following fields: European identity, and Basque culture, especially cultural changes in rural areas produced by the globalising process. His main publications include *Pueblos, ritos y montañas, Practicas vecinales y religiosas en el espacio y en el tiempo de la comunidad rural* (Bilbao: Desclée de Brouwer, 1996), and *La identidad reconstruida. Espacios y sociabilidad emergente en la ruralidad alavesa* (Vitoria-Gasteiz: Gobierno Vasco, 2002).

Jaro Stacul (PhD, Cambridge) is a research associate at the Wirth Institute for Austrian and Central European Studies, University of Alberta, Edmonton, Canada. He has held full-time positions in various academic institutions in Britain, Bulgaria, and Canada. He conducted research on local identity in the Italian Alps of Trentino in several spells between the mid 1990s and 2007, and analysed the ways in which ideas about private property and the natural environment form the background against which the 'ideologies' of regionalist political forces are debated and understood at the local level. His publications include *The Bounded Field: Localism and Local Identity in an Italian Alpine Valley* (Berghahn, 2003). Since 2008 he has been working on a research project on the redevelopment of post-industrial spaces in Poland, which involves fieldwork in the city of Gdańsk.

1

Alternative countrysides: anthropology and rural West Europe today

Jeremy MacClancy

I remember the moment well. I was doing fieldwork in Navarre, northern Spain, in the mid-1980s. Taking a weekend break, I was due to visit a commune in a hilly valley at the foot of the Pyrenees. Local friends had established it in a deserted village two years earlier. Before making the trek to their homes, my companion, who was from the area, wanted to show me Lakabe, the long-established, very successful commune on the other side of the narrow valley. As we walked down the valley's sole road, we met a group of some twenty youths, all carrying shovels, picks and hoes. 'They're a work party from the drug rehabilitation centre in the next village,' she said. 'And in the village after that, Buddhists from Bilbao are renovating the houses for a meditation centre.'

Her words made me realise, with a sudden flash, that almost the entire valley was being repopulated by a variety of alternatives: organic communards, Indophilic mystics, and addicts digging their way out of their habit. The indigenes had fled the area two decades before, for the sake of jobs in Pamplona. Now a new generation, of the disenchanted and the unemployed, had come in to renovate their collapsing houses, clear their fields, push the forest back, and start afresh. The Navarran regional government usually approved of this re-appropriation and would even consider giving them title to the lands they were working.

My second realisation was that this style of rural repopulation was relatively general and gravely understudied. Wright, in a 1992 review of recent ethnography on rural Britain, could only cite five examples, and only one of those (Strathern 1981) took the topic of incomers as a worthwhile theme (Wright 1992).The new arrivals into rurality were not given due space in contemporary studies. Other than some work by Edwin Ardener and a few of his Oxford students in the late 1970s, the topic appeared to have been neglected (e.g. Ardener 1985; Macdonald 1989). So I convened a conference, held at Oxford Brookes University, some of whose papers, appropriately revised, are included here.

In fact, the lack of interest in rurality went further than I originally realised. To my surprise, when I emailed a UK colleague inviting him to attend, he replied: 'The problem with "countryside studies" is that the latest trend is to study urban ethnic landscapes and not rural settings.' In France the shift is equally marked:

'Where interest was once focused on the village, it was now focused on members of Alcoholics Anonymous or the homeless who slept in the Paris metro' (Abélès 1998: 405; see also Rogers 2001: 492). To anthropologists of France, this geographical move was also one of temporality and development: 'out of the archaic countryside and into the present' (Rogers 2001: 494). European anthropology grew out of Mediterranean anthropology, a post-war endeavour primarily concerned with importing anthropological perspectives into the study of Southern Europe. Its pioneer anthropologists imitated their Africanist colleagues by deliberately seeking to live in small-scale rural communities. Even when their focus of interest began to extend beyond the village, they still tended to concentrate on rural regions, ones that lacked conurbations. With the rise of the European Union (EU), the decimation of peasantry in Western Europe (Macfarlane 1996: ix), and the increasing need to produce work that appeared socially relevant, anthropologists slowly switched their interest from the countryside to the city. Studies on immigration, racism, and interethnic conflict began to replace ones on kinship, honour, and property transmission. For example, a recent collection on the anthropology of the EU (Bellier and Wilson 2000) does not include anything on rural areas, the countryside, or the Common Agricultural Policy (CAP); another, on movement within and into Europe, is similarly silent on rural immigration (Stacul, Moutsou, and Kopnina 2006), while a review article on 'Europeanization' has almost nothing on the agricultural or rural policies of the EU and their effects (Borneman and Fowler 1997). As Marion Demossier, an anthropologist of rural France, puts it, this lack of anthropological interest into West European ruralities is 'puzzling' (Demossier 2011: 114). What happens in villages, it seems, no longer attracts the attention of many.

Moreover, those few anthropologists who have looked at rural issues in recent times have tended to concentrate on traditional populations. For example, de la Pradelle, in her delightful study of a Provençal farmers' market, focuses on the style of interaction between local buyers and established stallholders (de la Pradelle 2006). The newcomers, hippies, and African immigrants granted pitches are left on the very margins – of the market and her ethnography. Much of the academic work I refer to in this chapter thus comes from rural geographers, not anthropologists.

These negative attitudes towards rural realities, issues, and policies, by so many anthropologists of Europe, are misplaced. Just because cities concentrate people who continue to produce new and unexpected forms of social organisation does not mean rurality becomes the emptying home of a tired traditionalism.[1] Far from it. As our contributors demonstrate, the countryside remains a lively, contested site of new demographics, new social movements, new workplace patterns, new cross-ethnic mixes, and new conceptions of how life is to be lived. Since the city is only defined by opposition to the countryside, and since rural movements have urban effects, we cannot ignore the changes taking place in hamlets, villages, and rural towns throughout Western Europe. They are an integral part and parcel of life in Europe today.

The key aim of this book is to redress this academic imbalance, by examining some of the central changes in the rural zones of contemporary Western Europe. In particular, most contributors look at the newcomers to these areas and the rainbow variety of effects they are having. The 'alternative' in our title is to be understood broadly. The contributors are not just looking at the self-proclaimed alternatives (hippies, New Agers, back-to-nature types, etc.) but at labour migrants from outside Western Europe and affluent resettlers as well. Members of all these groups are, in their own way, contributing towards the construction of a non-traditional countryside. All of them help to maintain life in rural areas which would otherwise be emptying of residents. Of course, 'alternative' is itself a relative term, whose application is contextual and temporal. As several chapters demonstrate, much of what was considered alternative thirty years ago is now well on the way to becoming mainstream. Who knows what a book on 'alternative countrysides' published in thirty years' time might contain, or if that term would then make any sense?

Anthropologists are trained specialists in studying 'from the bottom up'. As such, they are particularly well-placed observers of rural evolution, providing critical, analytical accounts of what exactly is going on in West European villages in present times. It is above all thanks to the exploratory, open-ended nature of intensive fieldwork that they are able to question conventional knowledge about contemporary rurality, and to discuss its complexities: both local specificities and continental commonalities. In fine-grained studies based on long-term research, they are able to tease out the various discourses employed by relevant parties in different contexts. In other words, anthropologists strive to ascertain who says and does what, how, when, why, and to what effect. Carefully deployed, fieldwork is a very powerful and subtle mode of analysis, especially good at unearthing the unforeseen. As such, it is a particularly appropriate style of investigation for studying the varied realities and ramifications of rural life today.[2]

In this book we broach a range of interrelated themes which, for the sake of expository convenience, I have grouped into: ruralities, discourses, and practices; incomers from elsewhere in West Europe; and incomers from beyond West Europe.

Ruralities, discourses, and practices

We all have a notion of 'the rural' and of 'the city', whether analysed or not. Thanks to our upbringing in Western homes, we have all been reared on particular ideas of that contrastive set. Raymond Williams, in a classical study of this theme, demonstrated how historically grounded this pair of framing ideas is and how English understanding of the tension between the two has evolved over the last four hundred years. In the sixteenth and seventeenth centuries, the city was associated with money; the next century with wealth and luxury, then with the mob and the masses; and in the twentieth century with mobility and isolation. In turn '"the country" has at times meant everything from independence to deprivation', from settlement to rural retreat, from a home of cultivated 'honest' growth to the site of a wild, unspoiled, isolated nature (Williams 1973: 290–1). Similar, though locally inflected statements could well be made about the evolution of these conceptions in many other West European countries.

While what is meant by 'the rural' may change over times, it appears reassuringly unproblematic to most at any one time. In contrast, rural geographers have in recent decades questioned the ability to make a significant distinction between 'the rural' and 'the urban'. They query whether it is possible to define 'the rural' in an unambiguous, meaningful manner. They all, however, recognise the salience of the rural imagination in popular parlance, and the fact it is 'irredeemably contextual' (Halfacree, 2004: 303; see also Copp 1972; Hoggart 1990; Hillyard 2007). If 'the rural' cannot act as a precise conceptual category for purposes of academic comparison, the academics' job then becomes the investigation of what constitutes 'the rural' in different spaces and times, and the ways those ideas both structure and are structured by socio-economic conditions. We thus need to speak of 'ruralities' and not some singular concept.

The geographer Keith Halfacree, in a review of these positions, argues that the common turn to view the rural as residual, as that which is not yet urbanised, has to be resisted. Stressing that rural worlds are not relatively independent zones unto themselves, he contends that 'If urbanization is taken as a reasonable synonym for capitalism in its most highly developed guise, then rural places are as "urban" as the city' (Halfacree 2004: 303). The point is well made and underlines the common economic system that helps structure both types of space.

These literary and learned discourses of ruralities need to be placed alongside the corresponding political discourses. Since European nations are defined partly but importantly by territory, most nationalist ideologues have sung the praises of the land within their boundaries, especially the countryside and all they make it stand for. Thus Sabino Arana, the nineteenth-century prophet of Basque nationalism, extolled the mountains, hills, and valleys of his native Basqueland. For him and his followers, the local landscape sustained an exemplary, ethnic way of life which had maintained the moral values his movement held most dear. Nothing similar could be expected from city life (MacClancy 2007). Similarly, in Galicia, north-west Spain, local nationalists have made a traditional rurality so central to Galician cultural identity that today native urbanites with the money to do so perceive it their moral responsibility to buy and restore rural houses (Rodríguez 2008: 152–3, 167). In fact, it is hard to think of a European nationalism whose ideologues have not produced paeans about their countryside (e.g. on Ireland, see Goldring 1993: 63–74).

Jaro Stacul, in his contribution, gives an Italian example with an unexpected twist. He discusses the rise of the *Lega Nord* (Northern League) in the 1990s, a time of national disenchantment with established parties, then widely seen as deeply corrupt. Leaders of the populist *Lega* called for the recreation of a lost 'authenticity' and a traditional sense of community. They thus propagated an idea of a north Italian culture, denigrated southerners as lazy and parasitic, and criticised the State as the distant imposer of an alienating 'civilisation'. To these rhetoricians, it was the northern countryside which was the repository of laudatory values, in particular an ethic of hard work. To the Trentino villagers, with whom he did fieldwork and whose area had not been incorporated into Italy until the end of the First World War, the *Lega* was attractive because they regarded the State as remote, if not indeed foreign, and as responsible for creating a national park in their area. The State saw the park as a wild, public space; locals saw it as a restrictive regulation that curtailed the exercise of their traditional practices, such as hunting, which they had carried out on land they regarded as cultivated, in effect private property. This developed conception of land as cared for and controlled by locals chimed well with the privatisation policies then pursued by *Lega* politicians; thus both villagers and politicos could portray the state as a common enemy.

Until recently, West European governments regarded and spoke of the countryside as primarily a productive resource, for the cultivation of crops and rearing of livestock. To these governments, maintaining farms was essential for feeding the nation and to keep up at least a limited sense of national self-sufficiency. For successive French governments, national identity was so closely linked to the image of the small farmer that they assisted farmers with a range of state-sponsored forms of insurance (health, property, livestock, and crops). They also provided 'generous government credits, bonuses, tax breaks, and supervision and guarantees of farm loans' (Rogers 1991: 130). One consequence has been the strengthening of an allegedly archaic mode of agricultural organisation: the *ostal*, or stem-family farming household (Rogers 1991). The British government has been similarly concerned to assist small farmers in many areas, e.g. the hill farms of the Peak District, whose livelihoods would be gravely threatened without grants, and whose disappearance would radically change the local scene.

Today, the prominence of national governments has waned somewhat, thanks to the rise of the EU, with the European Commission (EC) long established as the major player in the evolution of rural Western Europe. From its beginning, the CAP has been a central component in the EU's budget. An enduring goal of the CAP has been social: to preserve family farms, seen as the condition of rural society, even at the cost of increasing efficiency (Gray 2000: 34). In recent times, evolving priorities, with the entrance of new members from Eastern Europe, have led to the progressive reduction of subsidies to farmers in Western Europe. Since most farms are today economically unviable without external support, agents of the EC have increasingly encouraged small farmers to diversify their sources of income: the farmer's wife turns their house into a B&B or *gîte*, or looks for an off-farm job. In the Basque provinces of France, some sell produce directly from the farm, identifying them with certified labels of origin or quality, in order to capitalise on new tourism markets (Welch-Devine and Murray 2011: 75).

The rural policies of the EU may seem relatively clear; their reception and interpretation are clearly not so. Many farmers have not simply accepted these policy changes with resignation but have taken great advantage of the opportunities offered, in ways not planned by the EU. While locals are guided by the offer of grants, they actively strive to steer them to their own benefit. As a Dubliner resettled in Connemara confessed, 'So deeply ingrained has the culture of grant aid become, in what the EC has determined as "Deprived Areas", it almost goes without saying that every action is influenced to an enormous extent by its eligibility for grant aid' (Williams 1998: 84). Some agriculturalists went further: for instance, in Greece, they learned to circumvent the Commission and criminally exploit its largesse to their own considerable gain. According to Christopher Lawrence, who did fieldwork in rural Greece,

> The early days of EU membership are still remembered fondly by agriculturalists in Argolida. Money was there for the taking. In a climate of large subsidies and lax controls, frauds and scams proliferated ... Since those early years controls over subsidy disbursements have increased, but defrauding EU subsidy programs remains an active sport. (Lawrence 2007: 150)

In 2009 one rural Irish entrepreneur told me the application forms for EU grants were so long and complex that 'one has to lie'.

With the development of global agro-business, the economic importance of local food production has declined greatly in West Europe. In consequence, the EC now views the countryside in multifunctional terms (Gray 2009; Heatherington 2011: 3). It has come to see farmers less as exploiters of agricultural potential, and more as 'guardians' or 'stewards' of the land they own, and who deserve to be subsidised accordingly. In this political discourse, rural zones become partly aesthetic resources, areas for the conservation of biodiversity and the management (if not invention) of heritage, to be exploited for the boosting of agro- and ecotourism and other leisure industries. Thus Elena Freire, in her contribution, shows how the Galician Autonomous Community, working in league with the EC, stimulated the revival of autochthonous pottery and paid for the unemployed to train as potters. Of course, as she demonstrates, the objects they turned might appear traditional and archetypally Galician but were in fact produced for non-traditional, decorative purposes for sale to those who wished to buy into a regionalist myth. By promoting a postmodern form of authenticity, the new potters, who did not come from the ranks of the traditional, long-established potter-families of the area, were selling a carefully managed dream of Galician rurality.

Balancing the different needs and desires of farmers, tourists, and others, brings its own problems in its train. For instance, the agendas of ecologists may, on occasion, be opposed to those of agriculturalists or fish farmers. Deliberately restocking wolf populations in north-west Spain is more attractive to wildlife spotters than to shepherds. In the French Pyrenees outdoor leisure activities have become so popular there is now conflict between recreational and traditional users of the area, particularly during the summer transhumance (Welch-Devine and Murray 2011: 81).

Rural emigration also led to increasing areas of former farmland gradually reverting towards a primordial state. Forests began to expand and encroach on villages. Thus in some places, faunal repopulation went hand in hand with rural depopulation. For instance, the number of wild boar is on the rise in many parts of Western Europe. In Tuscany today, local bodies and entrepreneurs are trying to take advantage of this increase by promoting wild boar cuisine. These recipes may be modern, but they are, or its main ingredient is, presented as traditional. Thus this initiative dovetails with the EU policy of stimulating rural economies by boosting the image of markedly local dishes. At the same time, the decimation of the gun-toting peasantry has had a further unintended effect: an animal once regarded as fit only for hunting has become a valued symbol of the edible wildness that urbanites seek on their time off. It adds a taste to their sense of rurality.

This new political discourse that aestheticises the countryside for mainly commercial reasons is not, however, as well-rooted as might at first appear. Thus increasing fears about the effects of climate change and global security have recently led some to calls for increasing agricultural productivity in the EU (Doward 2009). According to this line of argument, if governments are to be sure of feeding their populations, they must strive to meet these needs as much as possible from within their own borders. Political discourses of rurality are not stable, and it is the job of anthropologists to track and analyse their continuing evolution.

Incomers from elsewhere in West Europe

The new rural immigrants of recent decades are not a homogenous group but a variety of social types, each with their agendas. In the 1970s the sociologist Howard Newby, working in the English county of Suffolk, was able to categorise the incomers as simply middle class in background. They were mainly retired couples and second-homers seeking cheaper housing and the chance to live out their stereotype of an ossified rural idyll. Their arrival pushed up housing prices and divided villages, whose indigenous inhabitants were ready to accept agricultural change if it increased production. But by the 1990s, the colonising newcomers had become so varied that they could not be usefully classed as just 'middle class', but rather as coming from a range of different fractions from within that expanding class, broadly conceived (Cloke *et al.* 1995; Urry 1995).[3] On top of that, their increasing number had contributed in some cases to the destruction of the very rurality they sought.

In many cases these immigrants have come in a series of identifiably different waves, and they need to be distinguished as such. For instance while MacClancy, who worked in the west of Ireland, found that the majority of incomers there were patently alternative types fleeing the urban cultures of their upbringing, there are important distinctions within that general group: the hippies who came over in the early 1970s; the much more politicised 'crusties' who arrived a decade later; and the latest wave, which started in 1990s, of less radicalised urbanite escapees who strive to combine the value of living rurally with the benefits of information technology. Similarly Donald Macleod, who fieldworked on the island of La Gomera in the Canaries, differentiated between the German and the British settlers there. But keen not to overgeneralise, he underlined the variety within these two groups he had isolated (Macleod 2004).

In other areas the incomers may be of a different complexion. In the south-west of France, the majority of non-French incomers are not youthful alternatives but incomers seeking a base for holidays, a place to retire in or, more recently, a new home, usually grander than the one they sold in their native land. According to the sociologist Michaela Benson, who studied English incomers in the Lot, France, though these migrants could be generalised as chasing a rural vision that they considered increasingly hard to encounter in the UK, more significantly they could be subdivided into midlife, retirement, and family migrants. Their degree of integration into local communities did not necessarily improve, but could vary over time: those who had friends via contacts made through their children, might lose them when their offspring grew up and left the area. She found that successful integration depended less on learning French than on migrants' motivation and their pursuit of interests that they could share with locals (Benson 2009). In stark contrast, the French anthropologist Jean-Francois Baré, who has also done work in the Lot, observed a gentle clash of mutual misconceptions in social, cultural, linguistic, and economic spheres between polite middle-class Britons and their equally well-mannered indigenous neighbours. Moreover, by failing to speak a common language, the monolingual majority of both French and British local populations usually did not even realise the confusion they are causing (Baré n.d.). They resided in the same areas but occupied different worlds. It is as though, mutually unaware, they almost glided past one another. The same happened in the Mallorcan village of Deia, whose famous resident Robert Graves attracted a colony of expatriate artists. As one of the colony, who later became its ethnographer, stated: 'Unless something occurred which directly involved a local and a foreigner, everyone practised the adage "Live and let live". At times, it seemed as if each group carried on as though the other were not there' (Waldren 1996: 235).

In some areas incomers agglomerate into mononational or monolingual communities. The Mediterranean coastline of Spain is peppered with such colonies. The concentration of Norwegians in the Alicantine village of Altea, which even has its own Norwegian school funded by its home government, is perhaps an extreme example of these compatriot groupings. In many other cases diversity is the norm, and that diversity is growing. In the early 1990s, when one Briton went to live in a hamlet of the remote Las Alpurrajas region south of Granada, he found 'a few Danes and Dutch, and some English scattered thinly here and there'. By 2014 the incomer mix had become far more international and transregional:

> There are Algerians, Argentines, Americans, Chinese, French, Germans, Romanians, Czechs, Moroccans, Sahrawis, Poles, Dutch, Lebanese, Uzbeks, Iranians, English, Swedes, Danes, Bulgarians and Turks ... to say nothing of the more local *Zamoranos, Leoneses, Madrilenos, Jiennenses, Gaditanos* and *Onubenses*. (Stewart 2014: 268, orig. ital.)

Some people form what are termed 'intentional communities', with explicit lists of regulations. One of the most durable of these in Spain, Beneficio, is in the region Stewart describes. But self-formed communities are not necessarily all hippie in tone or style. Some may be Christians fleeing nearby cities for the silence of the countryside: for example, the Catholic community established in 1980s in Turballos, Muro de Alcoy, south-eastern Spain, dedicated to self-sufficiency, simplicity, and non-violence.[4] These communities may not all be on the left or leaning towards the liberal: in the mid-1990s, an international far-right organisation occupied a semi-abandoned hamlet near Valencia, east Spain, which they tried to turn into a neo-Nazi haven.[5] Some intentional communities may be formed by the villagers themselves: the long-established socialist utopia of Marinaleda, Andalusia, southern Spain, is so successful it has spawned imitators elsewhere in the region (Hancox 2013). What is striking about all these different settlements, founded from the late 1970s on, is that none appears to acknowledge their interwar predecessors, who had established their own ideologically grounded communities. It is as though utopia has to be created anew, without forebears, every time.

Incomers who have not committed themselves to intentional communities may leave open how long they will stay and how they regard their futures. Many of the British incomers to France should not be regarded as permanent resettlers, but as stopping over there in the course of their migrant trajectory. Since their main goal is a particular dream of rurality in an economic setting, they may well move on, or back if the cost of living rises, or the budget airline stops flights to their nearby airport. In recent years some have sold up for cheaper climes in Eastern Europe or North Africa (Ferbrache 2011). In the process, these lifestyle migrants become true transnationals.

Incomers need not come from afar. Some may be local returnees. In his chapter, Josetxu Martínez, an anthropologist of his home region, studied the evolving patterns of residency and sociability in the Basque province of Alava. Between the 1960s and 1980s, villagers left for the sake of jobs in the provincial city. But from the 1980s, in part stimulated by the local implementation of the EU's rural interventionist programmes, these same villagers started to make seasonal returns to their natal villages. Financially secure thanks to their urban employment, they now saw the countryside not as the site of ill-paid drudgery but as a recreational space in which to relax and socialise among their kin and affines. Though ageing locals saw them as outsiders because they were no longer tied to the soil, these urban escapees continued to regard themselves as in some sense insiders. They did not see themselves as returning to a home they had earlier abandoned because, Martínez argues, they were not aware of having ever left it. They had moved to the city physically, not emotionally. Thus he contends we should speak of a new rural-urban continuum in the area, which is replacing the previously well-established separation between the two.

At the same time, new forms of sociability are emerging, which transcend individual villages. Martínez discusses a recently invented ritual, which gathers the inhabitants of several villages within a recognised geographical area – the mountainous region of Alava. This novel style of community celebration shows that the space in which they socialise is no longer defined by the limits of their village but can encompass all the villages of their particular region. This space is doubly broadened for them, for of course at these rituals they share participation with the returnees who, sentimentally, feel they never went away.

Kepa Fernández de Larrinoa, a Basque anthropologist who now lives in the village he has studied since the 1970s, gives a more intricate case, and so underlines how multifaceted these evolutions can be. Alkiza is in a small mountainous valley twenty minutes' drive south of the coastal city of San Sebastián/Donostia. As in Martinez's study area, the distinction between rural and urban spaces is increasingly blurred, with villagers no longer understanding their identity in purely rural terms but in urban-rural ones. In the 1970s and 1980s, educated Basque urbanites moved in to participate in local activities and so live their ideal of cultural authenticity. But local forms of sociability are so narrowly organised that the only public events in which they could take part were the very ones they themselves created and which so define them. In the 1990s and 2000s the town hall recategorised some rural land as urban in a bid to retain the local population. However, many of the subsequent buildings were bought by city dwellers, forced out of San Sebastián by property speculation, and whose idea of a rural idyll does not include participation in local events. In the process a village whose inhabitants once upheld something approaching a unified local vision of the world is now the home of a much more complex, varied, and socially fractured reality.

Besides creating ceremonies, incomers can bring a variety of changes to their area of chosen residence: for example, restoring and revalorising old buildings; introducing new styles of architecture and farming (Figures 1.1 and 1.2); cultivating a much broader range of foods; augmenting local small-scale forms of production, such as cheesemaking; reviving abandoned modes of cooking; creating new artisanal products (such as different types of honey); establishing alternative schools; and maintaining non-conventional relationships (Bertran 1996; Cantarero 2002; Cáceres and Espeitx 2003; Robertson 2012; MacClancy this volume). In Puglia, south-eastern Italy, for example, well-to-do North Europeans have bought decaying *trulli*, distinctive conically roofed stone sheds, and then paid local craftsman to convert them into holiday homes. As one *trullaro* acknowledged, 'They gave us work and a bit of well-being – they brought our abandoned land back to life' (Mitzman 2013).

In La Gomera some made a potentially longer-lasting change, by marrying locals: they have both influenced local mores and in turn been influenced by them

Figure 1.1 Fairy-tale turreted house, for a blow-in cheesemaker, County Clare, west Ireland.

Figure 1.2 Locals thought this blow-in carpenter 'mad' to construct a wooden house in such a gale-swept area as County Clare, west Ireland. More than a decade later, the house still stood, in good shape.

(Macleod 2004). Moreover, it is often these North European immigrants who are among the first to exploit EU grants offered for rural development. In many cases, it tends to be the incomers who take the initiative, forming the groups necessary for a grant application. In Donegal, north-west Ireland, for instance, incomers and previously marginalised locals were able to form bodies which won EU LEADER[6] project money and so challenged the hitherto dominant 'Donegal mafia', a transgenerational coterie drawn from a few powerful families which had long controlled much of the county (Collinson 1999).

In some areas the predicament is so dire that town halls and estate agents are increasingly keen to attract outsiders with grand vision and deep pockets. I have already mentioned the disposition of the Deputation of Navarre to grant freehold to deserted villages to groups of serious migrants. In 2013, in Galicia, north-west Spain, the mayor of Cortegada put up for free an abandoned hamlet within the municipality to anyone with a viable project to restore and develop its buildings, as long as local jobs were generated in the process.[7] Some Spanish estate agents today have websites dedicated to the sale of whole, emptied villages, though they take care to forewarn the interested that buying a village is not the same as 'purchasing a packet of nibbles'.[8] Local historians are not far behind, producing for tourists and the curious illustrated blogs and books on the deserted villages in their area.[9]

Ethnographies/travelogues

Since anthropologists have written so relatively little about these areas, whether colonised by ex-hippies or ex-workers, I am forced to turn for further clues about the nature of life within them to the expatriate literature that has boomed on the British market in the last twenty years.

These exoticised accounts of life among not so very different others can yet provide further evidence for the sorts of changes incomers can bring: restoring old styles of new styles of naming farm animals; introducing sheep and mechanised sheep-shearing to a region; wanting to win the locals over to organic farming; and reviving old customs, such as parties at home of traditional music and dance (Williams 1987: ch. 12; 1989: 68–71; Stewart 1999: 97–110; 2002: 45; 2006: 26, 29; Jacobs 2003: 167). They also suggest the rainbow-like variety of groups that can colonise areas. Chris Stewart, resident in the Alpujarras, speaks of the variety of oriental religions upheld in the valley and of the local 'expat community engulfed in a raft of alternative diets, from straightforward vegetarianism through to vegan, ovo-lacto-vegan, macrobiotic and ayurvedic. There is also a small but significant minority of crudo-vegans, who eat only raw food' (Stewart 2002: 140; 2006: 176). These authors also show that conflict may arise not just between incomers and locals, but between different factions of the incomers, e.g. between hippies-turned-farmers and their eco-fundamentalist neighbours (Stewart 1999: 109–10). Most communes split apart, though their effects may linger. A British writer in the Valencian Sierra asks a local what happened to the one in that area: 'Oh, they all left', the man says. 'Sex scandal of some sort … Some of them still meet up here once a year, though. Get transformed into animal spirits – eagles and bears, that kind of thing: shamans' (Webster 2009: 61–2).

Further, if these authors are at least partially dependent on their writing to survive, then they are forced to turn their own lives and thus those around them into a literary product (see Williams 1995: 12). But if their works turn into bestsellers, then villagers, unwittingly or not, become involved in the process too: imposing tourists arrive to photograph the characters they have read so much about; businesses do well out of the increased trade; estate agents make money trumpeting the village as 'the one made famous by X's book'.[10] In the process the less entrepreneurial of the villagers become objects of visual consumption in a broadened context scripted by others and ever more alien to them. It is part of the quotidian surreality ever more common in today's countryside.

Resistance

There are, of course, ways for locals to resist the incomers, even those who learn the language, e.g. denigration, stereotyping, withdrawal, verbal aggression.[11] One local told Samantha Hurn, who did fieldwork in a west Wales sheep farming area:

> They [incomers] complain that they had to move away 'because of all the "foreigners" *[said in a fake Brummie accent]*: that they didn't feel safe going out at night. Then they move here and bring their prejudices and double standards with them. Can't they see that they're doing what they accuse blacks [sic] of doing in England? Taking over the place. (Quoted in Hurn forthcoming)

She found that those incomers who do not try to fit in, but are seen as intent on changing the local culture, are regarded in a hostile manner. Emma James, a Welsh-speaking sociologist who studied her natal community, uncovered similar attitudes and found that natives had complementary strategies for cutting down almost any immigrant. Those seen as unwilling to engage in village activities were condemned as antisocial, while those who did try to join in were branded as 'interfering' and 'overbearing'. Of course, the line between 'integration' and 'interference' could be very fine indeed, and where the locals chose to draw it at any one time was up to them (James 2003).

Modes of resistance may be seen as almost necessary here, by those who wish to retain their position or at least a modicum of dignity, against outsiders who may well be seen as socially or culturally superior, and who may think they can act as such. Even as early as 1986, a trio of geographers could describe Cornwall as 'swamped by a flood of middle-class, middle-aged, middle-browed city dwellers who effectively imposed their standards upon local society' (Perry, Dean, and Brown 1986: 129). The danger, of course, is that incomers may be scapegoated as the causes for a variety of contemporary social ills, just as tourists in Sri Lanka were blamed for social change, though in fact that process had begun some time before their arrival and continued in a somewhat independent manner afterwards (Crick 1994). For instance, in the rural areas of the province of Alicante, south-eastern Spain, where I have been conducting part-time fieldwork for several years, North European residents are often typed pejoratively as 'invaders', threatening or damaging diverse aspects of provincial social life. Usually excluded from membership of local moral communities, they are regarded as 'fair game' by many locals, to be exploited economically whenever the occasion arises.

It is important not to overgeneralise: not all locals engage in xenophobic discrimination or exploitative stereotyping. Many welcome or at least accept the incomers. These internal differences can create local tension, as one expatriate based in southern Spain related:

> My neighbour Domingo once went to town to buy some beans to sow. Our Dutch neighbour, Bernardo, asked him to buy a bag for him, too. Arriving at the seed merchants, Domingo said, 'Give me a kilo of beans and another for Bernardo.' The manager looked at him and said, 'I don't sell to foreigners.' 'OK,' said Domingo. 'Make that two kilos for me, then.' (Stewart 2014: 268)

Collinson, in his contribution, gives another twist to the stereotyping of incomers. Based on his fieldwork in Donegal, north-west Ireland, he shows that denizens deploy 'blow-in' as a derogatory term to castigate those they wish to crab. However, in a rural area like this where an extreme localism holds sway, just who is branded 'incomer' can take unexpected turns. Even a man born and bred in a Donegal village may be called an incomer just because his parents were products of a town all of thirty miles away. Collinson discusses a dispute between the residents' association of a rural housing estate, its estate-based opponents, and locally resident county councillors. Each tries to undercut the argument of the other by claiming that their adversaries are blow-ins, and that therefore their views have less weight. In contexts such as these, words like 'incomer' become flip-flop terms, whose meaning is ever open to interpretation; only its negative charge remains the same.

Stereotyping, of course, can be ignorantly deployed, especially when tourists join the social stage. One writer, relocated from the USA, discloses the postmodern confusions incomers can find themselves caught in. Based in Cork, south-west Ireland, he goes fishing one day,

> So I worked myself downstream ... Behind me, I discovered a pack of Aran sweater-bedecked Americans oohing and aahing and busily photographing my every move, as if I was now the embodiment of Ireland's timeless bucolic ways – the original postcard Celt. Such was the barminess that had taken over my identity. (Monaghan 2004: 112)

Occupation or cooperation?

It is all too easy for anthropologists, still fascinated by native systems of classification, to focus on definitional strategies. But it is just as important to examine cross-cutting modes of cooperation. Thus Hurn found that incomers who supported local agrarian culture were lauded, regardless of where they came from (Hurn forthcoming). MacClancy demonstrates that while indigenous Irish of Country Clare might at times separate themselves from those they label 'blow-ins', they are also ready to acknowledge that some can be relied upon to give a hand in times of need and that assistance can be as valued as rootedness (for a Hebridean example, see Kohn 2002). The geographers Scott Willis and Hugh Campbell recognise a similar phenomenon in the Parc National des Cévennes, southern France. There once free-loving hippies, the *Néos,* have captured the moral terrain and the grudging acceptance of locals, whether ageing residents or absentee indigenes, by their 'praxis of belonging'. For they are best placed to negotiate the local bureaucracy and administration; they occupy the land; 'they are the ones who produce "authentic" local goods, they are the ones who rebuild ruined farm houses in an authentic fashion, they are the ones who carry the vision of *patrimonie* ("heritage") held by both the Parc and the Absentees into praxis' (Willis and Campbell 2004: 327).[12] Willis and Campbell felicitously phrase the result a 'chestnut economy'. A long-term resident of the area recently argued that one reason so many from both groups here cohabit successfully is their mutual participation in a tradition of resisting the outside world. Though arising from different contexts they share an anti-progress ethic. In the words of one energetic but frustrated native, 'Some people would rather stay poor with a quiet life. They have got just enough to live on, so who can blame them?' (Bremner 2013).

On the Larzac Plateau, north-west of the Cévennes, the incomers have had an even greater effect. In 1970 locals who publicly opposed plans to expand massively a military camp there were joined by Maoists, anarchists, socialists, hippies, ecologists, revolutionaries, pacifists, intellectuals, and members of the Catholic clergy. The years of ultimately successful protest led to many activists finally residing there, and becoming a beacon of the antiglobalisation movement. The zone has today achieved a quasi-mythical status throughout Europe among members of the movement. Permanently based activists now outnumber indigenes (Williams 2008).

There is, however, a dark side to this repopulation, for the state may all too easily misunderstand the motives and actions of the politically inclined who chose to abandon the cities for a simpler, rural life. On November 2008, a squad of balaclava-clad gendarmes, backed up by helicopters, swooped on the small village of Tarnac, north of the Larzac Plateau, to arrest nine anticapitalists. Authorities considered them anarchist terrorists plotting to overthrow the state. The families of these middle-class graduates, villagers, and other supporters quickly helped raise international protests. All but one were soon released.[13] It is not just the agents of the state, but the locals as well who may choose to act against the incomers, moving beyond stereotyping strategies and taking matters into their own fists. The very successful Navarran commune I mentioned at the beginning had nearly burnt down the year before when a young man from nearby, disgruntled at the continued presence of these alternative activists, set the surrounding countryside alight. The flames had reached within a few metres of the buildings.

Political activity among incomers is not confined to the ranks of youthful rebels. Older, lifestyle migrants can also engage in patently political behaviour, enabling new coalitions. In 1994 on La Gomera, for the first time settlers and local left-wingers formed a coalition to successfully oppose development plans promoted by the area's right-wing elite (Macleod 2004).

The behaviour of some incomers also displays incipient signs of an emerging, grass-roots 'Euro-democracy', by getting elected to their village councils. This pattern, although still minor in national terms, is already electorally evident in a broad survey of French rural town halls (Collard 2010). Continuing fieldwork of my own in the Spanish province of Alicante evidences a similar development. Here though, local representatives of national parties may practise a hard-nosed strategy of recruiting foreign incomers in order to win their compatriots' votes. In at least one municipality this has even led to the election as councillors, of migrants who do not speak Spanish.

In some cases, corrupt indigenous practice can directly stimulate an agglomerating sense of common victimhood among incomers, who join hands with similarly afflicted locals. In the Valencian Autonomous Community of the late 1990s and early 2000s, thousands of expatriates suffered a swathe of expropriations, initiated by the regional government and extended by bankrupt town halls. In reaction threatened incomers from throughout the region formed cross-national coalitions to protest the legality of these land grabs. They deftly sidestepped the implementation of suddenly revived legislation from the early modern period of the area, by taking their case to the EU, which made further subsidies to the area dependent on revision of these outdated legalities. Also, during this period, a newly formed group of affected expatriates entered into coalition with local activists in one Alicantine municipality. Working together, they deliberately and explicitly got themselves elected as councillors in order to overturn the expropriative measures of the previous administration.

Out of common adversity, whether acting as exclusively expatriate groups or allying with aggrieved locals, incomers are beginning to organise themselves politically and to emerge as electoral forces in their own right.

Incomers from beyond West Europe

An English travel-writer is driving south through Italy in a carful of Italians:

> My eye is drawn to a bonfire burning in the middle of the field we're passing; and to the small group of people standing around it. Not just people; they're all women. And this is obviously a hallucination ... Because the women appear to me to be Black African women, dressed in traditional African clothing. There seem to be about a dozen of them, laughing and chatting among themselves, ebony skins gleaming in the firelight ... I check my fellow travellers for any sign that they too have just seen a clip from some documentary about African village life, inexplicably projected on to the Calabrian landscape ...

> 'Probably just there for the tomato harvest,' says Ciccio, as if it were the most natural thing in the world. 'Too late for the grapes, isn't it? But the Senegalese do the peaches around Cozena in June and July, definitively ...'
>
> Where are all the simple Southern farming folk you always imagine down in these parts? ... Was I really expecting to see troupes of olive-skinned damsels? ... Next time I open a tin of tomatoes, I shall make sure I concentrate on vizualising the much more modern and likely picture of a bunch of West African women standing at dusk around a bonfire in some strange Italian field, far, far from home. (Hawes 2005: 65–6)

It is not just neo-hippies and wealthy pensioners who are moving into the countryside. Labour migrants from beyond the borders of Western Europe are also rapidly increasing in number. Anthropologists of the area have long studied the labour migration of the original communities they have investigated, usually of South Europeans moving into urban Northern Europe (e.g. Davis 1977: 29–41; Brettell 1986). But it is only in the last decade that some have begun to examine the social consequences of the arrival of rural jobseekers from outside these countries. The almost continuous nature of this immigration and its high profile in the mass media only serve to make its anthropological investigation all the more urgent.

The reasons for this immigration are multiple. First must come the voluntary abandonment of agriculture by people whose predecessors were forced into farming labour. In my Navarran fieldsite in the 1980s, the decreasing profitability and prestige of tilling the land or husbanding livestock encouraged many young men to seek work elsewhere. Thanks to the great, recent expansion of State secondary and tertiary education, many had managed to gain the skills which got them salaried jobs outside the village. That way they also stood a better chance of marriage: few young women wished to marry an agriculturalist. As several of them stated to me, 'Farmers treat their cows better than their wives.' Lawrence argues that in rural Greece it is the women and children, previously dragooned into farm work, who have given up the drudgery of agricultural tasks for the sake of more attractive, less onerous alternatives. Women now enter the formal economy while children have become primarily consumers rather than juvenile workers contributing to the domestic economy (Lawrence 2007: 164).

Second, several ethnographers have argued that immigration controls are so weak that their governments implicitly enable these mass arrivals. Tacitly recognising the central role of the informal sector in their economies, they effectively allow non-EU immigrants to fill, if not boost, the ranks of this workforce. Trouble is, the legal status of the incomers is so uncertain and their desire for work so great that employers may exploit them savagely. Some of them do so. All too often these rural incomers do the jobs natives do not wish to, and at a lower cost to employers (Hanus 2013; Souchard 2013). They can be, as one anthropologist put it, a 'windfall' for the unscrupulous (Filhol 2013). What emerges from this systemised mess is a neo-feudalism in the modern age, where immigrants eager for long-term work permits are forced to become 'ritual supplicants' to the state, while rural bosses create a twenty-first-century clientelism, acting as patrons to foreign jobseekers who know they must be submissive, at times servile, to gain even a temporary income (Cole and Booth 2007; Lawrence 2007; see also Suárez-Navaz 2004). Multiply marginalised; they may be obliged to live in the dilapidated sections of ghettos, moving into the most derelict buildings, subject both to the intolerance of denizens and heightened levels of surveillance (Perrotta 2013; Zeneidi 2013). In effect immigrants, poor in rights, are made to fill the ranks of a new, rural underclass, one even weaker and more vulnerable than that of their indigenous predecessors (Mésini 2013). The natives, after all, cannot be threatened with deportation. As one migrant labourer put it, 'They made us work like *perros*. No, worse than dogs. I have never seen dogs treated the way they treated us on that farm' (Webster 2004: 46).

The rise of this migrant workforce has facilitated the remarkably rapid development of labour-intensive agriculture. Indeed some commentators claim there are now so many rural migrant labourers that, without their contribution, agriculture would simply stop in much of Western Europe today. It is not just that farming would fail to make any economic sense. There would also be far too few workers to tend and harvest the crops. The economic potential of exploiting these incomers is so great that it can exert a major influence on farmers' decisions over exactly which crops to plant and where to invest. Thus in Levantine Spain, some landowners have substituted fruit trees for cereal crops or draped their fields with polytunnels. Even though this switch means cheap migrant labour becomes essential to profitability – which may be very high – employers, by only offering short-term contracts and constantly renovating their workforce, can usually keep their employees docile and make them feel they are marginal, not central to their agribusiness (Martínez 2001; Cole and Booth 2007). Marx would not have been surprised.

If this situation is so dire yet so widespread, why has it been so little studied? Lawrence, for instance, refers to a 'paucity of material on the phenomenon' (Lawrence 2007: 68). One partial answer might be the illegal nature of so much of this labour migration, and some anthropologists' desire to steer clear of documenting shady practice for fear of not getting their research approved by their university's ethics committee. Another part answer might be the politically very sensitive nature of much of this material. This was highlighted in the (at times) heated debate within Spanish anthropology raised by the publication in 2001 by Basque anthropologist, Mikel Azurmendi, of a 'reportage' about relations between locals and migrant labourers in a rural town that had experienced a series of violent events (Azurmendi 2002; Martínez 2002; Hadji 2003. The original public statement against Azurmendi's book, signed by over sixty Spanish anthropologists, appeared in *Página Abierta*, 128, año 12:46–7). But both the fear of participant-observing illegal activity and of straying into polemical terrain are insufficient reasons why anthropologists have ignored this pattern of migration for so long. More satisfying answers so far elude me.

What is clear is that this style of immigration is not new. Only its present scale is novel. Thus Chantal Crenn, in her contribution, points out that Moroccans have resided in rural France for several decades. The original migrants came to work on vineyards, for which they now feel great affection. Their patent, learned skilfulness at tending the vines became a central part of their evolving, now transnational identity. But since the 1990s increasing mechanisation has made their livelihood ever more precarious. So their better-educated offspring today seek jobs in the nearby towns. Although several of this new generation marry locals, as a whole, the Moroccans are still regarded as outsiders. As Crenn found in her fieldwork, many of the locals continued to ignore them completely and 'were surprised by our theme of fieldwork on a minority they had never even considered as an identified group' (Crenn, ch. 4; Crenn 2003). To these denizens, the migrants in their midst, no matter how long established, were but long-term marginals unworthy of an identity.

The next stage in this tale came in 2002 when almost all EU States, bar the UK and Ireland, allowed citizens from certain Central European countries to enter without visas. However, they were only allowed to enter as tourists and for up to three months at a time. The predictable result was that hundreds of thousands of East European workers became 'labour tourists', outstaying their visas and gaining illegal, temporary employment at low rates. For instance, by 2013 in the polytunnels of Levantine Spain, Romanians had become the workers of choice for agri-farmers (Hartman 2008; on disgruntled Central Europeans working in the British countryside, see Ivancheva 2007). According to one observer, the Romanians, although they are exploited similarly to Africans and could therefore share an underclass consciousness, in fact deploy racist justifications to distance themselves as much as possible from their fellow workers, and so boost their own chances of employment (Potot 2008). One consequence is that North Africans, as they had feared, have been pushed down a rung of the racialised hierarchy of local employability. Another consequence is that the emigration of husband-and-wife pairs to the picking fields of Western Europe has in Romania led to the recognised phenomenon of 'strawberry orphans': children separated from their parents, brought up by aged kin or other carers, and maintained by remittances (Bilefsky 2009). In fact so many workers left the country that in 2008 Romanian ministers toured West European centres of compatriot emigration to persuade them to come home (Fabra 2008; Galán 2009). In Latvia so many rural emigrants have joined what is termed 'the great departure' that it is felt they have left the countryside 'empty', stripped of life, 'near apocalypse' (Dzenovska 2011; Dzenovska and Aistra 2013: 2). What is distinctive, at least in Britain and Spain, is that, unlike their West European predecessors who were usually uneducated and lowly skilled, many of these new rural incomers, whether from West or East Europe, are highly qualified (Potot 2008; Pina and Corkill 2010). This leads to the unusual sight of migrant doctors, teachers, and lawyers engaged in the '3 Ps': plucking, picking, and packing.

It is also noteworthy that there appears to be a geographical separation between the labour migrants and the back-to-nature types. The great majority of migrants go to work in areas of high agricultural production, of easy access for large trucks: there is money for farmers to make, and more offers of jobs. Hippies and other alternatives establish themselves in zones that are of low production and inaccessible to leviathan lorries: the land is cheaper; there is less competition, because of less profit for working it.

In recent years illuminating exceptions to many of these generalities have begun to emerge. Maybe we are witnessing the creation of a new dimension in rural complexity. For in several areas, migrant labour is now well regarded because of the range of benefits it is bringing. For instance, in contemporary rural Greece immigrant workers, especially Albanians, have revitalised the countryside economy. This supply of cheap labour has reversed the decline of agricultural production there and reinvigorated otherwise moribund villages. Albanians who manage to regularise their status can escape the neo-feudalist trap by working in both the fields and the construction industry, using cash raised to buy their own holdings, revive abandoned farms, or set up their own local businesses. Most villagers recognise their positive contribution. Some local males, otherwise fated to bachelordom, have married Albanian migrants, thus leading to the reopening of village schools (Kasimis 2008; Labriandis and Sykas 2009; Verinis 2011). Among rural migrants in West Europe today, these Albanians are the leading exemplars of upward mobility.

They are not alone. The mayor of one village in the Italian region of Calabria, which suffered race riots against incomer fruit pickers, has, since the late 1990s, turned around his hometown's otherwise terminal decline by accepting, not rejecting, migrants. The village is receiving government subsidies for doing so. The palazzo is now a 'welcome centre' for immigrants, setting them up with jobs, teaching Italian to their children, and distributing food tokens. This approach makes clear economic sense: for the central government it is four times cheaper to fund their stay in the village than foot the bill for their accommodation in a holding centre for refugees. In the process the school is kept open, thanks to the influx of immigrant children; formerly abandoned houses are reoccupied; and traditional trades are kept alive by incomers learning the necessary skills in artisanal workshops. In turn, their residence generates jobs in social services for the locals (Kington 2013).

Of course, these situations are forever fluid. The economic crisis that began in the late 2000s has had multiple, ongoing effects. In some areas educated but unemployed men are returning to work the ancestral lands they had earlier rejected for the sake of urban jobs and life. In many areas where unemployment has reached levels not seen in decades, more migrants are today going home than coming in, and in a striking reversal, some of the West Europeans are following them. On top of that, the progressive reductions in CAP subsidies planned by the EC imperil the futures of farmers who have until now benefited so well from Common Market policies. Watch this space?

Conclusion

Formerly many anthropologists of rural Europe scripted their manuscripts to a tone of lament, for the passing of a long-established way of life (e.g. Brody 1973; Du Boulay 1974; Kavanagh 1994; Tayler 1998). Their works became tomes of salvage ethnography, documentaries of old traditions about to disappear. Travel writers can indulge themselves similarly. One mourns the loss of local lore, in this case ethnobotanical: 'Sometimes the mountains felt like a drugstore where all the prescriptions had been lost and the pharmacists had died or gone into hiding' (Webster 2009: 102). The awkward truth for both these classes of authors is that some of those supposed traditions were not as long standing as they thought, and some of them did not die out, but were transformed for contemporary purposes.[14]

These blinkered chronicles of decline are today being belatedly replaced by much more multi-stranded ethnographies, alive to the variety of modern realities, where villages are now plural in composition and subject to accelerated change. It is this latter-day diversity and complexity that I have wished to emphasise here. Components of this complexity may include: an expanded variety of different discourses of rurality, where it is important to discern which is held by whom, when, why, where, to what effect; the countryside as a playground for the well-to-do, site of residence for the IT-savvy, or a place of confinement for the poor, unable to leave the area; the nature and consequences of government and EU interventions; the origin, desires, behaviours, and values of the incomers; their interactions, or lack of them, with locals, and the results for all concerned; racialisation and racial violence in rural areas, where ethnic minorities may be especially transitory and mobile (e.g. Ray and Reed 2005); organic food production, eco- and agro-tourism, and other novel farming practices; the diverse effects of the new information technologies (tele-cottaging, outsourcing, and shifting offices to remote areas whose regional authorities offer supportive grants); the renovation or re-creation of public space, for revitalised or freshly invented communal occasions (e.g. McCabe 2009). This novel degree of social complexity, refracted differently in different European settings, necessitates ethnographic studies in order to elucidate, in each case, the subtleties of its multiple strands and consequences, and so provide a potential basis for informed comparative generalisations.

In previous decades, anthropologists played a key role, unwittingly or not, in the construction of regional identities. For instance, work in the 1970s and 1980s by Spanish anthropologists on the multiple bonds between rural Galicians and their farmhouses had a direct effect on Galician identity (Rodríguez 2008: 152; for Basque examples, see MacClancy 2007). But what role can anthropologists play in today's countrysides? Fernández, observing the increasing importance of local ethnographic museums in development plans at all levels from the EU to regions classed as 'deprived', argues that anthropologists can act as highly effective advisors to the civil servants who implement and monitor these rural policies (Fernández 2006). Coca Pérez promotes the integrated deployment of anthropologists within rural development projects in order that local voices are heard and taken account of, that exclusively environmentalist criteria do not overshadow social issues, and that regional developers take note of contemporary social realities and not just folkloric dimensions of local heritage (Coca Pérez 2003). Given the sorts of changes discussed throughout this book, it is dangerously easy for regional administrators and centralised policymakers to become increasingly unaware of local actualities.

It is tempting to see today's countrysides as a land of everyday surrealities: where once-urban shamans now reside alongside ageing shepherds, former hippies fabricate new traditions, and EU policies promote postmodernist practices; while the sight of Senegalese around a bonfire signals the coming of the tomato harvest, and co-residents create mutual misunderstandings without even realising what they are doing, like an update of *Clochmerle* dubbed in Franglais. But these apparent surrealities are in fact but present day realities. If we are to understand the nature of social change within Western Europe, these are realities that cannot be ignored.

In this book, we have deliberately neglected topics of traditional interest to European anthropologists, such as kinship and property transmission, though in renovated forms they are still of importance. Also, we have not covered every topic of concern to anthropologists of contemporary rural Europe. For instance, we have not included studies of rural tourism, national parks, the social dimensions of re-introducing formerly extinct animals to wilderness areas (e.g. wolves in Scotland, large birds of prey in England, bears in the Pyrenees). Our goal was not to address every topic of rural relevance today. Rather, we wish to re-direct the attention of Europeanist colleagues towards the continuing significance of a vast geographical zone that they have learned to bypass. For the debates about, and within the West European countryside are themes too important for anthropologists to go on avoiding.

Acknowledgements

I thank my colleagues, especially Marc Brightman, in the Department of Anthropology, Oxford Brookes University, for their comments.

Notes

1 E.g. the St Briavels, Gloucestershire, Parish Grasslands Project which set up 'rent-a-cow' schemes for grazing small fields (Marren 2005; also available at www.parishgrasslandsproject.org.uk/web-content/images/pdf_files/Independent_article.pdf. Accessed 11 February 2010.

2 On the power of long-term fieldwork as a research method, see MacClancy 2002; MacClancy and Fuentes 2010.

3 It is also possible that Newby was unaware how diverse these Suffolk immigrants could be. The naturalist Roger Deakin, who went to live in the county in the 1970s, listed his fellow-incomers as 'quasi-hippies, pioneer immigrants, rough carpenters, dirt farmers, musicians, ditchdiggers, and drivers' (Deakin 2007: 4).

4 www.ciberiglesia.net/discipulos/04/04testimonio.htm. Accessed 23 June 2014.

5 'Neo-Nazis take over Spanish village', http://www.theguardian.com/world/1999/nov/20/vivekchaudhary; 'Las ruinas del sueno neonazi', http://www.interviu.es/reportajes/articulos/las-ruinas-del-sueno-neonazi. Both accessed 29 August 2014. I thank Peter Foster Macleod for information about this example.

6 Liaison Entre Actions de Développement de l'Economie Rurale (European Union Initiative for Rural Development).

7 www.bbc.co.uk/news/magazine-27034535. Accessed 17 June 2014.

8 E.g. www.aldeasabandonadas.com/venta-de-aldeas.html and www.pueblosabandonados.com/. Both accessed 11 June 2014.

9 E.g. www.verkami.com/projects/5993-llibre-pobles-valencians-abandonats-la-memoria-del-silenci/blog. Accessed 17 June 2014.

10 See e.g. the interview with Chris Stewart, www.wanderlust.co.uk/issues/issue52.html, accessed 2 February 2006; and the entry on the village of Frailes (which became the hometown of the late Michael Jacobs and discussed at length by him in Jacobs 2003), www.property-net-spain.com/provinces/jaen/sierra_sur.html. Accessed 25 September 2006.

11 See Boissevain 1996 for discussion of the strategies employed by European locals to mitigate the effects of mass tourism in their hometowns.

12 The terms 'praxis of belonging' come from Borneman 1992.

13 'Rural idyll or terrorist hub? The village that police say is a threat to the state. Nine deny anarchist plot saying they were just seeking the simple life', www.guardian.co.uk/world/2009/jan/03/france-terrorism-tarnac-anarchists. Accessed 2 February 2010.

14 E.g. on their misrepresentations of rural Ireland, see Wilson and Donnan 2006.

References

Abélès, Marc 1998 'How the anthropology of France has changed anthropology in France: assessing new directions in the field', *Cultural Anthropology*, 14: 3, August, 404–8.

Ardener, Edwin 1985 '"Remote areas": some theoretical considerations', in A. Jackson (ed.) *Anthropology at Home* (ASA monographs 24. London: Tavistock), 38–54.

Azurmendi, Mikel 2001 *Estampas de El Ejido. Un reportaje sobre la integración del inmigrante* (Madrid: Taurus).

——2002 'Quería que mi libro generase un debate, pero solo ha habido un embate y una descalificación', *Espacio Crítico, AIBR (Asociación de Antropólogos Iberoamericanos en Red)* (September), 22. www.aibr.org/antropologia/boant/criticos/SEP0201.html. Accessed 28 January 2009.

Baré, Jean-François n.d. *Britons in Rural France. Some Comments by an Anthropologist as a Quasi-native*. Unpublished paper.

Bellier, Irene and Thomas M. Wilson (eds) 2000 *An Anthropology of the European Union. Building, Imagining and Experiencing the New Europe* (Oxford: Berghahn).

Benson, Michaela 2009 'The context and trajectory of lifestyle migration', *European Societies*, 12: 1, 45–64.

Bertran, Xandri, C. 1996 'Los productos locales: entre la protección y la normalización (el caso del tupí)', *Agricultura y Sociedad*, 80–1, 258–88.

Bilefsky, Dan 2009 'Romanian exodus burdens the young', *The Observer, New York Times Supplement* London (22 February), 3.

Boissevain, Jeremy (ed.) 1996 *Coping with Tourists. European Reactions to Mass Tourism* (Oxford: Berghahn).

Borneman, John 1992 *Belonging in the Two Berlins. Kin, State and Nation* (Cambridge: Cambridge University Press).

Borneman, John and Nick Fowler 1997 'Europeanization', *Annual Review of Anthropology 1997*, 487–514

Bremner, Charles 2013 'From our correspondent: the Cévennes', *The Times* (29 April), 31.

Brettell, Caroline 1986 *Men who Migrate, Women who Wait. Population and History in a Portugese Parish* (Ithaca, NY: Princeton University Press).

Brody, Hugh 1973 *Inishkillane. Decline and Change in the West of Ireland* (London: Allen Lane).

Cáceres, Juanjo and Elena Espeitx 2003 'El papel de los productos alimentarios locales en las estrategias de desarrollo turístico del pirineo catalán', in *Cultura y política. Actas del IX Congreso de Antropología FAAEE. Junio de 2002* [CD Rom] (Barcelona).

Cantarero, Luis 2002 'Preferencias alimentarias y valores de los "neorurales". Un studio en Aineto, Ibort y Artosilla en el Serrablo Oscense', in M. G. Arnaiz (ed.) *Somos lo que Comemos* (Barcelona: Ariel), 151–77.

Cloke, Paul, Martin Phillips and Nigel Thrift 1995 'The new middle classes and the social constructs of rural living', in T. Butler and M. Savage (eds) *Social Change and the Middle Classes* (London: UCL Press), 220–40.

Coca Pérez, Agustin 2003 'Espacios naturales protegidos en Andalucía y desarollo rural. El patrimonio como recurso de desarollo', in *Cultura y política. Actas del IX Congreso de Antropología FAAEE. Junio de 2002.* [CD Rom], Barcelona.

Cole, Jeffrey E. and Sally S. Booth 2007 *Dirty Work. Immigrants in Domestic Service, Agriculture and Prostitution in Sicily* (Lanham: Rowan & Littlefield).

Collard, S. 2010 'French municipal democracy: cradle of European citizenship?', *Journal of Contemporary European Studies*, 18, 91–116.

Collinson, Paul 1999 *Development, Local Politics and the EU in County Donegal.* Unpublished PhD thesis (Oxford Brookes University).

Copp, J. 1972 'Rural sociology and rural development', *Rural Sociology*, 37, 515–33.

Crenn, Chantal 2003 'Des invisibles trop visibles? – Les ouvriers agricoles "marocains" dans les vignobles du Bordelais', *Revue Hommes et migrations*, 1301 (janvier-février-mars).

Crick, Malcolm 1994 *Resplendent Sites, Discordant Voices. Sri Lankans and International Tourism* (Chur, Switzerland: Harwood Academic).

Deakin, Roger 2007 *Wildwood. A Journey through Trees* (London: Hamish Hamilton).

De la Pradelle, Michèle 2006 *Market Day in Provence* (Chicago: University of Chicago Press).

Demossier, Marion 2011 'Anthropologists and the challenges of modernity', *Anthropological Journal of European Cultures*, 20:1, 111–31.

Doward, Jamie 2009 'Britain "must revive farms" to avoid grave food crisis', *The Observer* (1 February), 15.
Du Boulay, Juliet 1974 *Portrait of a Greek Mountain Village* (Oxford: Clarendon Press).
Dzenovska, Dace 2011 'Notes on emptiness and the importance of maintaining life', *Anthropology of East Europe Review* 29:2, 228–41.
Dzenovska, Dace and Guntra Aistara 2013 'Practices and policies of rural living in Latvia: an interdisciplinary view', *Journal of Baltic Studies*, DOI: 10.1080/01629778.2013.8368 27, 1–16.
Fabra, María 2008 'Rumania ofrece empleo para que sus ciudadanos vuelvan a casa', *El País*, suplemento 'Comunidad Valenciana' (8 April), 1.
Ferbrache, Fiona 2011 'British immigrants in France: issues and debates in a broadening research field', *Geography Compass*, 5:10, 737–49.
Fernández de Larrinoa, Kepa 2006 'Deterioro sociocultural y reconstrucción patrimonial: el fraude de la política económica y del patrimonio cultural inocentes', in K. Fernández de Larrinoa (ed.) *Intervención y vínculo. Reconstrucción social y peritaje antropológico en la administración pública e industria cultural del ocio* (San Sebastián: EHU-UPV), 13–57.
Filhol, Romain 2013 'Les travailleurs agricoles migrants en Italie du sud – entre incompréhension, instrumentalisation et solidarités locales', *Revue Hommes et Migrations*, 1301 (janvier-février-mars).
Galán, Lola 2009 'De vuelta a Rumania', *El País*, suplemento 'Domingo', (4 January), 8–9.
Goldring, Maurice 1993 *Pleasant the Scholar's life. Irish Intellectuals and the Construction of the Nation State* (London: Serif).
Gray, John 2000 'The Common Agricultural Policy and the re-invention of the rural in the European Community', *Sociologica Ruralis*, 40:1, 30–52.
——2009 'Rurality and rural space: the "policy effect" of the Common Agricultural Policy in the borders of Scotland', in F. Merlan and D. Raftery (eds) *Tracking Rural Change: Community, Policy and Technology in Australia, New Zealand and Europe* (Canberra: ANU E-Press), 15–40.
Hadji, Nathalie 2003 'El syndrome del converse. Comentarios sobre el análisis de la situación ejidense de Mikel Azurmendi', *Biblio 3W. Revista bibilográfica de geografía y ciencias sociales*, VIII: 437 (30 March). www.ub.es/geocrit/b3w-437.htm. Accessed 9 November 2014.
Halfacree, Keith 2004 'Rethinking "Rurality"', in T. Champion and G. Hugo (eds) *New Forms of Urbanization. Beyond the Urban-Rural Dichotomy* (Aldershot: Ashgate), 285–304.
Hancox, Dan 2013 *The Village Against the World* (London: Verso).
Hanus, Philippe 2013 'Trajectoires migratoires dans l'économie forestière de montagne – Du XIXe siècle à nos jours', *Revue Hommes et Migrations*, 1301 (janvier-février-mars).
Hartman, Tod 2008 'States, markets, and other unexceptional communities: informal Romanian labour in a Spanish agricultural town', *Journal of the Royal Anthropological Institute*, 14:3 (September), 496–514.
Hawes, Annie 2005 *Journey to the South. A Calabrian Homecoming* (London: Penguin).
Heatherington, Tracey 2011 'Remaking rural landscapes in twenty-first century Europe', *Anthropological Journal of European Cultures*, 20:1, 1–9.
Hillyard, Sam 2007 *The Sociology of Rural Life* (Oxford: Berg).
Hoggart, K. 1990 'Let's do away with rural', *Journal of Rural Studies*, 6, 245–57.

Hurn, S. n.d. *Clan of the Fox? Hunting Sub-culture in a Rural Welsh Farming Community* (Leiden: Brill, forthcoming).

Ivancheva, Mariya 2007 'Strawberry fields forever? Bulgarian and Romanian student workers in the UK', *Focaal. European Journal of Anthropology*, 49, 110–17.

Jacobs, Michael 2003 *The Factory of Light. Tales from my Andalusian village* (London: John Murray).

James, Emma 2003 'Research on your own doorstep: Welsh rural communities and the perceived effects of in-migration', in C. A. Davies and S. Jones (eds) *Welsh Communities. New Ethnographic Perspectives* (Cardiff: University of Wales Press), 49–79.

Kasimis, Charalambos 2008 'Survival and expansion: migrants in Greek rural regions', *Population, Space, Place*, 14, 511–24.

Kavanagh, William 1994 *Villagers of the Sierra de Gredos. Transhumant Cattle-raisers of Central Spain* (Oxford: Berg).

Kington, Tom 2013 'The tiny Italian village that opened its doors to migrants who braved the sea', *The Observer* (13 October), 27.

Kohn, Tamara 2002 'Becoming an islander through action in the Scottish Hebrides', *Journal of the Royal Anthropological Institute*, 8:1 March, 143–58.

Labriandis, Lois and Sykas, Theodosis 2009 'Migrants, economic mobility and socio-economic change in rural areas: the case of Greece', *European Urban and Regional Studies* 16:3, 237–56.

Lawrence, Christopher M. 2007 *Blood and Oranges. European Markets and Immigrant Labour in Rural Greece* (Oxford: Berghahn).

MacClancy, Jeremy 2002 'Taking people seriously', in J. MacClancy (ed.) *Exotic no More. Anthropology on the Front Lines* (Chicago: University of Chicago Press), 1–14.

——2007 *Expressing Identities in the Basque Arena* (Oxford: James Currey).

MacClancy, Jeremy and Agustín Fuentes 2010 'Centralizing fieldwork', in J. MacClancy and A. Fuentes (eds) *Centralizing Fieldwork* (Oxford: Berghahn), 1–26.

Macdonald, Maryon 1989 *'We are not French!': Language, Culture and Identity in Brittany* (London: Routledge).

Macfarlane, Alan 1996 'Preface' in C. Salazar, *A Sentimental Economy. Commodity and Community in Rural Ireland* (Oxford: Berghahn), ix–xii.

Macleod, Donald V. L. 2004 *Tourism, Globalisation and Cultural Change. An Island Community Perspective* (Clevedon: Channel View).

Marren, Peter 2005 'Field of dreams', *The Independent*, 'Magazine' supplement, (11 July), 32–7.

Martínez Veiga, Ubaldo 2001 *El Ejido. Discriminación, exclusión social y racism* (Madrid: Catarata).

——2002 Review of *Estampas de El Ejido* by Mikel Azurmendi, *Espacio Crítico, AIBR*, 21 (June). http://www.aibr.org/antropologia/boant/criticos/JUN0201.html. Accessed 28 January 2009.

McCabe, Scott 2009 'The making of community identity through historic festive practice: the case of Ashbourne Royal Shrovetide Football', in D. Picard and M. Robinson (eds) *Festivals, Tourism and Social Change. Remaking Worlds* (Clevedon: Channel View), 99–118.

Mésini, Béatrice 2013 'Mobiles, flexibles et reversible – Les travailleurs saisonniers latino-américans détachés', *Revue Hommes et Migrations*, 1301 (janvier-février-mars).

Mitzman, Dany 2013 'Italy's fantastical farmers' sheds turned holiday homes', *BBC News, Magazine* (20 October). www.bbc.co.uk/news/magazine-24567192. Accessed 21 October 2013.

Monaghan, David 2004 *Jaywalking with the Irish* (Melbourne: Lonely Planet).

Perrotta, Domenico 2013 'Les ouvriers agricoles étrangers dans l'Italie méridionale – Entre "seclusion" et action collective', *Revue Hommes et Migrations*, 130 (janvier-février-mars).

Perry, Ronald, Ken Dean, and Bryan Brown 1986 *Counterurbanisation* (Norwich: Geo Books).

Pina Almeida, Jose Carlos and David Corkill 2010 'Uma vida melhor? Portuguese migrant workers in a rural community', *Immigrants and minorities*, 28:1, 70–85.

Potot, Swanie 2008 'Strategies of visibility and invisibility: Rumanians and Moroccans in El Ejido, Spain', in S. Jansen and S. Lofving (eds) *Struggles for Home: Violence, Hope and the Movement of People* (Oxford: Berghahn), 109–28.

Ray, Larry and Kate Reed 2005 'Community, mobility and racism in a semi-rural areas: comparing minority experience in East Kent', *Ethnic and Racial Studies*, 28:2, 212–34.

Robertson, Alexander 2012 *Mieres Reborn. The Reinvention of a Catalan Community* (Tuscaloosa, AL: University of Alabama Press).

Rodríguez, Campos Xaquín 2008 'Negotiating urban post-modern identities in Galicia: the recovery of rural dwellings', *International Journal of Iberian Studies* 21:2,151–70.

Rogers, Susan Carol 1991 *Shaping Modern Times in Rural France. The Transformation and Reproduction of an Averyronnais Community* (Princeton: Princeton University Press).

——2001 'Anthropology in France', *Annual Review of Anthropology 2001*, 30, 481–504.

Souchard, Nadine 2013 'Entre capitation et subjectivation – Les travailleurs migrant-e-s et travailleurs délocalisé-e-s dans les abattoirs bretons', *Revue Hommes et Migrations*, 1301 (janvier-février-mars).

Stewart, Chris 1999 *Driving over Lemons. An Optimist in Andalucía* (London: Sort of Books).

——2002 *A Parrot in the Pepper Tree* (London: Sort of Books).

——2006 *The Almond Blossom Appreciation Society* (London: Sort of Books).

——2014 *Last Days of the Bus Club* (London: Sort of Books).

Stacul, J., C. Moutsou and H. Kopnina (eds) 2006 *Crossing European boundaries. Beyond Conventional Geographical Categories* (Oxford: Berghahn).

Strathern, Marilyn 1981 *Kinship at the Core. An Anthropology of Elmdon, a Village in North-west Essex in the Nineteen-Sixties* (Cambridge: Cambridge University Press).

Suárez-Navaz, Liliana 2004 *Rebordering the Mediterranean. Boundaries and Citizenship in Southern Europe* (Oxford: Berghahn).

Tayler, Donald 1998 *A Village in Asturias* (Oxford: Pitt-Rivers Museum).

Urry, John 1995 'A middle-class countryside?', in T. Butler and M. Savage (eds) *Social Change and the Middle Classes* (London: UCL Press), 205–39.

Verinis, James P. 2011 'New immigrants and neo-rural values. The small non-Greek farmers of global Greek countrysides', *Anthropological Journal on European Cultures*, 20:1, 48–68.

Waldren, Jacqueline 1996 *Insiders and Outsiders. Paradise and Reality in Mallorca* (Oxford: Berghahn).

Webster, Jason 2004 *Andalus. Unlocking the secrets of Moorish Spain* (London: Doubleday).

——2009 *Sacred Sierra. A Year on a Spanish Mountain* (London: Chatto & Windus).

Welch-Devine, Meredith and Seth Murray 2011 '"We're European farmers now!": transitions and transformations in Basque agricultural practices', *Anthropological Journal of European Cultures*, 20:1, 69–88.

Williams, Guy St John 1998 *A Year in Connemara* (Monasterevan, Co. Kildare: Daletta Press).

Williams, Gwyn 2008 *Struggles for an Alternative Globalization. An Ethnography of Counterpower in Southern France* (Farnham: Ashgate).

Williams, Niall 1987 *O Come ye Back to Ireland. Our First Year in County Clare* (New York: Soho).

——1995 *The Luck of the Irish. Our Life in County Clare* (New York: Soho).

Williams, Raymond 1973 *The Country and the City* (London: Chatto and Windus).

Willis, Scott and Hugh Campbell 2004 'The chestnut economy: the praxis of neo-peasantry in rural France', *Sociologia Ruralis*, 44:3, July, 317–31.

Wilson, Thomas M. and Hastings Donnan 2006 *The Anthropology of Ireland* (Oxford: Berg).

Wright, Susan 1992 'Image and analysis: new directions in community studies', in B. Short (ed.) *The English Rural Community. Image and Analysis* (Cambridge: Cambridge University Press).

Zeneidi, Djemila 2013 'L'enferment à la champagne? – Les conditions de vie des saisonnières marocaines dans la province de Huelva (Espagne), *Revue Hommes et Migrations*, 1301 (janvier-février-mars).

A 'private place'? Changing meanings of the countryside in northern Italy

Jaro Stacul

Introduction

The relationship between official discourses and the ways they are understood at different levels of the national community is one of the most intriguing issues in the social sciences. The study of competing discourses about the countryside in late modernity provides an opportunity for casting light on such relationship, and this chapter sets out to explore how meanings attached to the Italian countryside are affected by changing political ideologies, most notably by the political transformations Italy underwent in the 1990s and after. The last few years have seen considerable changes in theoretical approaches to the study of the countryside. Until quite recently the Marxist approach dominated theoretical debates. Central to this approach is the idea that the countryside represents the context for political action: in other words, it is the site for ethno-nationalist conflict and the context within which subaltern people resist the power of the 'centre' (e.g. the State).[1] This idea is taken on board by Nairn (1997) in an essay on the relationship between rurality and nationalism. In challenging Gellner's view (1983) that one of the preconditions of nationalism is the emergence of an industrial society, Nairn's essay pursues the argument that most ethno-nationalist conflicts go on recurring in predominantly rural situations (1997: 90). Thus, for Nairn, 'Ethnic nationalism is in essence a peasantry transmuted, at least in ideal terms, into a nation' (1997: 91; see also Wolf 1969). In arguing for the significance of rurality for nationalism, he shows that the countryside may be the social context embodying the forces of contemporary nationalism.

Yet with the decreasing popularity of Marxism, as a theoretical paradigm, the study of 'rebellious peasants' too became less popular, and rural emigration to urban centres was (tacitly) taken as evidence that the countryside cannot be politically relevant. The emphasis, in the social sciences, on the aestheticisation of everyday life (see e.g. Featherstone 1992) resulted instead in the social scientists' shift of focus from the exploration of the politicisation of the countryside to the study of its consumption and aestheticisation. In this sense, the countryside was no longer regarded as the context for political action (i.e. the 'periphery' as opposed to the 'centre' of economic and political power) but as a communal and 'visual' resource that everyone feels entitled to enjoy, whose aesthetic appeal is expected to be universal (Milton 1997: 20–6). It was turned into a 'visual' resource; something tourists want to feel, taste, and make things with (Franklin 2003: 8–9).

The countryside has so far been regarded as *either* the context for political action *or* an object of consumption and aesthetic contemplation, but a third possibility, i.e. whether the countryside can be a combination of both, has barely been allowed for.[2] Despite the differences between these approaches, I do not think that they are incompatible: if anything, the countryside may be an object of contemplation just as it represents the context for political action broadly defined and for resistance to the political establishment. In the discourses of many political leaders, for example, the rural world is still referred to as tantamount to stability, i.e. 'the roots to which one returns in periods of crisis' (Pratt 2003: 190). Moreover, a countryside conceived as 'landscape'[3] involves 'a definite history of property relations in which both the physical reality and collective recollection of rural dispossession lends backbone to the aesthetic and philosophical sensibility of loss' (Abramson 2000: 5).

While the countryside has been an object of intellectual debate of different kinds (Marxist, postmodern, etc.), still little is known about the ways hegemonic meanings attached to the countryside are understood by those who live and work in the countryside itself. Talking about a 'countryside culture' at a time of rural depopulation, when people move with a speed and frequency that were unthinkable a few years ago, may seem naive. Yet the fact that the theoretical significance of the countryside seems to be shifting from a site of resistance to the political establishment to a place fit for the gaze of tourists does not mean that those who are active in the countryside itself necessarily share all the meanings attached to it from the outside, i.e. by politicians or intellectuals. If anything, 'country people' may be caught between different understandings. What meanings, then, are attached to the countryside 'from within' as a reaction (or partial accommodation) to those superimposed 'from without'?

The study of the Italian countryside raises these issues, for rural areas have been transformed under the combined onslaught of postmodernity, rural depopulation,[4] the privatisation of leisure provision and the emphasis placed upon tourist developments (Barberis 1999; Camanni 2002). Although in Italy the countryside has been part of the leisure experience for a long time, we cannot assume that in late modernity it is looked upon as an object of aesthetic contemplation only: it may still emerge as the context in which State power is contested, both at the level of discourse and at the level of political action. While until recently in Italy the country and the city were seen as the ends of a tradition-modernity continuum (Davis 1969; Silverman 1975; see also Barberis 2009: 4–7), various factors challenged this idea. Among such factors the growth of family-based industry in the pre-Alpine countryside of the north, particularly after the 1950s, is one of the most significant (Bull and Corner 1993). Yet what also challenged the aforementioned dichotomy were the transformations in the political arena Italy underwent in the 1990s: the economic crisis and the corruption scandals that led to the demise of the governing Christian Democratic Party brought about a situation of political instability. Such changes were accompanied by the gradual decline of the Italian State as the main framework controlling the national economy and containing its citizens in terms of 'culture' and values.

Perhaps the most significant development that had an impact on conceptualisations of the countryside at different levels of the national community was the advent, in the Italian political arena, of the regionalist political force known as the *Lega Nord* (Northern League). When it came to the fore it contested the idea of national identity and the legitimacy of a State seen as corrupt (Diamanti 1996; Giordano 2000). It presented itself as populist in that it purported to recreate a lost 'authenticity' and a traditional 'community'. However, it also promised to protect the interests of entrepreneurs, had in its agenda an Italian version of Thatcherism, and achieved considerable appeal in rural areas in the north of the country.[5]

The Northern League championed the transformation of Italy into a federal state and, for some time, even the territorial division of the North from the South of the country. Its leader, Umberto Bossi, constructed northern Italy as a 'nation' in its own right partaking of a 'European culture' because of northerners' supposed propensity to hard work, as opposed to a 'Mediterranean' one of a putative lazy and State-subsidised South (Cento Bull 1996: 177; Giordano 200: 458–64), which was pointed to as the main cause of Italy's economic crisis. According to the Northern League's spokespersons, the 'northern Italian culture' was not just threatened by immigration from southern Italy, but also by the influx of migrants from non-European countries (Giordano 2000: 460).

Although in Italy political regionalism was not a novel phenomenon (Romanelli 1991), the advent of the Northern League brought to the fore the issue of northern Italian identity, and gave it a political dimension by essentialising the idea of a 'northern Italian culture'.[6] What also fostered the Northern League's success was the use of a language that can be easily understood, that differentiated itself from the political jargon used by most politicians. Thus, by presenting itself as an opposition movement, the Northern League chose a language that sought to bring politics 'down to the level of common people', even at the risk of sounding vulgar (Ruzza and Schmidtke 1996: 65). In the party's rhetoric, the northern countryside was constructed as the repository of the values (particularly a hard work ethic) that were believed to be lacking in the geographical and symbolic 'centre' of the Italian State. Thus, community and everyday culture and values became a banner to fly proudly as opposed to the 'civilisation' symbolised by the Italian nation state (Destro 1997: 371).

An Alpine valley

The Vanoi valley, an Alpine community in the Trentino region of northern Italy, is the context within which the political transformations just discussed had the effect of questioning some of the meanings attached to the countryside from the centres of political and economic power. The valley is located at the eastern edge of Trentino, and borders the Veneto region. It forms both an ecological and an administrative unit in that its ecological boundaries roughly coincide with the administrative ones, its territory falling within the limits of the municipality of Canal San Bovo.[7]

Until the 1960s its inhabitants lived by a combination of agriculture, forestry, and animal husbandry, but the population of the valley started dwindling with the demise of the agro-pastoral economy. Although over 4,000 people lived in the area in the 1940s, nowadays the valley has a population of scarcely 1,700 inhabitants and most of the locals who live there are foresters (mainly men), people who engage in various kinds of manual trades, and retired agriculturalists (predominantly women). However, despite the decline of agro-pastoralism, most of the locals still call themselves 'peasants' (*contadini*). While until a few years ago the valley was very difficult to access despite the economic significance of forestry and timber trade with the nearby Veneto region, nowadays, notwithstanding the improvement of roads, the valley is economically 'marginal'. Yet the rate of population decline is much slower than it was in the aftermath of the Second World War, and the valley is witnessing a period of some revitalisation, especially among younger families committed to preserving the social and cultural fabric of the local communities.

Given the limited availability of jobs in the valley, most of the able-bodied have an occupation elsewhere, and commute to other places on a weekly basis. Nowadays the 'human landscape' of the area includes locals who were born in the valley and have spent most of their lives there, and retirees from the nearby regions who acquired land and houses in the valley very cheaply, particularly between the 1960s and the 1980s. According to a survey conducted by the local credit institution in the mid-1990s, over 50 per cent of the houses in the valley were owned by people who do not have kinship ties in the area or reside there. At present the valley is dependent on outside capital and subsidies from the EU and especially from the regional council, which have undertaken various development projects in the area.

It is tempting to suggest that the valley is going through a transition from 'modernity' to 'postmodernity': phrased differently, while the term 'production' describes the productive role of the area (especially as regards forestry) in the 'old days', the decline of forestry[8] resulted in the valley's being turned into a commodity to be aestheticised. As Urry (1990: 98) has argued in this regard, 'To the extent to which contemporary appropriations of the countryside involve treating it as spectacle ... this can be seen as a postmodern attitude to the countryside, to be contrasted with an approach which emphasises its "use"'.

'Natural' or political landscape?

Concern over the countryside stems from the demise of agro-pastoral activities and from the subsequent disintegration of community life: agriculture is practised by very few (mainly in the form of horticulture), only a limited number of tiny patches are under cultivation, and the forested area is encroaching on the villages. Yet this concern was also the consequence of the alienation of a sizeable amount of land to the regional council on the one hand, and to retirees who spend the summer in the area on the other. However, it must also be stressed that such concerns also stemmed from the expansion and consolidation of the State's direct control over the valley and its resources through the implementation of protected areas (Stacul 2010: 232).

Thus, the decline of village life enhanced the advent of the Northern League (in the valley and elsewhere) that promised the reconstruction of the local community through its appeal to regional and local identity. Against the background of the decline of the nation state and the disintegration of community life, the Northern League's appeal to locality as a focus of identification was seen as a response to the changing political (and social) situation of the present, as it could meet the need for communal belonging that neither a putative anonymous and distant State, nor even the disappearing rural community, was believed to provide.[9]

The appeal that the party achieved had repercussions in the local political sphere: at a time of local elections, for example, the preservation of local identity and the necessity of preventing the land from being alienated to outsiders were high on the agenda of those running for election to the municipal council. One of the key points of the outgoing mayor during the 1995 mayoral campaign was that, in the event of re-election, he would endeavour to prevent the land's alienation to people who neither reside in the valley nor have kinship ties there. In making such promises he championed a political programme focused on the protection of locality and heralded a 'community' of the old days. Although he was not affiliated to any political force at that time, his messages drew upon those deployed by the Northern League, most notably upon the idea that people and things should stay in their own place of origin.

The emphasis placed by local politicians upon territorial identity mirrored some of the themes central to the propaganda of the Northern League, and had considerable impact on the inhabitants of the valley: a woman in her early seventies, for example, once told me that one of the advantages of living in a mountain village is that there are no foreign (i.e. non-European) immigrants around. Yet apart from a few people who shared this view, and despite the Northern League's crusade against immigration from non-European countries, most of the locals with whom I have conversed did not seem to worry too much about the few northern African ambulant traders who occasionally come to the area to sell their merchandise. Rather, they often expressed anxiety at the possibility that people from nearby villages or from other Italian regions could settle in the valley and acquire landed property there. In all likelihood this anxiety stemmed from the fact that while no African ambulant trader owns landed property in the area, several people from the nearby Italian regions do. While the Northern League used its rhetoric to champion the integrity of northern Italy vis-à-vis the south, or to oppose immigration from non-European countries, at the local level this rhetoric was effective for a different reason: it was seen as a response to one of the main concerns of the local people – the integrity and ideal autonomy of the community – for it was believed to address the issue of the protection of local boundaries from outsiders, irrespective of where they come from.

The integrity and ideal autonomy of the community became an issue of heated debate in the early 1990s, when the provincial park, the Parco Naturale Paneveggio-Pale di San Martino, established in 1967, gained jurisdiction over a substantial part of the forested area in the upper Vanoi valley. The consolidation of the park was part of an attempt, on the part of the provincial council of Trentino, to implement the 1992 EU Habitats Directive and subsequently designate the area as a Special Area of Conservation.[10] The rationale for choosing the Vanoi valley instead of another Alpine valley in Trentino is simple: first, 50.7 per cent of the territory is forested, and this area is distinctive for its biodiversity and for the white fir, a tree species that is disappearing throughout the Alpine region; second, the valley never became a ski resort; and third, the area does not boast 'authentic' foodstuffs or cultural traditions that can attract mass tourism.[11] As a result, the 'natural' beauty of the local landscape is the main resource that tourists can consume (Stacul 2010: 231).[12] Among the projects on the park's agenda was the creation of an open-air museum on land formerly farmed. While the museum was designed to attract visitors to the valley, its creation also involved turning a territory formerly accessed by locals only into an object of enjoyment or into a resort to be visually consumed by visitors. The consolidation of the regional park, then, resulted in local people's exposure to a different way of understanding and relating to landscape that reflects 'urban' views, i.e. as an intangible resource defined by its appearance. In other words, locals had to come to terms with a vision of the countryside as part of the leisure experience, something to be 'communally owned' as a source of enjoyment (Macnaghten and Urry 1998: 201).

Although the consolidation of the park was meant to revitalise the area and involve the people of the valley in the development projects that concern them, in fact its expansion was interpreted by many as an attempt, on the part of the provincial council, to impose legal restrictions on areas where in the past state and provincial legislation had limited restraining power on the everyday practices of local farmers (Stacul 2010: 232). Thus, the uproar caused by the consolidation of the park mobilised cultural oppositions between work and leisure, which are expressed by contrasting ways of conceiving the countryside as either 'land' or 'landscape' (Milton 1997: 17). What the debate threw into relief was also a concern over who had knowledge of the territory: the people who live on the land or an outside agency.

Although the idea of 'landscape' became an object of debate as a consequence of the shrinking of cultivated land, it also functions as a repository of group identity (Darby 2000: 283): it is an integral part of the political history of the valley, as the valley lies next to the regional border between Trentino and Veneto, which was the border between the Austro-Hungarian empire and Italy until 1918. Even nowadays many inhabitants of the valley describe the act of crossing the regional border as 'going to Italy'. At the end of the First World War, the valley (and especially the village of Caoria) became the heart of a monumental landscape connected with the arrival of the Italian army and the valley's annexation to Italy. The official, monumental time of the Italian nation state which is inscribed onto the physical landscape is expressed by the presence of monuments commemorating the Italian victory in the First World War (Cuaz 2005: 87–96). In this sense, the representation (and conceptualisation) of landscape is deeply embedded in relations of power and knowledge (Darby 2000: 9): while at that time the Italian nation state used to act as the dominant framework in the management of the historic landscape, nowadays its marks are hardly considered part of the 'local' landscape, or are looked upon as mere 'additions' to what is referred to as 'local'. Taking a hint from Herzfeld (1992), it is tempting to suggest that such monuments are 'indifferent' to the people of the valley just as the valley is 'indifferent' to the Italian nation state.

While the 'purity' of the physical and social landscape was the focus of the locals' complaints in the face of a declining community, the 'purity' of nature was instead the focus of the park and of the outsiders looking for a place they see as part of the leisure experience. The tourists and retirees I met in the valley made it clear that they wanted accessibility to places that they consider far from signs of 'modernity', that is to say woodland, meadowland or 'traditional' farms high on the mountainside. Yet their interest in the putative untamed nature of the Alps did not mean involvement in any form of environmental concern and responsibility. Rather, it entailed looking upon the countryside as an open space to which everybody has access simply because it is far from the constraints of urban life. It consists of a public space that many of these believe they have the right to enjoy; namely, a space embodied in practices that do not include work but walking, picking mushrooms and berries, fishing, etc. Even for those who were born and raised in the area, the valley is embedded in a set of social practices, and in the remainder of this chapter I will discuss how some of these practices affect past and present understandings of the countryside itself.

In the villages of Caoria and Ronco, locals evoke the social practices of the 'old days' when they complain about the fact that the place is no longer the same as it used to be, both in terms of physical appearance and in terms of social fabric. What characterises the countryside these days, one woman said, is decay (*degrado*). Locals relate this to depopulation on the one hand, and to the forest's encroaching on the inhabited area on the other. Pictures of the villages of the past seem to substantiate this view, and one cannot help noticing a stark difference between the communities of the 'old days', surrounded by terraced fields high on the mountainside, and those of the present surrounded by a huge forested area (Figures 2.1 and 2.2).

While for most outsiders who own a weekend house in the valley the huge forested area is beautiful, for locals it looks horrible. As two women said: 'E tutto selvatico qui adesso' ('Now it is all wild here') or 'It used to be cleared, open, now it is like a jail' (Noemi, b. 1926). The dividing line between the village and the forest, between the domesticated and the wild, has become blurred: 'There were not the

Figure 2.1 The 'cultural landscape' of the village of Caoria and its surroundings in the 1930s.

Figure 2.2 Caoria in 1992: the forest is encroaching on the village.

trees you see now. There used to be a footpath along which you could walk' (Virginia, 1910–2002). '(In the old days) there were fields in these villages. Everybody used to have goats, sheep, hens, rabbits, hogs ... we used to grow potatoes, beans, onions, wheat, barley ... then the forest started encroaching [on the village], and now nothing can be grown' (Assunta, b. 1931). If I were to take these statements at face value, there would be grounds for suggesting that the people's failure to cultivate their land broke the ecological balance established by the domestication of nature. Nowadays the natural landscape's going wild is associated with the community's (and valley's) 'moral fall': 'When the landscape becomes wild, humans too become wild and antisocial' (Daniele, b. 1930).

Most villagers vividly remember that in the 'old days' everybody used to have a very good knowledge of the natural environment that surrounded their village. It was 'their' place that they materially and symbolically cultivated until recently. Locals associate the cultivation of the place they live in with control over the environment in the sense that in cultivating land they were also the 'owners', and the 'wild' (and also outsiders) was kept at bay. The presence, in the past, of terraced garden patches, and the place names that distinguish each field and house suggested the existence of a 'cultural landscape' (Netting 1981: 3) used and modelled for generations by a resident human population. Likewise, footpaths are still believed to create a relationship between humans and the natural environment, and symbolise humans' appropriation of landscape: the more people have walked there, the greater the significance attached to this relationship. In this sense, what matters to locals is also to preserve a specific visual experience of the territory. In emphasising this, they focus on an immediate perception of the landscape as a reliable form of knowledge of the territory, which refers to personal experience of living on the land. This, in turn, defines a group of people who know the territory as an immediate object of experience.

According to the locals with whom I have conversed, the expansion of the regional park was the main cause of environmental decay. As a man, now deceased, said: 'When the park was established the forest started advancing' ('Arriva il parco e il bosco avanza'). According to him and to others I met, locals cannot now clear the land, fell trees and shoot game because of the restrictive laws imposed from outside agencies. That the landscape is no longer as 'clean' and 'tidy' as it used to be is interpreted as the result of the arrival of outsiders in the area.

In blaming the park and people who do not belong to the local community, locals draw a dichotomy between a shadowy and unspecified era of the past – when the State had limited power on local everyday practices – and the present when the management of the forested area is beyond local control. In other words, in the past people were 'autonomous' and could make their own rules by relying on their own means and through hard work, whereas in the present they can no longer do so, and have to abide by laws imposed by outside agencies; namely, the State, the provincial council, and the provincial park. Small wonder, then, that villagers contest the portrait of the valley, presented in the past by locally published tourist brochures, as

Figure 2.3 The material and symbolic cultivation of landscape: haymaking in Caoria in 1992.

'natural' and 'untamed' on the grounds that it is an image meant for the urban taste for 'wild' nature. In local discourse, by contrast, what looks 'untamed' and 'wild' is thought of as the consequence of the fact that few people fell trees, and even fewer cultivate the land (Figure 2.3).

In evoking a landscape of the old days, locals contest both a notion of landscape advocated by outsiders and by the park, and a vision of the countryside as an object of aesthetic contemplation, that is to say notions that cast the countryside itself not as workplace, but as part of the leisure experience. What is questioned, then, is the idea that a landscape gone wild is an object of aesthetic contemplation on the grounds that it is instead the outcome of environmental decay. As has been seen, the landscape evoked by locals is essentially a workplace, and the making of the landscape (in the form of cultivation or weed and scrub clearance) is described as a constant struggle (for a comparison with a Greek island, see Theodossopoulos 2003: 49). A landscape can be visually consumed if it is cultivated, that is to say, if it is worked. The object of contestation is not so much visual consumption, as the idea of beauty of a space open to everybody on the grounds that an open space cannot be cultivated, and so it is likely to become wild. Thus, beauty is conditional on economic viability. This view associates a visual landscape with a landscape managed by locals who were born and raised in the local community.

Very similar views inform the ways social actors talk about hunting, another practice in which the countryside is embodied. Formerly a subsistence activity, hunting is now a pastime which reveals much about the ways locals relate to the countryside.[13] It is significant because, unlike agriculture, it involves movement through an open space, and it seems antithetical to the cultivation of a 'closed space'. Yet hunting is also connected with humans' relations with nature and its appropriation. Interestingly, although local hunters have the right to shoot wildlife throughout the valley irrespective of where they live, in fact each hunter does so in an area that he knows very well. This area is usually handed down from father to son, even though this symbolic alienation does not entail legal rights to it, but simply social appropriation.

Because of the significance of such practices, hunting land is described as individual property, and is like a bounded field to which ideally only locals have access: 'The hunter is like a cultivator of animals, as it were, whereas the farmer grows plants, since he knows well his territory … If hunting is done properly, he may be able to increase the number of animals even though he kills them' (Raffaele, b. 1962). 'If you want to grow something, you have to cultivate it … so you watch if a roe-deer remains in the same area or moves in search of females … and from time to time you give him a piece of salt … You have to know your territory' (Federico, b. 1963). Hunting, then, 'produces' locality as it creates the boundaries within which hunters 'cultivate' their animals. It involves mastery of nature just as it establishes a relationship of sharing. Like the 'cultivator', who looks after his fields and crops, the hunter pursues his prey when the time is ripe, that is to say when the animals he intends to pursue have already reproduced themselves, so the life cycle goes on uninterrupted. Wildlife, from the above persons' standpoint, has to be 'cultivated' just like fields. The idea of 'cultivator' not only projects positive traits on those who materially and symbolically 'cultivate' the land, but also legitimates their actions. Implicit in this is the view that who 'knows' territory also 'owns' it: through its symbolic 'cultivation', territory is turned into 'private' or 'individual' property. By stating that who 'cultivates' the land has an implicit right to 'harvest', locals also define a 'moral order'. As Nando (b. 1918) said: 'Many people say that the hunter destroys. This is not true. The hunter protects too.'

The hunters I have interviewed described hunting as a traditional, local practice that underwent changes because of the actual enforcement of national and regional laws. In the old days all hunters used to have their own territory which they symbolically cultivated, however, now they have to abide by laws imposed from outside agencies. In the past they could control their own territory, now they have to move through areas they do not know well. Central to this view is the idea that those who control the land also keep it clean and tidy, whereas those who do not possess it (for example, outsiders, and tourists) cannot be interested in keeping it clear, simply because it does not 'belong' to them. In stating that, locals also evoke the image of a territory that was under local control and was eventually alienated to outside agencies (in terms of ownership or jurisdiction) that made it open to everybody.

It seems arguable, then, that in local discourses there are many parallels between cultivation and hunting: they both entail 'cultivation' (material and symbolic) of the territory and, implicitly, serve to assert possession and control by locals. Yet the idea of cultivation of the territory also casts light on the ways the countryside is conceptualised, because both agriculture and hunting map a bounded domain to which outsiders should not have access. By making use of an environmentalist idiom (epitomised by the idea of 'protection'), locals also avail themselves of the principle that keeping a place clean is a sign of civilisation, and that those who show disrespect by littering it are to be considered uncivilised or the 'other'. Such ideas reflect the opposition between a clean property managed by locals, and one controlled by outside agencies, to which everybody has access.

The difference between a 'cultivated' private property and a 'wild' public one is predicated both on visual experience and on ways of interacting with territory. This difference brings to mind the view, upheld by some theorists (e.g. Bender 1993; Hirsch 1995; Ingold 1995), that landscapes are constructed by people interacting with spatial areas. Ingold (1995), in particular, in developing his 'dwelling' perspective, has argued that landscape has to be understood as the world as *known* to those who have dwelt there, who do dwell there, who will dwell there: it is a place of memory and temporality. The interpenetration of past, present, and future centres on practices which produce the social character of any such landscape: these persist 'as long as people are actually engaged in the activities of dwelling' within that particular landscape (Ingold 1993: 161; see also Theodossopoulos 2003: 167). Yet dwelling in a physical space is not simply a matter of interacting with it: rather, as we have seen, it is also involved with the ways political identities are inscribed onto landscape itself, and with the ways political ideologies are accommodated to local-level discourses. The idea of a 'public space', to which the people of the valley became exposed, had to coexist with the significance attached to 'private property' as a result of the privatisation initiatives taking place all over the country and of the emphasis placed upon it by the Northern League.

Conclusion

Although in the 1990s the protection of locality against State agencies was at the forefront of locals' concerns, in the years that followed the people of the valley ended up accepting both the park and its environmentalist directive. There is little doubt that the decline, at the local level, of the Northern League's appeal played an important role in altering people's views. Yet what also played a crucial part in this change was depopulation, the passing of many elderly, formerly regarded as the repositories of 'local knowledge', who had strongly opposed the consolidation of the park, and young people's limited interest in their landholdings on the mountainside. In this sense, the account I have presented analyses a situation common to many post-peasant communities in Europe and throughout the world: it brings to mind a situation where a community of farmers is dispossessed by ruthless capitalist aggressors and evokes a better community of the old days when it is on the wane. This situation seems to highlight the dichotomy between peasant (or post-peasant) and urban values, and those between 'modernity' and 'postmodernity', and 'production' and 'consumption'. Yet if we were to take such dichotomies at face value we would have to infer that what is evoked is the countryside as a 'collective' space, as a resource that locals, as a collectivity, can use. The renewed stress upon the countryside as something 'made' by the people who own it conveys instead ideas of ownership, of exclusive rights. The idiom of cultivation of territory, which informs local discourses, does not mirror ideas of collective ownership, but evokes instead images of individual or family property.

What emerges, then, is a view of the countryside as an exclusive domain. It is exclusive because it is treated as property; and property, by its very nature, comes into being with the exclusion of others (Abramson 2000: 13). What local-level discourses about the countryside reveal is a conceptualisation of the territory built upon the dichotomy between public and private. What is perceived to be under threat is not a collectively owned resource, but individual property – a mosaic of privately owned lots ideally inaccessible to outsiders (including the Italian State). Nowadays the dichotomy between different ways of constructing landscape emerges as a political issue, as a result of the symbolic confrontation between the local community and the Italian State. The struggle over landscape, then, is caught in the symbolism of power relations: it was not so much environmentalism that was frowned upon, as the fact that conformity to an environmentalist directive entails the acceptance of rules imposed from people who do not belong to the local community. In other words, the main issue was not environmentalism per se, but *who* has the right to talk about it. On the one hand this debate reflected the dichotomy between an understanding of place as 'landscape' (i.e. an object of aesthetic contemplation) which all have the right to enjoy, and the idea of the countryside as 'land', that is to say private property and place of work (Milton 1997: 21). On the other hand, the debate revealed that an understanding of place as 'landscape' did not clash with the idea of private property: rather, these merge seamlessly and are intertwined in a transformative process. What at the local level is alluded to as 'landscape' is private property. Thus, landscape's being an object of aesthetic contemplation is conditional on its being worked and owned privately.

There is little doubt that this conceptualisation of the countryside reflects the significance that property has, in rural society, in shaping social relations. Yet it emerged as a political issue at a time of economic and social transformations, when privatisation initiatives took place all over the country, and when political forces with an Italian version of Thatcherism on their agenda achieved considerable appeal. While this conceptualisation embodies the values of a rural society, it also reconciles such values with those of Thatcherism, and does not necessarily stand in conceptual opposition to them. The emergence of a notion of the Alpine landscape as a 'private place' brings us back to the question asked at the outset, namely, what meanings are attached to the countryside 'from within' as a reaction to those superimposed 'from without'. While a rural society appeals to its values and produces this counter-discourse to come to terms with a rapidly changing world, it also draws selectively upon the values of the encompassing society. It draws upon the 'modern' concept of 'production' (i.e. the idea of a countryside 'made' by those who are active in it) to challenge a vision of their place as a 'postmodern' object of 'consumption' at the same time that it appropriates the idea of 'privatisation' for its own requirements.

In sum, what unites these conceptualisations is a vision of the social world and of a political landscape that casts the State as the 'outsider' and projects the values of a putative 'individualised' society onto the local social landscape. Thus, there is no automatic contradiction between an approach which examines the countryside as a context for political action and one which stresses its aestheticisation. If anything, it is the symbolic confrontation between different ways of defining the Alpine countryside as an object of aesthetic contemplation that forms the background against which the State is contested. It seems arguable, then, that local-level views about the countryside are the product of a transformative process and that they draw selectively upon different ideas, of which a vision of the countryside as 'privatised' is probably the most powerful.

Acknowledgements

This chapter is a revised and expanded version of a paper delivered at the conference 'Alternative Countrysides' held at Oxford Brookes, and is the result of research conducted in the Italian Alps in several spells between 1995 and 2007. I would like to thank the University of Trieste, the European Commission, the British Academy and the Accademia Nazionale dei Lincei for funding my research, and Renée Hirschon, Jeremy MacClancy, Dimitrios Theodossopoulos, Jackie Waldren, and two anonymous readers for their comments and constructive criticism on earlier versions of this work. Finally, my thanks are due to the Ente Parco Naturale Paneveggio – Pale di San Martino for allowing me to use photographic reproductions of its collection materials (Figure 2.1).

Notes

1 The literature on the countryside as a site of resistance is vast. See particularly Scott (1985) and Reed-Danahay (1993).

2 The last few years have seen an increasing interest in anthropology, and in the ways local communities resist attempts to turn rural areas into natural parks or 'heritage'. See, for example, Heatherington (2010).
3 See, for an examination of the concept of 'landscape', Hirsch (1995) and Stewart and Strathern (2003).
4 The 2001 census revealed that only 5.5 per cent of the employed Italian population engaged in agricultural activities (Merlo 2009: 87).
5 The Northern League's popularity has been failing as a result of a series of corruption scandals, and the party suffered humiliating defeats in local and European elections held between 2012 and 2014.
6 Despite the radical-right overtones of its political propaganda, the Northern League also succeeded in capturing the vote of former supporters of left-wing parties (for details see Cento Bull 2000: 18).
7 The territory of the municipality, whose shape is roughly that of an elongated oval, extends approximately 13 km from north to south and roughly 6 km from east to west. It has a total land area of 125.54 km^2, and numbers seven villages: Canal San Bovo (the municipal seat), Caoria, Cicona, Gobbera, Prade, Ronco, and Zortea. Only the two ends of the valley are inhabited; its central part, by contrast, is steep and narrow, uninhabitable, and too rocky even for pasturage. Both slopes rise sharply from the valley floor and differ greatly from each other in most respects. Because of its unfavourable orientation it is uninhabitable and covered with forest for the most part, and almost all the settlements lie on the eastern side. Mountains range in elevation from 2,000 to 2,500 m, and the average altitude of the valley floor is about 700 m.
8 The local sawmill was shut down in late 2002.
9 The Northern League created this community of values and meanings defined by regional 'ethnic' criteria. A curious aspect of northern 'ethnic' identity was that it was not defined by language, but by territory. The Northern League differentiated itself from most of the separatist movements of other parts of Europe, which stress language as a marker of differentiation, because it did not make use of language as a basis for the mobilisation of 'northern Italian consciousness'; more importantly, it succeeded in creating a myth of northern Italian identity even though being northern Italian had never been an issue before.
10 The municipal territory of Canal San Bovo is part of *Natura 2000*, a Europe-wide network of nature protected areas established in 1992.
11 See, for a discussion of this issue, Camanni (2002: 81–3).
12 It is not purely coincidence that in the early 1990s the valley was designated as the 'Trentino's green heart' (*Il cuore verde del Trentino*).
13 For details see Stacul (2003: 70–89).

References

Abramson, Allen 2000 'Mythical land, legal boundaries: wondering about landscape and other tracts', in A. Abramson and D. Theodossopoulos (eds) *Land, Law and Environment: Mythical Land, Legal Boundaries* (London: Pluto Press), 1–30.

Barberis, Corrado 1999 *Le campagne italiane dall'ottocento a oggi* (Bari: Laterza).

——2009 'Il mondo rurale dalla povertà al benessere', in C. Barberis (ed.) *La rivincita delle campagne: economie e culture del mondo rurale dalla povertà al benessere* (Rome: Donzelli), 3–28.

Bender, Barbara 1993 'Introduction: Landscape – meaning and action', in B. Bender (ed.) *Landscape: Politics and Perspectives* (Oxford: Berg), 1–17.

Bull, Anna and Corner, Philip 1993 *From Peasant to Entrepreneur: The Survival of Family Economy in Italy* (Oxford: Berg).

Camanni, Enrico 2002 *La nuova vita delle Alpi* (Turin: Bollati Boringhieri).

Cento Bull, Anna 1996 'Ethnicity, racism and the Northern League' in C. Levy (ed.) *Italian Regionalism: History, Identity and Politics* (Oxford: Berg), 171–88.

——2000 *Social Identities and Political Cultures in Italy: Catholic, Communist and Leghist Communities between Civicness and Localism* (Oxford: Berghahn).

Cuaz, Marco 2005 *Le Alpi* (Bologna: Il Mulino).

Darby, Wendy J. 2000 *Landscape and Identity: Geographies of Nation and Class in England* (Oxford: Berg).

Davis, John 1969 'Town and country', *Anthropological Quarterly*, 42, 171–85.

Destro, Adriana 1997 'A new era and new themes in Italian politics: the case of Padania', *Journal of Modern Italian Studies*, 2, 358–77.

Diamanti, Ilvo 1996 *Il male del nord: lega, localismo, secessione* (Rome: Donzelli).

Featherstone, Mike 1992 'Postmodernism and the aestheticisation of everyday life', in S. Lash and J. Friedman (eds) *Modernity and Identity* (Oxford: Blackwell), 265–90.

Franklin, Adrian 2003 *Tourism: An Introduction* (London: Sage).

Gellner, Ernest 1983 *Nations and Nationalism* (Oxford: Blackwell).

Giordano, Benito 2000 'Italian regionalism or "Padanian" nationalism: the political project of the *Lega Nord* in Italian politics', *Political Geography*, 19, 445–71.

Heatherington, Tracey 2010 *Wild Sardinia: Indigeneity and the Global Dreamtimes of Environmentalism* (Seattle: University of Washington Press).

Herzfeld, Michael 1992 *The Social Production of Indifference: Exploring the Symbolic Roots of Western Bureaucracy* (Chicago: University of Chicago Press).

Hirsch, Eric 1995 'Introduction. Landscape: between place and space', in E. Hirsch and M. O'Hanlon (eds) *The Anthropology of Landscape: Perspectives on Place and Space* (Oxford: Oxford University Press), 1–30.

Ingold, Tim 1993 'The temporality of the landscape'. *World Archaeology*, 25, 152–74.

——1995 'Building, dwelling, living: how animals and people make themselves at home in the world', in M. Strathern (ed.) *Shifting Contexts: Transformations in Anthropological Knowledge* (London: Routledge), 57–80.

Macnaghten, Phil and John Urry 1998 *Contested Natures* (London: Sage).

Merlo, Valerio 2009 'Un mercato del lavoro non più subalterno', in Corrado Barberis (ed.) *La rivincita delle campagne: economie e culture del mondo rurale dalla povertà al benessere* (Rome: Donzelli), 83–108.

Milton, Kay 1997 'Modernity and postmodernity in the Northern Irish countryside', in H. Donnan and G. McFarlane (eds) *Culture and Policy in Northern Ireland: Anthropology in the Public Arena* (Belfast: Institute of Irish Studies), 17–35.

Nairn, Tom 1997 *Faces of Nationalism: Janus Revisited* (London: Verso).

Netting, Robert 1981 *Balancing on an Alp: Ecological Change and Continuity in a Swiss Mountain Community* (Cambridge: Cambridge University Press).

Pratt, Jeff 2003 *Class, Nation and Identity: The Anthropology of Political Movements* (London: Pluto Press).

Reed-Danahay, Deborah 1993 'Talking about resistance: ethnography and theory in rural France', *Anthropological Quarterly*, 66, 221–9.

Romanelli, Raffaele 1991 'Le radici storiche del localismo italiano', *Il Mulino*, 40, 711–20.

Ruzza, Carlo and Oliver Schmidtke 1996 'The Northern League: changing friends and foes, and its political opportunity structure', in D. Cesarani and M. Fulbrook (eds) *Citizenship, Nationality and Migration in Europe* (London: Routledge), 179–208.

Scott, James 1985 *Weapons of the Weak: Everyday Forms of Peasant Resistance* (New Haven, CT: Yale University Press).

Silverman, Sydel 1975 *Three Bells of Civilization: The Life of an Italian Hill Town* (New York: Columbia University Press).

Stacul, Jaro 2003 *The Bounded Field: Localism and Local Identity in an Italian Alpine Valley* (Oxford: Berghahn).

——2010 'Contesting consumption: Changing meanings of landscape in northern Italy', in P. Stewart and A. Strathern (eds) *Landscape, Heritage, and Conservation: Farming Issues in the European Union* (Durham, NC: Carolina Academic Press), 225–41.

Stewart, Pamela and Andrew Strathern 2003 'Introduction', in Pamela Stewart and Andrew Strathern (eds) *Landscape, Memory and History: Anthropological Perspectives* (London: Pluto Press), 1–15.

Theodossopoulos, Dimitrios 2003 *Troubles With Turtles: Cultural Understandings of the Environment on a Greek island* (Oxford: Berghahn).

Urry, John 1990 *The Tourist Gaze: Leisure and Travel in Contemporary Societies* (London: Sage).

Wolf, Eric 1969 *Peasant Wars of the Twentieth Century* (London: Faber & Faber).

3

Environmental attitudes, community development, and local politics in Ireland

Paul Collinson

Anyone who has ever visited Ireland will be immediately struck by the natural beauty of the country. From the rugged uplands of the west, the golden beaches of Cork and Kerry, the rolling drumlins of the midlands to the sea cliffs of the north, Ireland is undoubtedly blessed with one of the richest and most diverse environmental endowments in Europe. Attracted by tourist brochures and advertisements which play heavily on images of Ireland as a rural paradise, tourists flock to the country each summer in their hundreds of thousands, hoping to discover the pristine, unspoiled countryside promised by the government's marketing campaigns.

However, the gap between image and reality in Ireland is growing ever wider. Much has been written about the deleterious effects the unprecedented economic growth of the 1990s and 2000s had on Ireland's environment (e.g. Meldon 1992; Dillon 1996; Deegan and Dineen 1997; Wickham and Lohan 2000; McDonagh 2007), and those who visit the country today to actively seek out what is promised in the tourist brochures may well return home disappointed – even though the famed 'Celtic Tiger' is, at the time of writing, dormant, and possibly extinct. The political rise of the Irish Green Party, which was in government since 2006 in coalition with Ireland's most dominant political party in the post-independence era, Fianna Fáil, and the party's subsequent spectacular fall (losing all its members of parliament in the 2011 election)[1] exemplifies the ambiguous and complex attitude which the Irish population have towards their environment.

The economic crisis of recent years has thrown into stark relief the impact on the environment of one of the most visible spin-offs of Ireland's erstwhile prosperity: the housing boom. In many areas of the country, a new phenomenon of the 'ghost' housing estate has emerged, characterised by row upon row of unsold new homes in which no one lives, often located in areas of the country where no one apparently wants to live either. One estimate calculated that Ireland's excess housing stock amounted to 136,000 homes in 2009 (DKM 2009), a quite staggering figure in a country with a total population of only around 4.5 million. Some have proposed that these estates should be bought by the government from developers and bulldozed back into agricultural land (*Irish Examiner* 2010).

In this chapter, I wish to explore some of these themes through an examination of development activity in County Donegal, Ireland's most northerly county. It is based largely on anthropological fieldwork conducted in the late 1990s (Collinson 1999), along with data collected during visits made to Ireland since then. My contention is that the historical neglect of environmental concerns in the overall development agenda in Ireland has above all a social basis, in the sense that it is manifested in the divisions which exist between community and environmental development groups – as well as with local councils – at local levels.

I begin with a survey of Irish attitudes to the environment, together with a consideration of how community and environmental development approaches are distinguished in the country. The research material that follows has been chosen to draw out some of the contrasts between those involved in each type of group by focusing on the social nexus in which each operates, and by comparing the different attitudes each holds towards the environment and environmental development in general.[2]

Irish attitudes to the environment

Attitude surveys have consistently demonstrated that the Irish population have, historically, a somewhat ambivalent approach to the environment. This is reflected in the number of people involved in environmental development groups. Motherway, Kelly, Faughnan, and Tovey's survey of environmental attitudes and behaviour among the population conducted in the early 2000s found that formal membership of environmental groups was low, at 3 per cent of the sample, with most people's engagement with environmental concerns largely confined to recycling (which had increased significantly over the previous ten years) and the periodic signing of petitions (Motherway *et al.* 2003: 46). The survey also found that concerns over the environment (and a willingness to pay for its protection) were strongly related to the wealth of a household (Motherway *et al.* 2003: 28). A similar survey by Kelly (2004) found the rate of membership of environmental groups in Ireland is among the lowest of European countries. Also, the Irish government itself was late to recognise the importance of environmental sustainability, in part through an incorporation of EU regulations and programmes focused on the environment (Coyle 1994; Tovey, Share, and Corcoran 2007).

These observations provide a partial explanation for the discernible dichotomy between 'community' and 'environmental' development in Ireland. Although the country has a strong tradition of community activism against the activities of potential polluters, predominantly multinationals, which has sometimes resulted in the relocation or closure of factories (Coyle 1994; Yearley 1995; Leonard 2007), until recently this has largely remained within the confines of 'NIMBYism'[3] and cannot be said to have emerged from a genuinely 'green' political movement. In Tovey's view:

> Much of the initial environmental protest in Ireland was exceptional in that it was directed at industrial pollution or associated mining and dumping; it was targeted to a large degree at foreign firms; and it involved local, usually community-based

organisations whose values had more to do with family and community than those of the international conservation movement. (Tovey 2007: 20–1)

The development debate in Ireland has historically been somewhat one-dimensional, economic considerations usually taking precedence over everything else (Tovey 2007). And while the concept of sustainable development is now established in the mainstream national development discourse, some argue that Ireland lags behind much of continental Europe in the way development itself is conceived (e.g. Kelly 2004; Barry and Doran 2009; Flynn 2009). There is little reference, for example, to the relationship between development and political change (Sklair 2009), which many would argue is a precondition for genuine sustainability (Varley 2009). The primacy of economics is unsurprising, given Ireland's history of 'under-development' and historic (and re-emerging) problems associated with emigration, long-term structural unemployment and social exclusion, but its legacy has been to marginalise environmental concerns.

Community development in Ireland

Ireland has a very strong tradition of local community development. It is rooted in ancient rural practises such as *cooring*, the sharing of agricultural labour, and *meitheal*, meaning community solidarity and mutual support. Community development emerged historically from the failure of the State to provide adequately for its citizens, and has therefore been seen as a local response to the inadequacy of centralised development planning (Curtin 1997). However – and at the risk of over-generalisation – much of it has virtually always been, and continues to be, couched around mainstream development models, prioritising the central tenets of the State's development goals and often acting in partnership with it (Tovey 2007).

Community development gained impetus during the 1940s and 1950s when a national rural development movement was established called *Muntir na Tir*, the aims of which were to combat the shocking poverty of the population and stem the tide of mass out-migration from the country. Founded by a Tipperary-based priest, Fr John Hayes, *Muntir na Tir*'s local organisation was based upon Catholic parishes, and social Catholicism represented its primary development model from the outset. While *Muntir na Tir* did attempt to develop self-reliance and local autonomy among the communities it worked in, it was always (and continues to be) dependent on state funding, articulated through a partnership approach to engagement with state bodies: a relationship that has since been replicated throughout much of the community development sector (Varley 2009).

This legacy, along with the long association of community development with rurality and agriculture, means that the environment has been seen largely as a resource to be exploited, and environmental concerns have never featured very strongly in the community development agenda traditionally; indeed, one could argue that it has been almost anti-environmentalist in its outlook (e.g. Skillington 1997; 1998; Peillon 2002). The main focus for most local groups is on private enterprise and attracting businesses to their area, whether this is through tourism initiatives, agricultural cooperatives or 'capacity building' programmes. In this respect, alternative conceptions of development, most of which have emerged from the environmental movement over the past three decades, have (with the odd exception) rarely been influential upon community development in Ireland.

'Locals' and 'incomers' in Donegal.

These observations are reflected in rural Donegal. All villages and towns contain a plethora of community groups, focused on almost all sectors of the population and encompassing numerous and very varied activities. As far as most of them are concerned, however, environmental development is not one of them, since this is generally considered to be of a far lower priority to social and economic development, and, in any case, is something which belongs in the natural ambit of the county council or the European Union. Environmental improvements are rarely pursued as ends in themselves; rather, they occur largely, if they occur at all, as by-products of other development projects.

I begin with a simple observation, namely that people involved in environmental groups in the area of eastern County Donegal where I worked were usually incomers. By environmental groups, I mean those set up for the specific purpose of pursuing environmental projects, along with the local branches of national charities, semi-state entities such as *An Taisca* (Ireland's equivalent of the UK's National Trust) or political parties (notably the Green Party). I have no firm statistical evidence that might support my observation, even if it were possible to generate any. Likewise, I do not know whether this is true of the rest of the county, nor indeed the rest of Ireland. However, research conducted nationally suggests that Donegal is by no means atypical in this respect. A survey of environmental activists conducted by Tovey, for example, found that in most groups, 'outsiders' were very much to the fore: with an over-representation of those from middle-class income categories and many having spent considerable time outside Ireland, something which Tovey neatly characterises as an experience of 'interrupted habitus' (2007: 111). Kelly (2004: 87–8) drew similar conclusions from the results of her focus groups conducted with representatives from various sectors of Irish society. Casey (2000) argues that such dominance by incomers in environmentally focused groups (particularly those with a tourist-oriented agenda) is inevitable: 'those without ... insight into the [tourist] market will be unable to realise the potential of the environment at their disposal. Moreover, they will show no interest in the resources themselves' (Casey 2000: 266).

I must also preface my material with a word of caution. In any European context, it is obviously difficult, in both practical and academic terms, to make a sharp distinction between 'locals' and 'incomers'. Not only do social groups fail to conform to the neat systems of classification which social researchers often like to define them by, but in employing such terms one is necessarily superimposing predetermined categories upon groups of people who may not actually share the researcher's view of who is indigenous to a particular area and who is not. In County Donegal, such a problem is compounded by the localism of population, in the sense that the majority of people tend to regard anyone who was not born and raised in the area where they live as incomers, regardless of where they are from. And sometimes even this is not enough to be regarded as truly indigenous. As an example, a friend of mine in the village in which I was based was regarded as an incomer by many of his neighbours, despite the fact that he had lived there for all of his life. The reason was that his parents were natives of a town thirty miles away, and had moved into the village after they were married. The fact that they chose to build their house on a plot which was originally regarded as 'common land' by the older inhabitants only served to reinforce his and his family's status as 'blow-ins'. ('Blow-in' is the Irish term for incomer.)

In the following discussion, I therefore make no attempt to categorise the population myself; rather, I employ the distinctions made by local people themselves, in order to illustrate the fact that the meaning of the concepts 'local' and 'incomer' vary significantly according to social and geographical context, and also reflect wider social tensions in Donegal.

Environmental groups in Donegal

The most prominent 'environmental' group in the Irish town or village is usually the Tidy Towns committee. The national Tidy Towns competition began in 1958 under the auspices of Bord Fáilte, the Irish Tourist board, and now attracts over 800 entrants each year. Since 1995, it has been administered by the Department of the Environment, Heritage and Local Government, and has moved away from being an enterprise driven primarily by tourism to become a more broadly based development initiative. According to the Tidy Towns handbook published by the department, the scheme is viewed as an example of the application of Agenda 21 principles established by the 1992 Rio Summit to local levels (Department of Environment, Heritage and Local Government 2002:17). An explicit link is also made between environmental, community, and economic development:

> Environmental improvement is a vital part of economic regeneration. Firms will not move into a blighted, uncared for town and tourism will not flourish there.
>
> The town or village that looks good has a better chance to thrive. The very act of environmental improvement creates jobs, raises property values and stimulates the local economy. (Department of Environment, Heritage and Local Government 2002:11)

Environmental improvement is also an essential component of local development programmes coordinated by the ADM Area Partnership groups and LEADER companies

> through their community development programmes. (Department of Environment, Heritage and Local Government 2002:17)

Although the government's efforts are undoubtedly laudable, and exemplify recognition of the importance of the social dimension in environmental initiatives, the contribution of the annual competition to improving Ireland's environment may be more questionable if one holds that sustainability necessarily involves political change. Moreover, in a survey of attitudes towards the competition carried out in 1999, Mercator Market Research suggested that enthusiasm among potential participants is likely to be inversely proportional to the prosperity of the town:

> If a town is prosperous there may be more of a predisposition to take part in the competition, buoyed by the ensuing local self-confidence. In areas with economic problems, however, there is less likelihood of people being interested in the competition. Thus, in areas with high unemployment and other social problems there is a sense of dislocation and exclusion from the competition. (Mercator Market Research n.d.: 3–4)

The authors also found that most Tidy Town committees that they examined were run – from the perspective of the majority of the population – by a clique of the 'same old faces'. An observation which could apply to some areas in Donegal.

In Donegal, the term Tidy Towns is actually a misnomer, since it is largely a rural scheme and almost every village has a Tidy Towns committee, even if not all enter the national competition. The important point for the theme of this chapter is that in the case of many of the villages where I did my fieldwork, the more active members of committees were incomers, or, more accurately, were perceived as such by those involved in other community groups. Moreover, the committees also tended, in the main, to be administered by the wealthier residents of an area, often those who had moved into rural Donegal from towns and cities in Ireland and beyond. Their focus was largely on the beautification of an area: litter collection, hedgerow trimming, and whitewashing, in preparation for the anonymous visits of the Tidy Town adjudicators, if the village was participating in the competition. Very few had interests which went beyond aesthetic considerations, into areas such as the relationship between environment and social development, or green politics, for example. Some of the members of community groups with a focus on social and economic issues, which was most of them, were actively disparaging about Tidy Towns committees and their activities. In the words of a chairman of one development group:

> The Tidy Towns committee do nothing for the people here. All they're interested in is how nice their own houses look, having nicer window boxes and lawns, and that. And this village isn't going to win anyway, no chance. We'd have to knock everything down and build it again.

If the government's aim in moving the competition away from an emphasis on mere aesthetics reflects a desire to make the committees more representative of local communities, and to encourage a greater degree of involvement from more traditional community groups in their activities, then the evidence from Donegal suggests that this is a harder task than it might first appear.

Apart from the Tidy Towns committees, there are few other groups with an explicit environmental agenda in Donegal. And, like the Tidy Towns committees, those that do exist tend to be run by incomers and have a focus on the aesthetics of their local area.

Mary Hegerty is the chairperson of a community development organisation based in a town in the south of the county. It was established in 1996 with the primary aim of acting as an umbrella group for the numerous community groups in the area, along with improving the environment in the town. Mary was born and raised over the border with the UK in Northern Ireland, and lived in England for twenty-two years. She moved to the town in the early 1990s. The various difficulties she has experienced in trying to attract support from the local community and raise funds for the group encapsulates the divide between incomers and indigenes in Donegal.

In 1997, her group attempted to buy a plot of land in the village, in order to build a children's play area. One of the motivations she had for developing the land was to improve the appearance of the village, as the land was overgrown and used by many residents as a dumping ground for rubbish. She approached a local EU-sponsored agency, which told her that she could apply for a grant to buy the land if the landowner was willing to sell it. After extensive enquiries, she eventually discovered that the land was owned by the Church. The group arranged a meeting with the priest, who told them he was not prepared to sell them the land because the price would be too cheap compared to selling it to a commercial buyer and that the group should not be spending money on such projects anyway which, in his view, were not beneficial to the whole community. In Mary's view, however, the priest's real reasons had more to do with the fact that she was not a practising Catholic and had never attended any of his services. In her words: 'In this town, power is in the hands of three people: the priest, the councillor, and the teacher. And you have to be in with all three to get anything done. But they're suspicious of me because they see me as an outsider, a blow-in.'

Another example comes from a town in the east of the county, and one particular public housing estate on its outskirts called Kilcarroll. The estate has had a long history. Although the first houses were built in the 1960s, the final phase was only completed in 1994. In 1997 it had 127 homes, with an estimated population of about 500. A residents association was established for the estate in 1995, principally in order to lobby the county council to make environmental improvements in the area, but a specific event also gave impetus to the group's activities.

Shortly after its formation, the group learned that a motion had been passed in the county council to sell a piece of land adjacent to the estate which had been earmarked as a children's play area in the original plans. A particular councillor for the town was behind the decision, and there were rumours at the time that he was acting as a broker between the council and the potential buyers of the land, and may have profited personally from the sale. A number of individual residents organised a petition, and collected 180 signatures from people on the estate. However, the council campaigned hard against the association, with a number of councillors alleging in the chamber that many of the names on the petition had been falsified by the Residents Association committee, which had, in any case, not been properly elected at a full public meeting. The Residents Association responded by taking the council to a planning appeal hearing, which resulted in the council overturning its decision and promising to build a children's play area on the land as originally planned.

This account was told to me by the chairman of the Residents Association, and the way it was couched says much about the importance of the local/incomer dichotomy in Donegal. First of all, the Residents Association argues that the environment in and around the estate has been neglected by the council for many years because no councillors live on it. In the chairman's words, 'They're not locals, they all live in the private houses at the other end of town, and never come down this way.' The council, for its part, argued that the Residents Association did not represent the views of the majority of people, and that the petition was made up of the signatories of 'strangers' who did not live there. Finally, although the Residents Association estimated that 80 per cent of the estate's residents were approving of its activities, they admitted that 20 per cent were opposed to everything they do. To quote the chairman again: 'The diehards we call them. They think it's all a waste of time. These are the people who moved into the first houses in the 1960s, and they have been there for such a long time. They think it's their estate and see us as the blow-ins.'

Some groups have moved beyond aesthetics in an attempt to pursue a more authentically 'green' agenda. One such group is the Inverkenny Development Association, an environmental group based in the north of the county. The group is concerned primarily with promoting the natural beauty of the area, by publishing brochures, running marketing campaigns and creating a network of walking trails, but is also hoping to move into the promotion of sustainable livelihoods among local residents. The chairman of the group, Gerry O'Leary, was born and raised in Northern Ireland, but lived in Canada for twenty-five years before returning to Ireland in the early 1990s. Around his large, eighteenth-century farmhouse he owns seventeen acres of land, which he uses for growing food for himself and his family, cutting hay and turf and exercising his four horses. Gerry tends to avoid supermarket shopping if he can, encouraging his family and friends to pursue a lifestyle based on an environmentally sustainable agenda, something which he argues is largely shared by members of his own group.

The townland he lives in has become a haven for immigrants, with a significant proportion of the population composed of people recently arrived in Donegal. They include a retired American army colonel, a former leader of Cork County Council, a German computer technician, and a white witch who used to live in Iran.[4] Many of them are involved in the development group. Gerry's attitude to development in the area is very much that of the outsider. He argues that most of the local 'native' population, whom he always refers to in the third person, do not really care about development, which he considers to be principally about the environment.

> You could plant an entire hillside with trees and no one in [the local village] would bat an eyelid. They don't realise that the acid that comes off them will pollute all the brooks around here. There's a plantation down the road owned by some guy from Leitrim. He's never even visited the place, just bought it as an investment. When the trees are harvested, they'll ship all the timber over to mills in the north and destroy all the roads on the way in the process. I wouldn't mind if there were mills round here that were creating jobs for local people, but there isn't. The guy'll get £50 a tonne for the wood, which will bring him a fortune. People round here should be campaigning against this sort of thing, but they couldn't give a damn.

The development association works largely autonomously and has few links with other community groups in the area (of which there are several). Gerry argues that the ecotourism approach which his group is promoting will only be beneficial to the local population in the long term, particularly by creating job opportunities, but has become increasingly frustrated by what he views as the lack of interest, and sometimes active hostility, shown by his indigenous neighbours towards his activities.

Local politicians

Some of the examples cited above hint at the often acrimonious relationship between the county council and local community groups in Donegal. Councillors view themselves as the authentic representatives of the population and are generally suspicious of most development groups in the county, which they see as undermining local democracy (Collinson 2005). And the fact that many environmental groups are led by incomers to the area only serves to heighten the antipathy they hold towards them, particularly as incomers are often blamed for having a distorting effect on the economy of the county by pushing up the price of housing (at least until the economic crash of 2007–08). The vast majority of councillors are also farmers or businessmen, something which further colours their perspective on environmental issues. Finally, they are largely male,[5] in contrast to the majority of development groups which tend to be dominated by females. There is thus an additional gender-based dimension to the divide between councillors and community groups, with economic and community (including, indeed especially, environmental) development being associated respectively with male and female spheres of activity.

Councillors obviously represent the public face of the council, and inevitably get the blame if their constituents feel that their area is being neglected. There is, however, a clear division between councillors and the county council executive, particularly in relation to environmental matters. Although the executive has several environmental programmes and initiatives in place (see, for example, Donegal County Council 2006), for most councillors improving the environment usually takes very much a secondary role to economic considerations. Councillors have few real powers in Ireland, and their main roles are focused on a fairly narrow set of concerns which surround securing benefits for their constituents, such as planning approvals, grants, employment with the council, social security and medical cards, and school placements.

Environmental matters, when they are raised in the council chamber, are largely related to issues such as improvements to the water, drainage, and sewage infrastructure of the county. Councillors sometimes raise motions relating to the aesthetic appearance of particular areas, but it is notable that these are rarely targeted at the effects of economic development:

> Cleaning up refuse and scrap left by travelling people ... Clr ... asked that the council considered closing the road at Ray, Manorcunningham, where a particularly bad problem existed with travelling people.[6]

> That this council take immediate action to resolve the problem for the people of Magherecar, Bundoran, caused by the period parking in that area of large groups of mobile travelling families and the subsequent rubbish accumulation that occurs as a result of their stay.[7,8]

Despite their relative impotence, councillors have traditionally had one particular instrument by which they can exert power over the county council executive, which is something known as the Section Four motion. In theory, this is a measure by which councillors can force the executive to carry out their wishes, as long as at least three quarters of the elected members support a proposal. In the late 1990s the instrument was invoked on a regular basis in the council chamber in Donegal. It was usually applied in relation to housing, instructing the council to grant planning permission for new houses, extensions, etc., and its use was particularly prevalent at election time.

A number of high profile legal rulings in favour of county managers in the early 2000s led to the demise of the use of the Section Four motion in most local authorities, including Donegal (Sheehy 2003: 134–5). But the motion partly explains the often haphazard way in which housing development was pursued in Ireland until recently, and the apparent lack of planning controls there were upon it. In the words of one councillor: 'In the past, if you were in with the right people on the council, you could build a house in the middle of the street if you wanted to.'

Despite the demise of the Section Four motion, tensions still arise between the executive and the council in relation to planning applications, as in this exchange regarding a proposed housing development in the east of the County:

> [Senior Planner's report] It is considered that the proposed development is located on visually sensitive lands on the lake shore where development would both intrude significantly on and materially alter the view to be had from the adjoining National Secondary road. Accordingly, the proposed development contravenes the aforementioned provision of the County Development Plan, 2000 (as varied) and would, therefore, be contrary to the proper planning and sustainable development of the area.

> Clr ... advised that the development would in no way impede the view of [the lake]. Vision lines, he stated, were adequate and the applicants had confirmed that every effort would be made to ensure that overgrowth etc. was curtailed. A number of members highlighted the fact that the applicant was a member of the indigenous community and building on family land.[9]

This exchange also serves to highlight views on the attitude of councillors to indigenes versus 'blow-ins'. In this respect, as in relation to attitudes to the environment, there is likely to be a strong correspondence between the views of councillors and those of the general population.

Conclusion

The evidence presented here suggests that there is a complex range of attitudes to the environment on the part of those involved in development in Donegal. Assuming that national surveys are representative of the population of the county, economic considerations take precedence over the environment issues for most people, something which is only likely to have deepened during the recent recession. Local councillors tend to reflect this view. Community groups also by and large focus on socio-economic issues, with environmental development only weakly articulated in the county and concentrating largely on aesthetics (e.g. in the case of the Tidy Towns committees). Finally, there are a small number of groups which are attempting to pursue a more authentically 'green' agenda, exemplified by the Inverkenny Development Association. The proportion of 'incomers' (even though they may not see themselves as such) compared with 'indigenous' participants tends to increase with a greater emphasis on environmental issues. Of course, not all incomers are only interested in the environment, and many are very active in other types of community groups as well. But the difficulties some incomers have in integrating fully with the local population, and being accepted by them, is an experience which is shared across groups.[10]

So, what does all this tell us? That the Irish don't care about the environment? No, certainly not. The concerns of the Kilcarroll residents regarding the appearance of their estate are just as strongly held as those of the chairman of the Inverkenny Development Association about the natural environment in his area. But there is certainly a tension between those who see the environment in purely aesthetic terms and those who have a more conservationist approach (see Tovey *et al.* 2007: 533). It is also clear that environmental attitudes are strongly related to social background, with incomers (who are often wealthier than 'indigenes') much more likely to be involved in environmental activism. It follows from this that the environment means very different things to different people in Ireland, and there are different discourses pertaining to it. This provides a partial explanation for the observation that in Donegal, and probably elsewhere in Ireland, environmental development tends to fall between several stools, with the result that it has been historically neglected in the overall development agenda.

Mary Kelly (2007) identifies a number of types of discourses relating to the environment in Ireland, drawing from her research on environmental attitudes among a number of different sectors of the population. She argues that there are six principal discourses, which she characterises as moral, radical, political, romantic, scientific, and regulatory. While none of the group discussed above fits neatly into these categories, it could be argued that a number of environment development groups in Donegal are associated with a moral discourse frame: an ethical desire to preserve the environment for the benefit of the community and future generations (Kelly 2007: 16–17). Some, most notably the Inverkenny Development Association, are probably also driven by romantic notions of Ireland as well, and their 'emotional response' (Kelly 2007: 88) to the landscape, and perhaps by a radical political agenda too. But most development groups, and certainly the county council, fall into the regulatory discourse frame, characterised by a focus on the pursuit of economic growth in conjunction with environmental protection. Kelly notes that this was the dominant discourse among all the groups she studied, with most participants acknowledging the inherent tensions embedded in this relationship (Kelly 2007: 37).

As I hope to have shown here, there are also specific social tensions which underlie these different discourses. Incomers to rural areas in Donegal have often moved in specifically because of the beauty of the natural environment. In the main, they are more affluent and better-educated than the native population, and have therefore more inclination to become involved in development projects that have a specific environmental focus. They are more likely to have a 'green' political outlook, growing their own food, recycling rubbish, using cycles instead of cars, etc. For people who have been born and bred in Donegal on the other hand, participation in development activities tends to be motivated by their own everyday concerns: employment, training and education, agricultural development, family welfare, social inclusion, and so on. Only in urban public housing estates like Kilcarroll do community groups tend to have both a social and an environmental agenda, but here the environment is conceived simply in terms of physical appearance, with nothing of the extra accoutrements such as green politics which is the case among some of the incomers in rural Donegal. And in rural areas, groups operate separately, just as incomers and locals are largely separated into their respective social – and often geographical – ambits, which further serves to compound the piecemeal nature of the development process. As Tovey points out:

> The environmental movement in Ireland is composed of groups of 'competent actors', acting within an existing social and cultural context, to whom their own engagement appears a reasonable course of action given their personal formation as individuals, their frameworks of meaning and their social situations. (Tovey 2007: 184)

The economic crisis which has gripped Ireland since 2008 has focused attention on the deleterious effects of the boom years of the preceding decade or so. Some in the environmental movement in Ireland may argue that the economic crash is a blessing in disguise, putting a halt to what they see as Ireland's unsustainable over-development. However, others may take the view a reversion to the bad old days of mass unemployment, social exclusion, and emigration is a heavy price to pay for environmental protection. The tensions between sustainability and economic reality continue to frame the environmental debate in Ireland and serve to shape competing discourses of development, the latter firmly rooted in, informed by and impacting upon social relationships between different groups of local actors.

Notes

1 The Green Party now (2014) has no members in the Irish parliament (*Dáil Éireann*) for the first time since 1989.
2 All personal and place names have been changed to protect the anonymity of informants.
3 NIMBY means 'not in my backyard'.
4 It is worth noting that the environmental activists interviewed by Tovey for her 2007 study display a similar eclecticism.
5 Of the twenty-nine members of the council elected in the 2009 election, only three were female.
6 Donegal County Council Minutes of Meetings, 24 February 1992.
7 Donegal County Council Minutes of Meetings, 25 January 1993.
8 An increase in the number of permanent sites for travelling people during the past ten years and the instigation of the Donegal Local Traveller Accommodation Consultative Committee in 2002, which includes three representatives from the community, appear to have curtailed the raising of the type of motions cited above.
9 Donegal County Council minutes of meetings, 25 January 2005.
10 It is notable that this observation stands in contrast to the findings of Ruth Casey, in her study of the pseudonymous village of Ballygannive in western Ireland, where incomers are perceived as having stimulated a culture of environmental activism in the area and are lauded for this (Casey 2000: 264–7).

References

Barry, John and Peter Doran 2009 'Environmental Movements in Ireland: North and South', in J. McDonagh, T. Varley, and S. Shortall (eds) *A Living Countryside? The Politics of Sustainable Development in Rural Ireland* (Farnham: Ashgate), 321–40.

Casey, Ruth 2000 'Virtual locality', in E. Slater and M. Peillon (eds) *Memories of the Present. A Sociological Chronology of Ireland 1997–8* (Dublin: Institute of Public Administration), 259–71.

Collinson, Paul 1999 *Development, Local Politics and the 'New Europe' in County Donegal* Unpublished PhD Thesis (Oxford Brookes University).

——2005 'Development, democracy and the New Europe in the Irish Borderlands', in T. M. Wilson and H. Donnan (eds) *Culture and Power at the Edges of the State* (Munster: Lit Verlag), 289–320.

Coyle, Carmel 1994 'Administrative capacity and the implementation of EU environmental policy in Ireland', in S. Baker, K. Milton, and S. Yearly (eds) *Protecting the Periphery. Environmental Policy in Peripheral Regions of the European Union* (Newbury Park: Frank Cass), 62–79.

Curtin, Chris 1997 'Community development in Ireland: an historical overview', Paper presented at IRDL Conference on Cross-Border Cooperation (Moville, 10 May).

Deegan, J. and D. A. Dineen 1997 *Tourism Policy and Performance: The Irish Experience* (London: International Thomson Business Press).

Department for Environment, Heritage and Local Government 2002 *Tidy Towns Handbook* (Dublin: Department for Environment, Heritage and Local Government).

Dillon, Sara 1996 'Vulnerable landscapes and the inadequacies of the Irish planning acts', *Dublin University Law Journal*, 102, 102–25.

DKM Economic Consultants 2009 *Review of the Construction Industry 2008 and Outlook 2009–2011* (Dublin: Department of the Environment, Heritage and Local Government).

Donegal County Council 2006 *County Development Plan 2006–2012* (Lifford: Donegal County Council). Published at www.donegalcoco.ie/services/planningeconomicdevelopment/Central+Planning+Unit/countydevplan.htm. Accessed 12 July 2011.

Flynn, Brendan 2009 'Environmental lessons for rural Ireland from the European Union: how great expectations in Brussels get dashed in Bangor and Belmullet', in J. McDonagh, T. Varley, and S. Shortall (eds) *A Living Countryside? The Politics of Sustainable Development in Rural Ireland* (Farnham: Ashgate), 53–68.

Irish Examiner 2010 'Unfinished business' (6 April). Published at www.examiner.ie/ireland. Accessed 26 April 2010.

Kelly, Mary 2004 *Environmental Attitudes and Behaviours: Ireland in Comparative European Perspective: Third Report of National Survey Data* (Dublin: Social Sciences Research Centre, UCD).

——2007 *Environmental Debates and the Public in Ireland* (Dublin: Institute of Public Administration).

Leonard, Liam 2007 *The Environmental Movement in Ireland* (Galway: Social Sciences Research Centre, National University of Ireland / Springer).

McDonagh, John 2007 'Rural development in Ireland – retrospect and prospect', in B. Bartley and R. Kitchin (eds) *Understanding Contemporary Ireland* (Pluto Press), 88–99.

McDonagh, John, Tony Varley, and Sally Shortall (eds) 2009 *A Living Countryside? The Politics of Sustainable Development in Rural Ireland* (Farnham: Ashgate).

Meldon, J. 1992 *Structural Funds and the Environment: Problems and Prospects* (Dublin: An Taisce).

Mercator Market Research n.d. *Attitudes to Tidy Towns*. Published at www.environ.ie/en/Environment/TidyTowns/PublicationsDocuments/FileDownLoad,2390,en.doc. Accessed 3 April 2010.

Motherway, Brian, Mary Kelly, Pauline Faughnan, and Hilary Tovey 2003 *Trends in Irish Environmental Attitudes between 1993 and 2002. First Report of National Survey Data* (Dublin: Environmental Protection Agency).

Peillon, Michel 2002 'Culture and the state in Ireland's new economy', in P. Kearby, L. Gibbons, and M. Cronin (eds) *Reinventing Ireland: Culture, Society and the Global Economy* (London: Pluto), 38–53.

Sheehy, E. 2003 'City and county management', in M. Callahan and J. F. Keogan (eds) *Local Government in Ireland: Inside Out* (Dublin: Institute of Public Administration), 123–42.

Skillington, Tracey 1997 'Politics and the struggle to define: a discourse analysis of the framing strategies of competing actors in a 'new' participatory forum', *British Journal of Sociology*, 48:3, 493–513.

——1998 'The city as text: constructing Dublin's identity through discourse on transportation and urban regeneration in the press', *British Journal of Sociology*, 49:3, 456–73.

Sklair, Leslie 2009 'The transnational capitalist class and the politics of capitalist globalization', in S. Dasgupta and J. N. Pieterse (eds) *Politics of Globalization* (New Delhi: SAGE), 82–97.

Tovey, Hilary 2007 *Environmentalism in Ireland. Movement and Activists* (Dublin: Institute of Public Administration).

Tovey, Hilary, Perry Share, and Mary P. Corcoran, 2007 *A Sociology of Ireland* (Dublin: Gill and Macmillan, 3rd edn).

Varley, Tony 2009 'Populism and the politics of community survival in rural Ireland', in J. McDonagh, T. Varley, and S. Shortall (eds) *A Living Countryside? The Politics of Sustainable Development in Rural Ireland* (Farnham: Ashgate), 341–60.

Wickham, James and Maria Lohan 2000 'Dublin's car system', in E. Slater and M. Peillon (eds) *Memories of the Present. A Sociological Chronology of Ireland 1997–8* (Dublin: Institute of Public Administration),77–9.

Yearley, Stephen 1995 'The social shaping of the environmental movement', in P. Clancy, S. Drudy, K. Lynch, and L. O'Dowd (eds) *Irish Society. Sociological Perspectives* (Dublin: Institute of Public Administration), 652–74.

4

Ethnic identity, power, compromise, and territory: 'locals' and 'Moroccans' in the Sainte-Foy-Bordeaux vineyards

Chantal Crenn

This contribution concerns the process of dynamic construction of the concept of territory, stressing its variations and instabilities. We take as the definition of 'territory' the whole of inhabited landscape and the collective representations of it by the humans who live within it (Simon 1981). At the same time it is produced by them and incorporated into their history and their culture. In this particular way it pertains to ethnic identity, a phenomenon with multiple dimensions: certainly geographical, but also historical, cultural, symbolic, and maybe even poetical. In this chapter, we will mention, in addition to those who call themselves native, not only the peoples who came mainly from Morocco to work as farm workers in some of the Bordeaux vineyards in the 1960s and 1970s, but also those from Tunisia or Algeria. These workers settled there, and their families remain to this day.

It is interesting to note that in the field of interethnic relations and international migration, the countryside has been neglected, both in the recent history of French anthropology, and from the viewpoint of relevant public policies. Thus, for an anthropology trying to find its place in Western societies in the contemporary world, the rural ambit is ignored because it is too marked by a memorial anthropology; that is, the protection of a disappearing world. From the standpoint of public policies and researchers, the countryside is seen as idyllic with 'no problems', without 'immigrants', without suburbs, thus with no need for research on these issues. Migrants from North Africa and the Sahara are rarely taken into account in policy research on the rural world. Just as they are neglected by anthropologists, in public policy they also remain invisible, only being considered in relation to the tasks they perform in the vineyards and not as members of the community.

In opposition to this neglect, this chapter will take into account the ethnic identity of 'Moroccan' farm workers as an additional possibility of organising their relation to others on the territory of vineyards. We place inverted commas round the word 'Moroccans' because it is a demeaning cultural categorisation employed by the rulers who call them this way even though they can hold French nationality. However, in order not to make the text unwieldy, we won't systematically bracket the word with commas. But it is important to remember that these migrants can also be Algerian or Tunisian. If Algerian, they come from the region of Sidi Brahim; if Tunisian, from Thelpete. For those who actually come from Morocco, most originate from the region of Garb. Initially farmers, they came from the countryside surrounding the city of Meknes, but some first migrated to the city of Meknes before leaving Morocco. Others come from Rabat or Casablanca, and worked on farms in the south-east of France before settling in the south-west, thanks to a network of mutual acquaintances and the labour needs of the French State, which links residence and employment. In this wine area, the high number of people from Morocco is quite significant and has an impact on the way the other North Africans establish their presence.

That these immigrants are still labelled 'Moroccan' today, however, highlights their marked exteriority to the French nation, and in this case particularly to the vineyards. The French urban population thinks it is the responsibility of vineyards to testify to a 'pure' 'authentic' past. The vineyard is part of the attributes designated by the then Minister for Industry, Eric Besson (2009), to refer to the French national identity. However, the wine world has much in common with the urban environment. Here we're talking about the French gaze, which sees in the formerly colonised populations a radical, indeed irreducible, otherness between East and West. It is crystallised in religion, the status of women, and eating practices. At lunch time in the vineyards, the fact that Moroccans neither drink wine nor eat pork pâté is regarded by their fellow workers and bosses, who consider themselves 'native French' or 'European', as an additional boundary. As we will see, racism suffered by these workers is not confined to the lower classes. The town councillors themselves are no exception, pejoratively calling their small town 'Marrakech'. The installation of video surveillance cameras, requested by the inhabitants of Sainte-Foy-la-Grande because of the imagined presence of the Moroccans' children (often adults) on the streets at night, further strengthens the process of ethnicisation in this wine territory. In addition, middle-class families bypass their local school to avoid their children mixing with Moroccan children.

Ethnic boundaries not only take shape in relation to the majority, but also among minority populations (in the sociological sense). With so-called Gypsies or Romany, relations are contentious. The members of these two groups set the Moroccans apart from the wine territory because of the latter's alleged affiliation to Islam and their relatively recent presence; unlike those (Christians) who have been settled there for generations.

The mobility of groups of individuals and their fitting into a given space reveals their processes of participation in social spaces. In the case of Moroccan workers employed in the vineyards, their social itinerary (migratory, professional, religious, etc.) will relate to the spatial and temporal dimensions of that itinerary.

As we can began to perceive, ethnic identity is not a natural layer on which community life can be established. It is in fact produced by it. This study on the identity of Moroccans in the French countryside concerns the actual situation of the group claiming this identity. This chapter therefore leads us to analyse their situation as a minority in the wine-producing environment and to specify the objective social relations that it establishes. Beyond the everyday racism experienced, we will see that the feeling of social exclusion felt by these populations is also due to the fact that they hold the lowest place in the wine sphere.

It is why we need to insist on the political and socio-economic contexts (we could say 'exogenous factors') of this particular rural space, enmeshed as it is in national and international logics. Although these elements might appear external to the Moroccan group, in fact they cannot ignore or avoid them, because these elements, among other things, influence not only social and geographical mobility, and processes of differentiation, but also endogenous factors. These endogenous factors influence both the institution of the group's collective organisation (e.g. power relations, leadership, ethnic trade, occupation of territory, collective happenings in public space) and its interpretation within individual trajectories.

We will first present the historical and economic context of the vineyard around Sainte-Foy-la-Grande and the processes of distinctions; identifications that profoundly involve the situations of interethnic relations; and the definition, which those who consider themselves indigenous, give to Moroccans. We will then discuss the rural–urban continuum in which the vineyard and Moroccan families are situated. Finally, we will see that, by their own occupation of the wine territory, Moroccan ethnic identity is not reducible to external labelling. We will also see how it is involved, in turn, in the building of the country surrounding Sainte-Foy. The eating practices of the Moroccans occupy a very interesting place in this rural location.

Vineyards reinvented or 'cultivated difference'

Sainte-Foy-la-Grande is situated at the eastern end of the Gironde department, 70 km from Bordeaux, 20 km from Bergerac and 15 km from Duras in the Lot et Garonne. It almost forms an enclave in the Dordogne department. This *bastide* (fortified town from the Hundred Years War) built in 1255 on a previously inhabited area has long been a refuge for freed serfs, Albigensian heretics, Huguenots, Spanish republicans, some 300 citizens from Longwy during the Second World War, and finally Malagasy nationalists, exiled after the 1947 revolt. Migrations have always played a major part in the establishment and shape of its population. From 1870 to 1970 the area also witnessed the establishment of various foreign groups: Italians, Spaniards, Portuguese, and French migrants such as Bretons from Brittany, French Muslims (*Harkis*), or French from Algeria (*Pieds Noir*). More recently two types of foreign populations have come in: Moroccan vineyard workers, and many British people. On top of that, in the 1980s numerous French people chose to make their homes there, and they represent a sizeable neo-rural population.

Wine and Protestantism

The all-important economic activity of the area has been and still is wine production, even though, according to our informants, its economic future is not as bright as it used to be; viticulture and its local history are therefore a sure source of identity.

As can be seen from historical research on the region, the vineyard, its production and its trade have established local economic and symbolic activity for centuries. If the charter granted to Sainte-Foy by Alphonse of Poitiers in 1256 alluded to wine only twice, its confirmation by Louis XII in 1498 was much more explicit. Like those in Bordeaux, the vine-growing inhabitants of Sainte-Foy were granted the privilege of being the only ones allowed to harvest their wine before St Martin in winter (on 11 November). The charter then provides information on the many taxes to pay to bring in, leave, or sell their wines in the city. The abundance of texts about wine available for the entire jurisdiction until 1756, stressed the spatial importance of the vine not only in this area but also in the local economy. Wine was then the great cash crop of the region and, as such, a major source of enrichment. This was reflected particularly by the weight of taxes and the emergence or strengthening of a sense of belonging to a 'Sainte-Foy country' which was organised by the control of the production and especially the marketing of wine.

Wine and its production were responsible for the construction of a vast Sainte-Foy-country, between Bergerac and Libourne, probably thanks to its port and its local trading where, as in Bergerac, Protestantism played a prominent role. Its existence continues beyond the revolutionary period, and by the end of the nineteenth century around Sainte-Foy, there was a wine country producing Bergerac-type sweet white wine, called the Little Sauterne from Libourne.

In this region, once known – and even today by some local scholars – as the 'country of the new conquest', the local story written by Protestants about their seeking refuge in the area from the sixteenth century is still used today to forge a contemporary professional identity, via wine cooperatives and trade unions. It is also the struggle between Protestants and Catholics in the vineyard that characterises the borders of this territory in the collective imagination. Tales of the Hundred Years War, of cloistered monks and anarchistic geographers punctuate family conversations on wine estates.

The Catholic Italians: social rise thanks to the vine

The Italians, who arrived from the 1920s on, also have a central place in the wine area, in so far as the topic we are interested in (Guillaume 1990). Settling in great numbers decades before the Moroccans, the Italians were employed either as sharecroppers or as agricultural or domestic labourers on mixed farming properties. Regardless of the native region, unemployment in the Italian countryside influenced the decision to emigrate. High birth rate, low economic activity, and familiarisation with immigration thus prompted whole branches to leave the family farm, relieving the father and also any brother who had migrated, to settle where a job awaited them in Switzerland, Austria, or France.

There was great demand for agricultural workers in France after the 1914–18 war. The country lacked a work force and much of the land lay fallow. However, even prior to that at the end of the nineteenth century in south-west France, re-establishing the vines after the phylloxera plague had required much labour. Furthermore, during this period there was a heightened indigenous emigration from the area. Farms were deserted and passed on to Italian sharecroppers. However, for many of these sharecroppers what was left to them after giving the owner his dues provided only a meagre salary.

Poverty and deprivation are very obvious in the stories of these Italian sharecroppers' descendants. Community life oscillated between two activities: church and family gatherings. Similar to their dedication to working the land, church was at the centre of people's life stories, and they regularly attended church services outside working hours. Religion was an important factor for acceptance by some of the local population, that is, the Catholics among them. But it was also an obstacle to overcome if they were to achieve the social rise expected in a Protestant land. After the Second World War, some of these immigrants bought agricultural properties (not only vineyards, because mixed farming was then the norm in the region), when indigenous exodus was the rule and when economic conditions were unfavourable to the wine trade. Thus, today they think it is by their selfless work in agriculture, particularly through their investment in the production of the vine, that they have 'deservedly' legitimated their presence in the region and have competed with the religious and political power of the local Protestants. Few evoke the racism that they and their parents suffered. The grandparents have done everything to avoid being treated as 'Macaronis' by their work and fervent religiosity. Thus the arrival of the Moroccans revived the threat of being stigmatised, and of being reduced to immigrant workforce status.

Heritage, label and wine: a feeling of belonging for whom?

Yet the vineyards are places that have been recruiting foreign labour for a long time and it is where the Moroccan workers have been traditionally employed. These workers usually followed 'a boss', the French owner of a vineyard in Morocco, Tunisia, or Algeria, back to France at the end of the French protectorate in Morocco in 1956. Also, some came because they heard of possibilities by word of mouth; they sought a better economic situation than in Morocco, and sometimes joined parents already on site.

For the most part, the Moroccans are salaried by private vineyard owners or by cooperatives, formed by 'new agriculturalists' and which try to create a new driving force via the union of several young producers of organic wine. These also succeeded in reviving the Sainte-Foy-Bordeaux label (*Appellation d'origine contrôlée*), which dates from 1937 (Crenn and Téchouèyres 2004). However, the label was abandoned after the Second World War because it was no longer economically viable; it had become more profitable to sell the wine under the Bordeaux Supérieur label. The Sainte-Foy-Bordeaux label was reinstated in a global context in 1999, to distinguish it from the labels of Saint-Emilion and the great Bordeaux. What we have here, therefore, is a meeting between political and economic interests, as the appellation is being used by the local council to develop tourism in the area. At the same time, it is interesting to note that the region is experiencing a strong sociological change because many people are now working in Bordeaux, Paris, or London and do not depend directly on the wine industry.

To approach agricultural workers through the medium of wine offers a threefold interest. First, it allows us to understand the appropriation of the Sainte-Foy territory by the wine-producing community and the establishment of its rules for the whole of the local population. Second, it shows us the professional world in which the Moroccans try to fit: a world characterised by transmission of know-how, professional culture, social hierarchy, interethnic relationships, racism, etc. We notice for example that the Moroccan agricultural workers are totally absent from the agriculturalists' discourse about the vine and the 'land'. The professional world they belong to tends to completely ignore the Moroccans. Indeed, the agriculturalists were surprised by our theme of fieldwork on a minority that they had never even considered as an identified group who would have brought something to the wine community: their skills, availability, and flexibility. If they *are* described, it is to expose their shortcomings: poor attendance at work, and lack of compatibility with the dominant social and cultural norms. Third, this approach allows us to analyse the extension of the concept of 'heritage' (local term meaning, here, 'national heritage') in two areas: (a) a technical scientific one, heritage being supposed to provide protection from the excesses of modernity on the environment and humans; and (b) the preservation of elements of a culture, thought to be disappearing (Di Méo 1996: 247–69).

In this context, the interlocutors who define themselves as 'Protestant wine growers' are at the same time both marginals and local wine industry leaders. In our opinion, they always insist on their innovative and free spirit. They want to appear as avant-garde, compared to the other Sainte-Foy inhabitants, that is, 'Catholics'. The values held by these interlocutors are also those of commercial companies, of success, of the spirit of independence, and of adaptation; values that, according to them, have necessarily produced local leaders for the vineyards. Their central role in the erection of the regional cooperative wineries and their commitment to the rebirth of the Sainte-Foy-Bordeaux Union by adopting a 'reasoned wine growing' is also meant to show their sense of individual and collective responsibilities.

In the same way, these interlocutors see the place of 'Moroccan migrants' (i.e. minorities) as being associated with their ancestors seeking refuge in this area in the past. As a result, 'Protestants' strive to appear to be more tolerant in their attitude towards the Moroccans, but in reality they do very little to help them settle. For instance, the Protestants only speak about them when directly questioned by the anthropologist. They openly denounce the racism that the Moroccans suffer, but they do not interact with them on a daily basis.

The Protestant heritage has become a lever used by these actors to legitimise wine production in the area and thus to claim a unique identity locally speaking, but also faced with the globalisation of wine markets. Mechanised harvesting, bottling using microbullage (the measured oxygenation of wine), other modern winemaking techniques, the most appropriate dosage of fermentation, and wine marketing via the internet are all being developed. However, in addition, the Protestant winemakers we met use the *Nuits du Patrimoine* (nights when, throughout France, the local architectural heritage is celebrated) to promote their properties and wine to local inhabitants and to the large number of passing tourists. Elements of the past are selected to meet the current trends of consumption: the search for authenticity and quality by consumers. In a manner akin to the exploitation of the concept of '*terroir*' (Trubek 2008; Demossier 2010), the 'making of heritage' is here deployed as a category which structures ways of understanding 'how to drink properly' and 'how to be in harmony with its social and natural environment'.

This relationship, which the Protestant growers articulate between local land and local heritage, seemed to meet the expectations of the French urban population facing their 'natural' environment but also appears to be in agreement with a mythicised past. The reactivation of the Sainte-Foy-Bordeaux Union and the establishment of a brotherhood with its own costume, the re-introduction of the 'harvest meal' (though they are now almost non-existent in the majority of estates) at the time of the *Vituriales* (the feast of the Sainte-Foy-Bordeaux Union on the first weekend in August), reflect the symbolic motives available to these elite and economic resources, which give it the ability to promote its identity locally. By presenting the quality of their wine in this way, the quartet of winemaker, land, heritage, and global market has found a place where the individual relationship to consumers is central and where the Protestant affiliation is mobilised.

For this reason, the Sainte-Foy-Bordeaux Union has a problem of recognition locally by the whole population. It is usually associated with a rather Protestant elite; though even if many Protestants are in the Union, not all its members are Protestant. Many winegrowers do not join the Sainte-Foy-Bordeaux Union; precisely those (mainly Catholics) who worked to accomplish the huge modernisation effort cannot recognise themselves in a professional identity which, according to them, values the stereotypes of the past. They cannot recognise themselves in a local identity centred only on Protestant heritage. They do not want to belong to the Sainte-Foy-Bordeaux Syndicate just because the economic and symbolic consequences of membership in the *Bordeaux Supérieur Appellation* have previously borne fruit. They therefore claim their places as actors of wine production outside of the Union. Moreover, if the Union struggles for recognition of a specificity of the Sainte-Foy land through geological surveys and a common denominator in the characterisation of wine when it is tasted, many producers are not fooled and think that basically 'willingness is necessary to find the nuances'.

In this context of upheaval, where Protestant Christian history is strongly claimed, 'Moroccan farm workers' struggle to find their place despite the rather tolerant speech (in front of the anthropologist) of the 'Protestant elite'. As we have seen, the concepts of common heritage and respect for the environment are today very evident in the vineyards where the Moroccans work, and they have a noteworthy impact not only on their way of life but also on their ethnicity. Among the new uses inscribed in this rural space is the importance of the Moroccan workers' presence in the area for over thirty years. We can thus ask: What is their position? How are they seen by others? What is their impact on wine production? How are their cultural differences perceived?

At the centre of the urban–rural continuum: 'Moroccan workers' and their families

The Moroccans in the vineyards are in the middle of a complex history process. The old dichotomy town/country is not yet totally erased. But it has changed shape. If it is always possible to define a rural space as opposed to an urban one, the forms taken by the Moroccans' interaction are new. The idea of an urban domination is being slowly replaced by that of a continuum between these two worlds where the notion of rurality is now valued.

The way in which the Moroccans have been established locally has changed over the twenty to thirty years. In the past, the men (without their wives, who were left in Morocco) were housed collectively in makeshift shelters on the property. Following the urbanisation–modernisation programme of the countryside, and after the law favouring family regrouping was passed and implemented in 1976 by President Valéry Giscard D'Estaing, they were housed with their families (wives and children came from Morocco) in low-rent council housing recently built on the periphery of the small town of Sainte-Foy (population 3,000). Sited near a motorway, these buildings, together with the construction of nearby shopping areas and petrol stations, as well as a tourist information office, considerably changed the landscape, creating an urban space within a broader rural one.

It is not just that merchandise and urban fashions have invaded the countryside, thanks in particular to the creation of new circuits of distribution, headed by hypermarket chains such as Leader Price (especially popular among the Moroccan families). Significant, additional factors have included the changes to the organising modes of management activities, as well as in distribution and work patterns. In this wine-growing zone where the Protestant elite has, since the nineteenth century, attempted to reduce the frontier between traditional rural culture and scientific culture, the new technological processes were adopted quickly in wine production. Harvesting is now carried out by machines, and specialists take over the wine making, both of which have important consequences on the possible 'career' of the Moroccan workers who, today, are only allowed to perform basic menial tasks along the production line.

In the early 2000s, despite the mechanisation of tasks and less use of manual labour at harvest time, a new direction became apparent. Some Moroccan families invested in real estate: in building lots in the middle of the surrounding countryside, and constructing their own houses, 'each family helping the others' (Brahim, aged 60). These lots are situated on the opposite bank of the river, in Port-Sainte-Foy, facing Sainte-Foy. The new direction has much to do with the fact that a mosque was raised in this area. Also, the land is cheaper, and being there does not brand the inhabitants as 'those of the fairground' (Brahim), i.e. the very low-class suburban area. In these labourers' migrant itinerary, access to private property was essential, as it allowed them to recreate a home in a familiar half-rural, half-urban environment. The particularly well-tended vegetable gardens display mint and coriander borders, attesting to the presence of Moroccan gardeners. These are about the only exterior signs of the Moroccan identity of the inhabitants although, inside, their homes conform to the norms of Moroccan housing. As far as vegetable and animal production is concerned, the local farming culture is sufficiently close to their own, so that they can reappropriate it without changing its meaning. Thus their settling outside of town and not in council buildings was realised in a manner of apparent total freedom.

New technologies of distribution and communication have also contributed to the change of their rural landscape. Indeed, these new technologies bring into their homes the very heart of economic globalisation. All the families have television, telephone, and radio. Satellite TV allows them access to television news other than those of the Western channels and to follow 'Arab' events of the day thanks to the Al-Jazeera channel (for example, during the Iraq war). Furthermore, satellite TV also allows them to access the same news and information as their family in Morocco. Of course, they also share with the locals the great sporting events and other important programmes on local or international TV (Abélès 1996: 9). With this media input, the Moroccans' construction of identity is no longer produced within the traditional game of opposition between Self and Other, between the interior and the exterior. Instead, these migrants and their families are creating for themselves a specific rural world, making use of all the images presented in the media. In the process, they construct for themselves 'an imagined Arab community' akin to 'the imagined community' of Benedict Anderson ([1983]; 2006). Through the media they are presented with images from all domains: economy, politics, fiction, sport, etc. These images enable the collective appropriation, in different ways, of a 'public sphere of exiles'. Locally, and in their situation as 'outsiders', this imagined Arab community appears to be, above all, a means of resistance towards the dominating local population.

Seen from this point of view, the rural territories of the Moroccans should not be confused with enclaves. They are rather spaces of circulation, recognised by the migrants who set up a network of complementary, functionally differentiated spaces. We have identified here, as in urban areas, the same Moroccan capacity at constructing the countryside, not as a succession of different spaces, but as a network of broadly connected, topographic and social circuits.

The Moroccans have thus contributed to the transformation of the French countryside. Despite the complexity of their cultural and adaptive references, we can consider them as rooted in the area. The families have taken over the rural space without completely transforming it. They did not attempt to reduce it into a simple prop for a community life closed in upon itself. Instead, like Lévi-Strauss's *bricoleurs*, they 'invented' their occupation of the land as something between Morocco, the imagined Arab community, and the local and national context.

In spite of the complexity of their references, one can here speak of an 'anchoring', to the extent that most of the young born or raised in France remain in the area, very often after having married locals. Those who have found work elsewhere come back every weekend. They may express their attachment to the place of their childhood by renting a house not far from that of their parents, or by continuing to participate in local activities, for example the football team, whose president is a descendant of Tunisian rural workers.

For those who have invested in their own individual house, return-trips to Morocco, Algeria, or Tunisia were less frequent when they were working but, once retired, they made return-trips on a regular basis, at least as long as they were in good health. The choice of their final home is debatable, which reflects the difficulty of choosing between the country of departure and arrival. Besides, the concepts of 'arrival' and 'departure' are relative and, for these individuals who have lived longer in France than in Morocco, depend on where they are currently living.

This strong feeling of belonging to the vineyard land of Sainte-Foy but also to the Moroccan countryside can perhaps be explained by the construction of Moroccan identity as rooted in the countryside: first in Morocco, then in France. Most of the families are from rural Morocco where vines are still cultivated. Indeed, for many years, the proceeds from emigration have served not just to put up beautiful houses emblematic of migrants' economic success, but at the same time to enlarge familial estates: a strategy until then reserved for some rich families (Crenn 2003). However, even if they have funded the expansion of familial property in Morocco, they have worked all their lives in the Sainte-Foy countryside. Financing the family property over there, enriching the wine region through their work here: they have a sense of belonging to both at the same time.

We notice that the Moroccan image of the vineyards fits into a transnational context. They are producing their very own 'locality' in a moving context. The identity of this group is not fixed. It makes use of elements, coming sometimes from other cultures, and sometimes from the local vine-growing culture. However, this identity is also built within the framework imposed by the structural constraints of the vineyard.

The ideological context of the vineyard: the exploitation

In the vineyards, to be categorised 'Moroccan' is to be seen as poor, uneducated, a Muslim, and having no respect for women: 'Here we say that a good Moroccan is a Moroccan who does not understand French, who does not know their rights as employees' (Protestant wine worker, aged 55). Thus the figure of the (male) migrant farm worker exploited at will, without knowledge of his rights or not seeking to benefit from them, is still relevant in the wine sphere, and is a point that interests us. Incidentally, a number of growers and agricultural businesses are still looking for such employees, in search of unskilled and docile labour. However, those already settled for thirty years constitute a population that no longer quite fits these criteria. The Moroccans face competition from Polish and Spanish workers or 'Andalusian Moroccan'. The wine business is, in this region, still in need of secondary workers, who are numerous but seasonal; few people now enjoy permanent contracts.

Some of those interviewed worked on several farms over the last twenty or thirty years to complete various activities, the most common being cleaning and pruning the stems and '*tirer les bois*' (removing the dead wood). Some of the workers were seasonally hired as 'permanent' but then dismissed for economic reasons or sometimes in favour of a stepson or brother of the owner, who was in search of employment.

> One day my boss told me: 'I have bad news for you, my son- in-law does not work, I decided to hire him, because of family solidarity, you can understand that?' Of course I understood but it was hard ... well, I received my dismissal indemnities as it should be, but I had no more fixed workplace. (Brahim, 58)

Others are laid off and replaced with seasonal, rather than permanent workers, who are sent by flourishing agricultural contractors in the region. Permanent workers were called 'the Arab' or 'the Moroccan' of such-and-such.

> I was the first in the village to hire a real North African, and everybody told me: you're going to invade us with 'your' Moroccans ... So when I sold them a piece of land to build their house, it was the revolution. (Protestant winemaker, 57)

His former employee Mohammed, now seasonal, recalls being called 'the Arab of the Maubastit'.

Those who are lucky enough to remain permanent still face the same labelling. However, in general, when the oldest of them reminisce, they usually show their attachment to the property on which they worked the longest. A kind of scattering emerges from their interviews too. 'Before being hired fifteen years at X's, I did a season with so and so, then another at another's. By the way, this one never called me back.' Walking in the vineyard one of them said, 'Look, I grafted a year in this plot of land that belonged to X then the one next door.' According to Moroccan workers, it was difficult to establish friendly relations in this context of movement and instability. These statements are confirmed by the winegrowers, who do not know the individual identity of their seasonal workers. This is reinforced today when they delegate the maintenance of the vines to a company. They no longer have any direct contact with the workers. However, those who benefited from a permanent contract have fond memories of the links forged between 'them' and their boss and experienced the modernisation and economic difficulties of the vineyard as if it were their own. Among the oldest employees, who had brought their wives along with them in the 1970s adventure and now find themselves back with their first status (i.e. seasonal worker) bitterness is perceptible. Their children's unemployment forced the workers to migrate to town when they themselves feel threatened by unemployment (because they are increasingly excluded even from the simplest tasks), which makes ageing difficult. And their eviction from the vineyards causes a form of nostalgia.

Women also establish a difference between the urban and wine-growing areas: 'In the vineyard, we were free, no one was aggressive towards us, we could wear the veil or not. It's not like in town where people do not hesitate to make racist remarks' (Fatima, 57). Their stories are those of the vineyard and, paradoxically, 'the love of the vine'. All these life stories also show an ambiguous feeling of love/disgust for the 'bosses of the vine' who provide economic resources. They regard their work as a real form of participation in the local economy, a professional identity, and the hope of a final integration, but which also offers poor working conditions and discrimination.

> Many of us are unemployed or seasonal, sometimes I work two months, sometimes seven ... It's hard. But I am not complaining like those who have lost their jobs after an accident at work and have never been able to have the fault of the employer recognised: employers who, until then, cherished them as they were good vine pruners, born leaders, or simply exploited at will! (Karim, a seasonal worker, 54)

Indeed, accidents at work are numerous, and in these times of conflict they reveal the social status given to these workers. Brahim, aged 57, who lost two fingers of his right hand, states:

> I was considered like his son. With my wife, we had housing just for us. He gave me responsibilities. I do not know why he treated me better than my fellow workers who were housed in groups on beaten earth. Maybe because I was working well. But the day I cut my fingers, we had to go to court ... But here I lost. He knew all the judges ... He won and I have a ridiculous disablement pension ... I cannot work any more.

Others discovered that once dismissed and at the time of retirement, their boss had not declared them during the first years of their contract, preventing them from claiming their full retirement pension. Contempt towards their boss at the way in which they were managed is therefore understandable. Halema (aged 50) bitterly recalls the long waiting hours by the phone when it was time to thin out, and remove the dead wood: 'Last year I worked on a farm in Saint-Emilion. They were very satisfied with my services, and they said "Next year, we will call you back." They never called back ... They preferred a Moroccan from Morocco without her papers!' For some, like Halema's husband, the situation is considered a little less precarious, as he is 'rehired' every year by the same boss but also 'laid off' by the end of the season. This entitles him to claim unemployment benefits. This precarious status will continue throughout their working lives. However, some, like Ahmed, have fond memories of the time when, as a permanent worker, he participated along with his boss in all stages of winemaking from the vine to the wine storehouse. He had got what he wanted: a permanent contract, but only for a while:

> When I was at B's, an organic winemaker, and Protestant, we were as much in the cellar as in the vineyard. So, we knew what was happening ... The office was next door to the wine cases ... Sometimes I was going to the trade fairs because I had got my truck licence. He told us everything. Now my new boss sells everything to the wine cooperative and I am relegated only to the upkeep of the vines. So I'm less informed. I do not see anything anymore.

Brahim recalls how initially their lives were devoted only to work and expresses what Sayad (1999) called 'the truth of immigration':

> When I got married in Morocco, under duress by the way, I came here with my wife. We had only one thing in mind: to work and earn money. In Morocco nothing was waiting for us. I could not live on my uncle's farm or my stepfather's. Then we came here. My wife, I introduced her to my employer and she was immediately hired. We ate on site. I remember we did not cook as much as now. We ate what was prepared. Halal didn't exist! When our children were born, we had them looked after by a French woman, so that Djema could continue working. Our whole life was organised around our job and the vines. Nevertheless, my boss let me go the day I had an accident at work.

They would have accepted anything, endured everything for a final status, a little recognition, and a fixed salary. By dint of non-recognition, mistrust and the internalisation of a negative identity against bosses – and by extension French people – is evident in their words. Ahmed: 'Even those who call themselves Protestant and more tolerant, they are racist towards us'.

Many remember the precarious conditions in which they were subjected in their house. Nadya (aged 51) recalls the days when her family lived in the 'free' house of the employer, located near the wine land: 'The wind came in. It was wet, there was no heating, no bathroom either. The children were always sick, just like us!' Before Nadya's arrival, the rooms had been used to store equipment or agricultural products. To make them into dwelling places, the few changes made were mostly limited to the division of the space into several parts: a common room, a room used as a bedroom, and a kitchen. The lack of insulation and openings, plus broken, unrepaired tiles, resulted, they remember, in the walls becoming saturated with water. According to a doctor from the Mutualité Sociale Agricole at the time, parasites and humidity caused chronic coughs and skin diseases. Some fathers, who suffered regularly and were forced to take an increasing amount of sick leave, had their jobs threatened. Sheikh (aged 63): 'The boss always finds someone else, and we ended up on the street, jobless, homeless.' These statements were corroborated by a Mutualité Sociale Agricole factory inspector working in the Libourne region. He informed us that this type of housing was still available in the 2000s and that there were still unfair dismissals if the employees were considered to be taking sick leave too frequently. According to employers, the move to bring the work and rest places closer together offered the migrant workers the opportunity to own a home free of charge and to get to work without a vehicle, thus masking material and symbolic dependencies and the lack of basic necessities. Unhealthiness associated with the feeling of 'being ill-housed', migrants said, could not be completely eradicated by individual home ownership, because the shift to apartments in the housing project has not completely removed the impression of 'malaise'. In the same way, living in the *bastide* of Sainte-Foy-la-Grande contributes to their feeling of exclusion, because the town centre is today deserted by the French middle classes. Therefore, to be 'ill-housed' is as much a feeling of social exclusion as living in unhealthy conditions. Yet migrants believe that they have everything in place to try to find a social balance through work. Some of them have already achieved this on account of '*un bon patron*', but this is rare.

Despite the subordinate tasks the Moroccans were given, they found a special meaning in their work. For instance, pruning – a particularly valued part of the job – was made a symbol of success when they became known for their ability. The women, who are affected by the division of labour (they are usually given less valued tasks than pruning) and by the periods of insolvency, symbolically revalue their jobs. As Colette Pétonnet wrote in her ethnography of French suburbs, no worker can be expected to conduct a job just to earn a living (Pétonnet 1979). In this way these women give a sense of purpose, a positive value to their occasional presence in the vineyards. They try to keep their dignity and to oppose the negative representation, or worse, the silence that the majority have of their work. These women bring to their labour a specific family meaning: 'My father worked in the vineyards in Morocco, I always accompanied him in his duties. I am extending a family know-how.' Another: 'This vine is like my child. I have planted it, cared for it, watched it grow. It is part of my life.' They reinterpret the precariousness of employment as a positive virtue: that of free time organised as they please. 'The piecework for us women is better. We organise our time as we want, and the boss has confidence in us. As long as the job is done, it's good!'

In the anthropologist's eyes, at a discursive level, men and women can make their presence essential – depending on the timescale. In the current appreciation of the 'handmade', they attribute the guarantee of quality to their actions in the vineyard: 'If mechanisation, chemistry does the work for us, the consumer will lose out. He will not have the quality in his glass.' They reinterpret their relegation on farms according to the crisis in the wine sector in France: 'We discuss the price of wine with the boss. We understand that, given the competition, he has trouble keeping us.' Trust between 'them' (the bosses) and 'us' (the workers), based on the assurance of a job well done, punctuates their speech about the vines, leaving the ethnic variable aside. 'The boss, he leaves us alone to work, evidence that he has confidence in us.' 'He hires us every year, because he knows he can rely on us and, above all, we work faster than the Gypsies.' Their professional pride is at stake.

At the same time, if this work of symbolic self-appreciation can help them to withstand the concrete reality of work or the lack of it, they are not fooled. They know full well that it is a symbolic device. We can say that this trick worked until the demise of permanent employment. But now their status as 'seasonal' sticks; this symbolic work is less and less effective because the majority (national employers and employees) does not 'work anymore'. There is no possible progress, although there are a few exceptions of young Moroccans who have become cellar masters. Absenteeism becomes, then, a defence mechanism. Faced with the impossibility of social climbing through skilled work on the vines, 'to let them down' is experienced as a way of organising their time to their advantage (e.g. family matters, doctor's appointment) or as a weapon against the powers of work organisation. Finally, to be absent is experienced by some as a way to go on strike individually, because ever more frequent compulsory free time conveys to them their uselessness. They live the paradox of 'the unemployed immigrant', who cannot go back home without having succeeded, yet can no longer justify his presence in front of the majority of the immigrant society. Unemployment doubles the internalisation of a negative identity.

However, none of them moves to try to find a job elsewhere. They all say they belong in Sainte-Foy, and they regard the landscape of vines with joy when they come back from Morocco, Algeria, or Tunisia after the summer holiday. Leaving the area would be experienced as a new uprooting. Until then, their use in the vineyards justified their presence in the eyes of the majority in the vineyard. But the economic difficulties in the vineyards, along with the bad press attendant on 'Islamic' terrorism, expose them to a widespread racism found in the wine-producing towns and in French society in general.

Vineyards as 'one's own territory'

Despite precarious living conditions (e.g. seasonal employment, undeclared work, housing, racism), the Moroccans feel they share with their vine-growing employers, a know-how of the agricultural 'land' and particularly of wine making. Their attachment and belonging to Sainte-Foy manifests itself in the wine production; but at the same time they also feel strong links with a Muslim country, where drinking alcohol is prohibited.

In Sainte-Foy, before the arrival of mechanisation, they remember having participated in all the scheduled events leading to the wine production, and thus felt an affinity with the vineyard and its running. Even if things have changed, their family life is still punctuated by the different phases, which they recite as a litany, of vine cultivation and wine production. For them, their future as men and women depends on it. Their children's early familiarisation with the vines will be a way to learn and internalise what the French call a '*terroir*' (Trubeck 2008), in all its complexities and subtleties. The various plots managed by their parents are defined as specific entities, and through precise characteristics pertaining to soil, geographical situation, age of the vine, and so on.

The transmission of this know-how requires the unpaid physical work of the children, which is supposed also to develop their sense of effort. If the parents do not wish their children to work in the vines, as they have, it is still the case that some of these youths go on to replace a retired relative, usually their father. As a cultural marker, work presides over all transmission, and it is essential for young workers to prove themselves in this professional milieu in order to take the relative's place. For example, thirty-year-old Ahmed became '*maître de chais*', or winery technical manager, after the retirement of his father from the same estate. Others establish agricultural businesses, based on the knowledge transmitted by their previous, unpaid physical work.

In the workers' discourse, this professional knowledge emphasises the idea of local rootedness. They speak of the vine as their 'infant' which they have planted and raised. The very landscape is constitutive of their social identity. The description of a vine requires a specific gaze on its general appearance, of the rows of vines, of the plot. This evaluation is concerned with its strength, colour, and cleanliness: the whole has to be considered. In conversations, the concept of work well done, of beautifully tended vines, keeps on coming up:

> Haléma (aged 38): 'When I come back from Morocco and that I see once more the hills with the vines, it moves me.'
>
> Ahmed (aged 60): 'When I am not in the vines, I think about them, how will they grow … We love beautiful vines.'
>
> Fatima (aged 55): 'The vines are here, all around us. I planted them. I look at them grow, my beautiful vines.'

Pruning is established as a supreme model of social recognition. Each of them has a tale showing off his or her particular pruning technique. When visiting vines, they can never resist evaluating the quality of work done by colleagues, and they will stop to assess the vineyards in detail. The youngest take part in pruning contests in the area and they do not hesitate to compete in national events.

When the wine-producing profession has to be defended, they are at one, they say, with the winery owners. In these times of crisis they stress the importance of the '*terroir*', against massive Australian and South American production. Over the course of their lives, they have marked out the Foy territory from Bergerac to Saint-Emilion, and recognise the excellence of the Saint-Emilion wines. They explain precisely the differences between the appellations: differences in pruning, cleaning, tending, harvesting, etc. For them the wine from Saint-Emilion has all the noble qualities because of the amount of manual labour involved in its production. They condemn mechanisation as it is now practised around Sainte-Foy because, according to them, it goes against the production of real 'quality'.

Since the 1990s the Moroccans have witnessed, with fear and consternation, their gradual exclusion from the sphere of wine production; their relegation to subaltern and episodic tasks. This is, of course, mainly due to mechanisation, and the economic expansion of the area, to which they have largely contributed. Yet they have a feeling that this contribution is not recognised either by their employers or by the townspeople with whom they share a territory. From time to time they are employed on properties within a radius of 50 km from the village; but they do not move from the area of Sainte-Foy, where they feel they belong.

In the vineyards, indigenous categories reveal, in this respect, social antagonisms. French locals tend to distinguish the 'old ones' (Italians) from the 'new ones' (Moroccans). We can add 'rooted' and 'stranger' to this dichotomy, which reflects the marginal position the Moroccans are given today in local economic development. As a minority group they crystallise the economic difficulties of the vineyard world. Their decreasing participation or 'disinvestment' is badly understood and misinterpreted. 'Why are they absent when we have need of them? They go off to the doctor instead of coming to work' (Jean Claude, 45, vineyard owner).

The professional precariousness that is affecting some of these Moroccans questions the established order, so often universally presented as a constructor of legitimate identities: the attachment to a place, to the various hierarchies it generates, and so on. The 'economic valorisation' of the territory, to which they actively participate, is poorly recognised or not recognised at all by their employers who continue to give them precarious and seasonal employment. This leads some of the workers to develop further what we have already mentioned: a type of transnational collectivity, whether that be imaginary or real.[1]

Spaces of one's own: a permanent construction

In the face of this marginalisation in the professional and public sphere, these now part-time agricultural workers have found ways of redefining their identities, as consumers. The older ones know that they will obtain nothing more from the locals. Thus they act in other spheres.

They are creating specific links and spaces through their production, distribution, and consumption of food. The study of these initiatives, which include establishing a network of meat provision (with farmers to buy sheep or cattle), the creation of a halal label of quality, and the setting up of ethnic businesses, illustrates the construction of identities in response to local conditions of integration and social division (Bertheleu 2001).

We have considered here the environment in its social meaning, since we want to examine the relationship established by these migrants with their new surroundings through the acquisition of food. In this rural world a specific 'Moroccan' but also 'Algerian', or 'Tunisian', network of food production and distribution has been established, more particularly concerning fruit, vegetables, and halal meat. (Inverted commas are placed around these terms for the same reasons that they frame our use of 'Moroccans'; these are indigenous mainland-French terms exposing a hierarchical culturalist categorisation of others resident in France, who went to live there either because of mass recruitment organised by the French State on decolonisation in 1960, or because they followed a French patron during the same period.). The average 'shopping basket' seemed to us able to define borders within a territorial entity, itself generating identity. Organising food provisions, cooking in a context of migration, which may be regarded as facts expressing identity, can open up perspectives on the question of multiple constructions and the crossing of territories.

The choice of a so-called Moroccan grocer, of a vegetable grower from the Lot et Garonne, of a producer of 'Blonde d'Aquitaine' cattle, and of the slaughter house in La Réole or Bergerac, each with its own Muslim sacrificer approved by the Paris mosque and able to bleed the animals 'as one should', allows them to express not only the values of their group but also the different ways of belonging to this particular rural area of France. The way they shop for foods is inspired by the various components present at the local level, therefore reflecting their own structuring of the territory of Sainte-Foy. They go to the various supermarkets (e.g. Leclerc, Leader Price, Intermarché) choosing them not only for the nature of the shopping, but also for the prices – the women exchange information on the day's bargains. The Saturday morning market has also become a not-to-be-missed event in the week, to such an extent that an Arabic language teacher has had to change the schedule of her courses to accommodate it.

Immigrant women used to visit a kosher butcher's shop in Lamonzie Saint Martin once a week for stocking up on meat for the family's freezers. They are now using halal butchers that have opened in the villages of Sainte-Foy-la-Grande itself, or Grand Frais in Bergerac. Buying from these stores gives them the certainty of eating not only halal meat, but also a safe and healthy meat. 'It has the stamp on it, it's marked on the meat ... Like that at least we know what we are eating' (Fatima, 50).

'Moroccan' stalls at the local weekly market cater for Moroccans of course, but also for locals increasingly curious of 'foreign' cuisines. Three small shish kebab restaurants have opened in Sainte-Foy, thus allowing the locals to explore and share specific foods. School fairs also are scenes of 'exchanges' between 'French' and 'Moroccans', through pastry stands and other foods produced by the Moroccan women. As one of them expressed it:

> When we have a pastry stand at the fair, they look at us more positively, but otherwise, in the public spaces of Sainte-Foy, it's hate and contempt. I know that I have French nationality, but they don't look on me as French. With our sweet pastries, we try to soften things. (Haléma, 38)

It is mostly through food that they try to establish contact with the locals. Invited to a town hall meeting on the participation of Moroccans in the local festive events of Sainte-Foy, the representatives of the mosque suggested giving a lamb to the college for the festival of Eid el Kabir. This provoked sharp reactions among the members of the town council who, given the long-standing secular tradition of the French State, were opposed to any display of religiosity within the schools.

Through eating habits, the various operations of appropriations of the environment show how individuals can transform it according to their general interests, both practical and symbolic, not only in function of local but also national constraints.

The healthy eating 'heritage': between Morocco and France, an idealised rurality?

This research has shown that new ideas about nutrition are emerging among these families while at the same time, as Moroccans, they are being accorded a very unequal position in the social relationships that shape their working life in the vineyards. Despite this, for both parents and children, the 'vine-growing territory' is considered their 'natural' environment, one favourable for the production of good food, and for the maintenance of good health, through self-production, direct purchase of vegetables and meat, and the possibility of an appropriate lifestyle. Following the general evolution of the representation of what constitutes 'good nutrition', industrial foods are a particular theme on which they openly voice their fears (Hubert 2000).

We have tried to show here how the Moroccans of the vineyards reintegrate the discourse and representations of the majority on the contemporary craze for a 'reassuring and healthy countryside', whether Moroccan or French, in a search for 'authenticity' and 'tradition' (Lenclud 1987). In 1990 the Moroccans thought that this order had been disrupted by the Westerners who gave animal products to herbivores. They therefore think that Muslim practice will give them a greater control over their foods and thereby their health. Ethnic, religious, and health requisites are intertwined here.

We have also shown how 'Moroccan' and 'rural' identities are valued to justify healthy diets, or put aside to signify a belonging to urban France and a well-balanced lifestyle. Nevertheless, the discourse, as noted above, should not make us think that these populations only consume 'local products' and halal. They also consume products of the agro-food industry, but oscillate between these three poles, valuing their rurality and their Muslim faith in the present context of valorisation of '*terroir*' but also of political edginess towards Muslims. Studies of eating habits show how these minorities transform their territory according to their practical and symbolic interests and also to economic and political constraints.

Thus, in a changing countryside, globalisation, migration, imaginary projections, rural and urban territories, ethnic interactions and cultural identity are all linked, giving each other meaning in an ever changing pattern. At the same time, the study of cultures and territories must be placed within the political environment of societies – themselves part of a world system. In this case, like the Protestants, the Moroccans appropriate this rural territory, making it their own through their history and their work in the vines. The so-called Moroccans of this wine-growing area, despite being excluded from the professional field, invest in the local area by building houses and developing a local food network, for example a halal butcher or their own vegetable gardens. What is interesting to note, is that they develop the same ideas of this territory: a territory which they consider to be their own, 'authentic' and 'pure', in contrast to the town.

Note

1 For some young people, comings and goings between France and Morocco develop into commercial activities (Tarrius 2001).

References

Abélès, Marc in A. Appadurai (ed.) 2005 *Après le colonialisme. Les conséquences culturelles de la globalisation* (Paris: Payot, coll. 'Petite bibliothèque payot'. Orig. pub. *Modernity at Large: Cultural Dimensions of Globalization*. 1996).

Anderson, Benedict 2006 *L'Imaginaire national réflexions sur l'origine et l'essor du nationalisme* (Paris: La découverte. Orig. pub. 1983).

Bertheleu, Hélène 2001 *Identifications ethniques: rapports de pouvoir, compromis, territoire* (Paris: L'Harmattan).

Besson, Eric 2009 *Grand débat sur l'identité nationale: 18 November*. www.gouvernement.fr/gouvernement grand-débat-sur-l-identité-nationale-25-000-contributions-recues-des-la-premiere-semaine. Accessed 10 June 2013.

Crenn, Chantal 2003 'Alimentation et santé des familles d'émigrants au Maroc: acculturation et ethnicité', in I. Gobatto (ed.) *Dynamiques locales de la mondialisation: les Afriques en perspective* (Paris: MSHA/Kathala),167–202.

Crenn, Chantal 2013 'Des invisibles trop visibles? Les ouvriers agricoles "marocains" dans les vignobles du Bordelais', *Revue Hommes et migrations*, sp. issue 'Migrations et mondes ruraux', 130 (January–February–March): http://www.hommes-et migrations.fr/index.php?/numeros/migrations-et-mondes-ruraux/7080-des-invisibles-trop-visibles. Accessed 3 April 2013.

Crenn, Chantal and Isabelle Téchoueyres 2004 'Enracinement, production de la différence et nécessités du marché; l'exemple du président du syndicat Ste Foy-Bordeaux', *Anthropology of food* [Online], 3 December, http://aof.revues.org. Accessed 26 June 2013.

Démossier, Marion 2010 'Le point de vue de l'anthropologue', in *La Gouvernance des terroirs du vin* (Bordeaux, Edition Feret), 201–09.

DiMéo, Guy 1996 'Production des identités et attachement au lieu', in Lamy Yvon *L'Alchimie du patrimoine, discours et politiques* (Talence: MSHA), 247–69.

Guillaume, Pierre 1990 *Étrangers en Aquitaine* (Talence: MSHA)

Hubert, Annie 2000 'Alimentation santé: la science et l'imaginaire', *Cahier de nutrition et de diététique*, 35:5, 353–6.

Lenclud, Gérard 1987 'La Tradition n'est plus ce qu'elle était…', *Terrain*, 9, (October) http://terrain.revues.org/index3195.html. Accessed 25 June 2013.

Pétonnet, Colette 1979 *On est tous dans le brouillard. Ethnologie des banlieues* (Paris: Galilée).

Sayad, A. 1999 *La Double absence. Des illusions de l'émigré aux souffrances de l'immigré* (Paris: Le Seuil, coll. 'Liber').

Simon, Pierre-Jean 1981 'Minorités et territoires', *Pluriel débat*, 25, 35–7.

Tarrius, Alain 1992 *Les Fourmis d'Europe* (Paris: L'Harmattan).

Trubek, Amy 2008 *The Taste of Place: A Cultural Journey into 'Terroir'* (Berkeley, CA: University of California Press).

5

The new rural residents: emerging sociabilities in Alava, Basque Country

Josetxu Martínez Montoya

The traditional habitat

Alava is one of seven territories of the Basque Country, with an approximate population of three hundred thousand, most living in the capital, Vitoria-Gazteiz, and in a few other urban centres. The rest of the territory is formed by about four hundred villages, most composed of a small number of households (four to five in the smaller villages, twenty to thirty in the larger ones).

Traditionally, Alava was inhabited by local communities formed by peasant families, organised under a council of neighbours, and structured by age, gender, and kinship. Its corporative character was manifest in socio-religious associations (*cofradías*) and in the tight control of territory through geographical limits and spatial and social rituals. Freeman (1968) characterised these associations as 'mass-feast-meeting-complexes'. As used to be said in the villages, *'No hay misa sin mesa, y no hay vereda sin colación así como no hay romería sin cura y sin fiesta'* ('There is no mass without table, no common work without lunch, and no pilgrimage without priest and party'). Celebrating belonging gathers together aspects of local society concerned with the sharing of daily issues at the bar, playing cards, visiting the ill or the elderly, and celebrating and enjoying the fruits of labour and the land.

In the recent past communities were strongly localised, deeply rooted in their territory, in which the control of behaviour and thought, of the use of community space and time was one of the main defining features (Martínez Montoya 1996; 2004). Group solidarity was based on respect of tradition and adaptation to the productive and reproductive cycles of the community. Community cooperation, social responsibility, and the resultant way of thinking were a product of this adaptation.

Delocalisation, relocalisation

These long-established territorial units of social organisation began to experience significant destructuring between the 1960s and 1980s. There were at least three important consequences of the deagrarisation and deruralisation that they suffered: the progressive abandonment of agriculture; migration towards the cities; and the decline of a traditional means of management and normatisation of rural communities. The rural environment was delocalised. Vitoria-Gasteiz swelled with rural emigrants, producing a population vacuum, which had severe consequences ecologically (environmental impact and imbalance), socially (ageing population), and culturally (loss of heritage and traditional values). Neither domestic nor productive units were renovated. The sense that villages were disappearing became acute, since the traditional means of territorial management were no longer being reproduced.

However, today, the rural environment seems to be showing new signs of vitality. Many regional institutions are becoming interested in the rural environment, while many of its inhabitants who left in the past are now coming back, married and with children, to remodel and reuse the old family house, or to build a new life. Social life is rebuilt; new socio-economic and sociocultural projects emerge.

The Alavan countryside is being reoccupied. Today's neo-rurals are playing a significant role in the changing demographic profile of the till-now ageing rural population. Rural Alava has no longer a mainly peasant population; territory is no longer primarily defined in agricultural terms, but by a variety of functions: residential, recreational, as well as agricultural. These require different, alternative and in many cases, competitive logistics.

The territory has stopped becoming a demographic desert, but has turned into something quite the opposite, for the relationship between the human group and the territory – space – is being redefined. A new sociocultural model for the rural environment is under construction.

The independent variable

Sociologically, the new basic fact in the composition of the new rural populations is the return to the rural environment and its occupation by seasonal or permanent residents whose main activity is not primarily agricultural. At the same time, institutions are implementing a strong interventionist policy to promote the complementarity of primary activities with extra-agricultural activities. The aim is to produce a renovated form of pluriactivity for the rurality and so attempt to correct the pernicious effects of the uniformalising and productivist policies of the 1960s. Since the 1980s the EU, troubled by the abandoning of rural areas, has created a programme for the economic, social, and cultural revitalisation of rural areas. This programme is intended to check the ageing of the rural population and rural emigration by promoting sustainable development based on fostering small enterprises and tourism, and by improving local habitats and rural services. These policies, together with the back-to-the-country movement of those who once lived there, have resulted in permanent and seasonal reoccupation of rural areas. The policies of the institutions and the aims of the returnees are, however, not primarily based on agricultural activity but on leisure and recreation.

This powerful push towards rural regeneration over the last two decades is the consequence of three sociological realities: (a) the continuing modernisation of the traditional rural project; (b) the reconversion, powered mainly by institutions, of rural space to multifunctional space; and (c) a new sociability linked to a new conception of habitat: 'neo-rurality'. The villages found in the traditional rural space of Alava are, today, the result of those three factors. The greater or lesser influence of any of the three explains the diversity of village identities in Alava today. It is clear, however, that the rural environment has itself been profoundly changed. Today 'rural' could be defined not so much by the concept of community as of locality. The contemporary rural space is a space of multiple presences and functions, in which the management of what is local is both competitive and complementary.

This phenomenon can be best understood by analysing the concerns of rural inhabitants. Until the 1960s life was difficult, they say, and the most important thing was to get ahead and find a good position for one's children (through a job, marriage, etc.). In the 1980s, ageing locals were becoming increasingly worried by the emptying of their village squares. Today, in contrast, worries centre around urban, social, and cultural projects which are perceived as different, and often as aggressive and disrespectful of identity and tradition.

But not all is bad. Many of the immigrants were in fact born or grew up in the villages. Their concerns, presence, and projects give motivation, life, and continuity to what seemed to be dying out. They are the agents of the new sociability and the regenerators of a millennial culture which seemed to have reached its end.

The management of the new rural sociability

I here focus on the management of rural sociability, which was very rich in the past but declined during the years between 1960 and 1980: secular traditions disappeared, forms of social cohesion controlled by religion weakened, community councils faced difficulties trying to maintain the normative schemes of the past. The rural environment, broadly understood, was no longer capable of managing its own sociability, since the territory was losing its more dynamic elements. In effect, machines were chewing up villages' rich organisational tradition.

Nevertheless, as social anthropological work can show in a detailed manner, the territory continues to offer spaces and places of intense conviviality which may foster the growth of a deep sense of belonging. It is here where the new cultural associations, replacing old *cofradías* (religious confraternities) have a key role in energising rural sociability. In particular, festivities are the occasions where the new community comes together and manifests itself, in traditional spaces. Unlike their ritual precursors, these festivities are not linked to fostering fertility, or to the local, cosmological circular logic. Rather, they reveal the felt need to end the decay of social life and conviviality caused by the rise of a competitive and individualist society. 'Natural, ecological life' and 'community life' are in turn the new myths which the promoters of these rituals attempt to rescue and utilise as energisers of the felt need for social life experienced by members of Alava's new generations.

After a long period of social and normative de-structuration, the social space of the community finds new referents for social legitimacy and makes them appear, or (in the language of Clifford Geertz) textualises them, in the practice of shared sociability and rituality. What, if not this, are communal dinners, community feasts, festivals, the celebration of neighbourhood festivities, the rituals of hunting parties, or other local festivities? Through these rituals, rural immigrants, who were estranged from the spaces of traditional life, can participate in those spaces, and in the process reconstruct and resocialise them in a new manner. In doing so, they rely on memory (heritage) and the spaces of sacredness (which serve to rebond with the cultural past) to insert themselves into the chain of community sociability, otherwise broken by machines and urban progress. The rotations and circuits which once marked the identity of villagers have now to accommodate the new sociability – goods circulation networks, in which traditional spaces can be used to solder the ruptures and the abandonment of spaces in the economic, social, and cultural life of the past.

Why do people come back to the village to perform the rites of passage of their children (e.g. first Holy Communion, confirmation), to live the dream of a life of commitment and happiness (marriage), or to be buried in their grandparents' land, that is to say, in the genealogy of the community? Why do people find identity, personal prestige, and collective identification with people and places which still symbolise to many sacrifice, poverty, inferior status, and the impossibility of realising a full life, things which may, after all, be found in the city?[1]

New conflicts in the rural environment: the plaza as a way of life, integration, and resistance

Between January and June 1992 the *Plaza Irekita* (Open Square) Association of the Alava Mountain region held a series of meetings, one apiece in eight villages of the region, so that the new rural residents could share their experiences with the traditional community members. These meetings sought to be an opportunity for new and old residents of the villages to reflect on how they perceived the new situation of their villages, their composition and the degree of integration they enjoyed.

The initiative arose from a basic concern: the need, felt by association members, to be more aware of the new social situation of the villages in the territory and the degree of social integration they possessed. In particular, the permanent presence of neo-rurals in the villages brought an unavoidable challenge: is it possible to live in the village in such a way that it remains an open space? The objective of the *Plaza Irekita* initiative was to bring out these new ways of living in the village expressed in the name of the project: 'Open Plaza: the different ways of living in a village'.

The encounters revealed that the presence of new residents is both conflictive and enriching. In some instances newcomers integrated into the local community; in others, they replaced it, and provided alternatives to traditional rural social life. It became clear that a simple dichotomy of old and new residents did not shed much light and failed to reflect the varied social and cultural situations of current rural populations. Alavan villages are today populated by residents whose interests and ways of life and thinking are very diverse (farmers, retired people, technical managers, seasonal residents, etc.) They are all part of the villages, in different ways. They all occupy a space and care for and manage it in different ways. Without older adults, there would be no functioning churches, and without youth, few hopes for the future and no new projects. Without farmers, roads would become unusable, and houses uninhabitable. In the same way, without those who come back periodically, many projects would be untenable and sociabilisation severely damaged. And we mustn't forget services, social programmes for the elderly and development projects, or more important, the permanent institutions which manage communities and make it possible for them to survive. These villages are the result of all these presences. For the young, the village is boring; for a mayor, it's a bag of trouble; for the vacationer, a paradise; and for those who come back after living elsewhere for a long time, a place to be revitalised.

Sometimes these practices collide because they are perceived as problematic and the richness they bring to the community is ignored. The wealth of the villages today lies in this diversity, and in the recognition and valuing of differing practices and ways of living the plaza. There is, however, a presence that is seen by some as problematic: the weekend residents. As some of the returnees complain:

Outsiders are seen as invaders; insiders are closed-minded.
It is difficult to be part of the community, they are very closed-minded people.
It was only when my child went to school that I began to be part of the group.
There are no welcoming or integration committees … they ignore us.

These are expressions of a deeply rooted tendency in the rural environment: resistance to the non-resident, who is seen as alien. When these non-residents are perceived as a group, stereotypes and barriers of identification and exclusion emerge. There is a kind of patrimonialisation of the territory and a fear that the outsiders are coming to order people around and impose their authority.

And yet, many of those who come back have never been strangers to the village. They think of it as their village; they are its children. Culturally speaking, in their terms, there has been no rupture in the many years they have been physically absent. That is why it is so easy for them to link again into everyday life in the village and also make it richer, because they value and need it to develop fully as individuals. While, as individuals, they are not perceived as strangers (they are children of a home everyone has known all their lives), when they are seen as part of a different, alternate group, they are perceived as strangers against whom local society reacts to defend itself. This explains the strength of the 'insider/outsider' perception that exists, and even seems prevalent in many villages.

However, such a dualist vision hides a reality which is increasingly present and defining of what constitutes a contemporary village: a place of life, work and residence of differentiated collectivities, with different rhythms and very varied degrees of integration. Today there is a mismatch between perception and sociological reality: we have a population that is increasingly diversified and heterogeneous, but highly polarised and focused on the insider/outsider opposition, due, in part, to what may be called a conflictive management of local identities. Villages are increasingly relationship networks, i.e. something built and permanently renovated. In the minds of their traditional dwellers and some of the newcomers, the corporative vision has primacy. This way of thinking comes out strongly at election times, but is also expressed in the management of sociability and of community spaces and times: church congregations, festivities, bars, etc.

Roots, or the consciousness of belonging

The testimonies gathered in the encounters organised by Open Plaza demonstrated the importance that a sense of roots and belonging have for these people. Those who left their home village are not aware of having ever left it. Their experiences, their close ties with the place, family, friends, and memories all make them feel part of the place (*heimat*), of the village where they were born and had to leave physically but not sentimentally. Those who have come back remember that they left because they had no alternative or because they were seeking a better future for their children.

The new residents are really family or friends who once left the village. Now they return to a space and a community they feel part of. They reintegrate into something that they feel as their own and want to update because they care about it. They take part in activities, old and new, that the village offers, with no sense of rupture. They find the space they left and seek to reproduce it after years of crisis and abandonment. They experienced a distancing, but not a cultural rupture. Being from a village has been with them all their lives, and their return is for them, a reintegration into a way of being and living, into a culture: forms of relationships, behaviours, attitudes, feelings, and perception of group life.

However, the classification given to neo-rural people, *domingueros* (Sunday visitors), is not casual, for they do have one foot in the village, and the other outside. That is why some people think that newcomers are simply taking advantage of finding a nice place, which the permanent residents have maintained through the years. But newcomers, in turn, feel they never abandoned the home village. And not only that: having returned, they have helped regenerate the village. And that is difficult to dispute.

There is a strong feeling that living in the village is integrating into it. And so, those who return, having once belonged and having had the village as their reference point, have hardly any difficulty in being accepted, and feel like members of the large extended family that is the community. They feel at home, and able to exercise their right to it. They are part of the village's history; its past is their past; their shared life experiences make them co-participants of the memory of the place and its particular history.

At the same time, there is a strong cultural resistance against accepting neighbours, residents or inhabitants who use the village as a dormitory or place of leisure, and as nothing else. They exclude themselves from the plaza and its cohesive, centripetal, and formulating powers of group behaviour. They are seen as visitors, i.e. living in the village means being part of the plaza, perhaps in a different way today than in the past, but definitely part of it. And this means working for the village, collaborating and participating in its activities, being integrated into the dynamic of ruling community time and space. The commitment to place assumes that the person feels part of it and is capable of entering the plaza and its integrating dynamic.

It could be said that the village is what people do every day. Today, these everyday activities follow several rhythms. What some say when speaking of a particular village, Lagran, is true – there are three speed gears to living:

- first, Sunday afternoon when visitors leave and the grandparents are at last able to rest, because with the visitors go the noise and the rush.
- second, Friday afternoon when, oppressed by loneliness, grandparents anxiously await the arrival of visitors and the time when the village's population seems to double.
- third, summer when the investment is secure: the village's population will triple.

These three rhythms express three ways of living in the village:

- the first defines the village in terms of management and concern. It is the work of the permanent members of the community, some aged, such as grandparents; others dedicated to the everyday work of agriculture and farming, care of the house and domestic work.
- people who come during the weekend 'live the village' primarily in terms of representation, i.e. as something to be built, or a gap to be filled according to nostalgic models. This way of living the village has been enriched by the presence of seasonal residents, who come with a great desire to relive what they have lost and find again the community in which they were born. This is a two-fold desire: both social and cultural. The richness of the past, the signs of which are still present (festivities, places, monuments, art, etc.) and which acquire special importance; they are endowed with the ability to channel the construction of a new community which is integrated into traditional space, but which, at the same time, partially replaces it. This helps to explain why some people say with complete candour that they have never really left the village and have always lived in it; they carried it with them and as soon as they were able, they returned.

- a third rhythm is the one that takes place during the summer and the longer holidays. In this case, there may be no other element apart from consuming (tourism, leisure, rest).

Villages are made up of all three rhythms. The village square, however, requires that representation and consumerism guarantee management, or it may not be able to survive.

From these three distinct rhythms we are able to see (a) the diversity of presences in village life; (b) the importance people place on living the plaza, on the culture of the plaza, and on the renovation and reconstruction of the plaza as a place of shared expression of culture. Given this, we may talk of different ways of living in the village; but, at a more profound level, the plaza in fact imposes a style, a way of being and sharing that is similar for all. Underlying the concept of Open Plaza is a deeply rooted cultural tendency which limits belonging-to-the-community to those who share residency or those to whom this category is extended, that is, the elements of cohesion and formulation in group behaviour seem to be defined by this criterion.

Thus, although we find different rhythms and presences, or (to put it another way) different ways of living and feeling the village, there exists only one commonly accepted way. How the plaza and the social relations with which it is filled are understood does not seem to leave much room for diverse sensibilities.

The cultural logic of the village as a construction model for a more extended social life

The model of life and integration into the plaza in the village is so deeply rooted that its cultural dynamic is reproduced, at a larger level; in this case at the construction of a new socio-economic project, the reconversion of the Alava Mountain region[2] into a new space of development.

Each year, the Alava Mountain region celebrates a special day (The Day of the Alava Mountain) to remind everyone that they must work together to achieve integral development in the region. This region more than others has suffered the socio-economic decline within the province of Alava. One particularly depressed municipality, Lagran, was chosen as the site for the celebration in the summer of 1999. Here I analyse this special day in the context in which it took place and the expectations it generated.

The Day is a festive manifestation that celebrates belonging under a new sociological reality, a territorial management construct: that is, a territory subject to external intervention. Because of the imbalance caused by agricultural specialisation during the 1960s, local authorities implemented a number of programmes and actions based on the developmentist philosophy 'integral rural development': in other words, economic pluriactivity, residential viability, fulfilment of services, and social and cultural revitalisation. The geographical framework of intervention is dubbed a region or shire (see Chaussier 1998). The Alava Mountain was one of those regions.

People from all walks of life became involved in this project (politicians, entrepreneurs, farmers, intellectuals, organisation leaders, etc.), with a single common objective: make the region live, and do so within the logic of continuation and renovation. All of this was done for the purpose of generating an imagined, but also inherited, idea that a landscape, a set of traditions, a mode of social organisation, and a project are shared: in sum, an identity.

Lagran had suffered severe population decline in the 1960s and 1970s, and is an example of the effort that institutions and neo-residents are carrying out to revitalise the village's social life. Regardless of the good quality of its products, younger generations seem unwilling to take on the same occupation as their parents. But even when they have moved to the city, they are not abandoning the village. Lagran does not look like a forgotten place. Houses, buildings, and infrastructure do not speak of decline; rather, of well-being. The children of those who migrated to the city are coming back. They repair the granaries and the houses of elderly parents, or construct newer buildings, so life appears renovated and the buildings well maintained. But this is not all. The golf course in Lagran and Urturi and the recreational complex of the latter (e.g. agro-tourism, restaurants, golf course) have helped re-route development and the possibilities of a region in which potato cultivation renovated the generating capacity of traditional life (coal and cattle), and in which another motor (tourism and seasonal or weekend residence) is attempting to return life to the area again.[3]

Given these changes, the Day becomes a reflection on what the region aspires to achieve: the construction of a regional space with an identity of its own, which gathers around a common project its six constituent municipalities, in order to energise development programmes. The message communicated by the celebration of this festive ritual within the space of traditional social life, of the village's plaza, is significant. The intention is to inscribe in this space a regional project that overflows but doesn't supplant or replace the village's space. Rather, it follows the logic of community cooperation and reciprocity.

The space of the celebration

The space chosen for the activities of the Day of the Mountain is a good indicator to understand what the organisers sought to express and achieve.

Sunday mass at the parish church opened the Day. It continued in the village's central plaza with folkloric Basque dances and music: *fanfarria* (fanfares played by brass and percussive ensembles), *trikitixas* (accordionists), and *txistularis* (fluteplayers). In the village park, a Basque-speaking troupe engaged children in traditional games. Near the sports centre there were exhibitions and activities of crafts and handmade products: honey, pastries, beans, cheese, and black pudding, each from a specific village, along with local artisans displaying their products, ready to discuss their manufacture; i.e. the ages-old wisdom of artisanship and the new farming products were the main attractions at the celebration.

Contemporary rural society is manifest in this kind of ritual performance as shown by analysis of three closely intertwined aspects: the human group, the space, and the ritual. The group's ritual activities, temporarily regulated, are marked in the space of everyday sociability and are, here, full of shared meanings. The inhabited space (as opposed to the productive or the natural space) is privileged in this ritual. It engraves the idea of constructing a new community around the spaces of the past to signal the beginning of a desired new reality: the development and recuperation of the population of the region. The location of the activities on this day suggests that the new socio-economic project seeks to be inserted in the form, the spaces, and the cultural logic that used to regulate the traditional life of the villages. This explains why the Church and the Plaza are integrated and take a central role in the festivity, as they used to do in the past and continue doing today in the village's sociability.

These spaces are related to the agricultural world, whose management is simultaneously productive, communal, and cosmological, in the circular community logic. However, this economic foundation is today unable to reproduce the life of human habitat and to maintain territory. The new realities that are emerging (golf course, agro-toursim, restaurants, children and Euskara, handmade products and agricultural elements brought in from outside) speak of emerging realities invading the mountain space. Tradition is not replaced but transformed into a tool to build the new sociability, i.e. into a model and image of social behaviours and cultural tendencies to be transmitted. The presence of traditional artisans and vintage photographs at or near the sports centre communicates the message of the integration of two worlds, one of which is yielding to the other without traumatic ruptures, and makes real, through ritual, the message being communicated.

It is interesting to note that the symbols appearing in this celebration are not those linked to farming (potatoes, cattle) but generated by the new emergent activities of the region. They are, however, symbols and activities that, by integrating into the spaces and rituals of traditional sociability, express and realise at a symbolic level something that the festivities and rituals linked to the villages realise in an exemplary way: local community. This is the performative dimension of the celebration: its success at making the region like a village, in which community members reproduce the solidarity rituals which villages still conserve. This, however, would be impossible to do only through the aged population that inhabits the region permanently, or with the sociability of the *cofradías* and other socio-religious institutions that used to keep the village alive. These do not exist anymore. Setting the new project in action requires new managers and new agents: these are the cultural institutions or associations.

It is through this new social-organising reality of the villages of Alava that the success of the celebration can be explained. It was the work of the local government, together with the cultural associations of Villaverde, Lagran, and Pipaon, which made possible the realisation of this new ritual, with its new messages and the new language in which they are expressed.

The agents of the new sociability

The cultural associations are a new phenomenon in the rural life of Alava. They respond to the reality of a seasonal population that chose to energise the life in the villages and recover the traditions of the past, and to transform these human habitats into centres of sociability and the celebration of leisure time (weekends). In this sense, these associations have replaced the old *cofradías* in their role of giving cohesion to the community life of the villages (Martínez Montoya 1995).

It is thanks to them and through their mediation that physical closeness is transformed into social closeness. This is not just a village-centred closeness but an inter-village one, which in the past was upheld by common use of sanctuaries and mountain hermitages. In this sense the close relationship between cultural associations of the three villages of Lagran, through activities (such as inter-village competitions, fairs, choir, and group excursions) that are staged along the annual cycle, with particular emphasis on important holiday periods (Christmas, Easter, and summer) is remarkable. Activities are not, however, limited to those periods, but continue throughout the year: *Lardero* Thursdays (the last Thursday before Lent), walks to Laguardia and Estíbaliz, special feast days (San Kiliz, Day of the Pensioners, Nature day, Potato Day), talks, etc.

The associations, regarded in cultural terms, have become remarkable global alternatives of sociability. The sociability they energise is based on recovering tradition, heritage, and the cultural scheme of the past while integrating environmental, patrimonial, and relational elements. Those who come back on a seasonal basis seek not only to enjoy a day of leisure, or take advantage of nature, but to recover a way of life that belonged to their elders, and in which many of them were born. Traditional culture and space have been capable of hosting the reconstruction of the deteriorated social situation engendered by years of productivism.

This seems to be the logic of the Mountain Day's celebration. The model is the village; the emerging new sociability, the region; the fuelling agents are the cultural associations; the symbols are as multiple as the uses of space, but remarkable among them are the leisure activities through which the cultural associations express themselves. To summarise, it is companionship, the old and renovated ritual of community cohesion, always present in a system in which commensality seals new and old solidarities, which is wrought in the urban-rural space of our territory.

The idea of building a regional community is expressed though the formerly village-based model of circular, reciprocal relationships. This is marked in space and transferred to current socio-economic and sociocultural ways of life that are inserted into the dynamics of the plaza.

Conclusion

In rural Alava, the decade of the 1980s marked a significant turning point. It is a period in which new elements began to consolidate a social and cultural process. One of the most significant elements was the permanent (although seasonal) presence of new rural residents who chose to return to the way of life to which they were born, and to transform it in a space of social and ritual practices which take into account the local traditions, heritage and identity of each village. These villages have had a culture based on valuing permanent residence and consciousness of belonging to a rotating community chain of duties and dues.

The socio-economic changes of the 1960s had broken this cultural logic. Two decades later, new community members – to a large degree children of the village – returned on a seasonal basis and remade social and ritual life based on similar values. The first of these values, permanent residence, is a factor against them: they are seen as alien and invasive. But all in all, progress and economic development have shortened the distances between the rural and urban spaces and transformed them into a spatial continuum of sorts. The classic dichotomy between rural and urban has blurred. It is still there, however, as we have seen, in the resistance to emerging sociabilities, but the new special conditions of the well-communicated Alava territory are beginning to dissolve them. In contrast, the second value, the recovery of tradition and heritage, is these returnees' best card in the strategy they pursue: to rebuild the past's sociability in the space of their elders, reproducing in this manner cultural tradition.

However, neither the identity nor the culture of these new members of the community is the same. The new communities are not defined by adaptation to the productive and biological cycles, as were the communities of the past. We find, in contrast, multiple and fragmented identities. Participation in sociability associations is fragile and elective. Rural festivities and rituals reproduce a time and space that did not condition the behaviour and mentality of individuals. They do not reproduce a community of tradition. The signification of the multiple activities and ritualisations in which the rural environment acts as the subject has to be found in something other than traditional rural logic, which used to reproduce the biological cycle around circular times and spaces (see Martínez Montoya 2001).

The activities of new residents show the cultural tendencies towards the construction of identities in times and spaces that aim to recreate community in a renovated mode. These are times and spaces in which individualism and competition have no place. The new members are not bound to the times and spaces of the past. The bond that links them does not chain their lives around corporative duties. Their times and spaces are urban; however, they have found villages, whether their ancestor's or otherwise, which welcome them and allow them to develop worlds of meaning, which in turn strengthen their otherwise fragile identity. They are in search of ontological security (Revill 1993), and find it via re-traditionalisation

(Thompson 1996), i.e. social phenomena generated by the dynamic of social change through which social groups can re-mould their life projects and fill them with guiding meanings.

Notes

1 For an analysis of this re-symbolisation process of rurality, see Martínez Montoya, 2003.

2 This is a region of the Historical Territory of Alava. With only a little more than three thousand inhabitants and forty-seven population centres, its traditional activity used to be farming (grains, potato, and cattle). For almost two decades it has been the subject of institutional intervention to revitalise its socio-economic development.

3 Post-industrial society seems to be oriented, in our territory, towards a tertiarisation process in which there is a clear separation between residence and work and in which the new rurality is emptied of productive activities to constitute itself as ecological, leisure, labelled, and identity celebration spaces. The relationship between the human group and territory has gone through a significant transformation. The latter appears as a privileged place of multiple and differentiated practices in order to satisfy the new demands of the rural-urban society which inhabits it.

References

Chaussier, Jean-Daniel 1998 'La question territoriale en Pays Basque de France (Exception irréductible ou laboratoire du pluralisme?)', in F. Letamendia (ed.) *La construcción del espacio vasco-aquitano. Un estudio multidisciplinar* (Leioa: EHU-UPV), 257–74.

Freeman, Susan Tax 1968 'Religious aspects of the social organization of a Castilian village', *American Anthropologist*, 70:1–3, 34–40.

Martínez Montoya, Josetxu 1995 'Asociaciones culturales. La gestión de la sociabilidad rural', *Okoa Kultur Elkartearen Aldiskaria*, 4, 24–5.

——1996 *Pueblos, ritos y montañas. Prácticas vecinales y religiosas en el tiempo y en el espacio de la comunidad rural, Valle de Arana (Araba, Euskal Herria)* (Bilbao: Desclée de Brouwer).

——2001 'La nueva ruralidad: de la comunidad a lo local', *Inguruak*, 30, 205–16.

——2003 *La identidad reconstruida. Espacios y sociabilidades emergentes en la ruralidad alavesa* (Vitoria-Gasteiz: Gobierno Vasco/Eusko Jaurlaritza),139–56.

—— 2004 'La fiesta patronal como ritual performativo, iniciático e identitario. La celebración de la comunidad vecinal como lugar de dependencia, de pertenencia y de permanencia', *Zaiñak, Cuadernos de Antropología-Etnografía*, 26, 347–67.

Revill, George 1993 'Reading Rosehill: community, identity and inner-city Derby', in M. Keith and S. Pile (eds) *Place and the Politics of Identity* (London: Routledge), 117–40.

Thompson, John B. 1996 'Tradition and self in a mediated world', in P. Heelas, S. Lash and P. Morris (eds) *Detraditionalization. Critical Reflections on Authority and Identity* (Oxford: Blackwell), 89–108.

6

Farms, flats, and villas: senses of country living in a Basque-speaking village

Kepa Fernández de Larrinoa

This chapter focuses on how peasants from a particular Basque village articulate their understandings of the country and the city during two periods: first, the late 1970s and the early 1980s; second, the beginning of the twenty-first century. The first corresponds to a high point in the process of national modernisation in Spain, which was based on industrial development. The second is occurring during a shift to Europe-oriented policies, and a growth of discourses on rural development and welfare. Both periods echo substantial changes in rural Basque society. To better understand those changes from a peasant's perspective, it is necessary to start from indigenous concepts of the country and the city. Thus, I discuss several words which Basque-speaking peasants refer to when locating themselves in the dialectics between the countryside and the city. To this end, first I briefly describe the village; then, I portray several traditional and newly cultural models with which villagers express concepts of social belonging or rejection; finally, in order to explain how residents interpret social change in the village in relation to those cultural models, I focus on the local school and the open party that parents have organised annually since the early 1990s. For, where there was once something approaching a unified local vision of the world, the present reality is much more complex, varied, and socially fractured.

All my remarks and information are based on the intensive fieldwork I carried out in the village between 1982 and 1985, followed by repeated visits in the following years; since 2000 I have resided there permanently.

Views of the village and the city

Alkiza is a Basque village in the province of Guipúzcoa, Spain. It has a population of almost four hundred people. It is 28 km to San Sebastián, capital of the province, and 8 km to Tolosa, the county's capital (Fernández de Larrinoa 1991; Aranburu Ugartemendia 2001). Some of the residents are still farming, which was the area's main activity until recently. Others have partially or totally abandoned farming for alternative activities. It is significant that there is an increase in the referents with which people identify when they decide to live in the countryside.

Among the rural residents of Europe today, farming and peasant identity are certainly no longer determining factors. Thus, the more inclusive term 'rural society' has come to substitute the former 'peasant society'; a term which referred only to one social segment of the several that exist in the countryside. While 'peasant society' referred to a segment that today is in explicit decline, the social segments it excluded are precisely those now thriving (Kearney 1996; Cloke and Little 1997).

As in other parts of Europe, farming in Alkiza is in decline, while the construction of apartment buildings and the conversion of old farmhouses into residential houses is proliferating. The globalisation of the economy is fuelling the development of agro-industrial research and enterprise (Clunies-Ross and Hilyard 1992; Goering, Norberg-Hodge, and Page 1993), and the peasantry has become a vestige of what it was before, at least in terms of being a singular, small-scale, family-based activity with distinctive cultural features (Franklin 1969).

Current residents in Alkiza show differing forms of identity. But it is of particular relevance that many of those who come from farming homes strongly identify with peasant activities, although they no longer make their living from agricultural business. Moreover, a very small number of houses in Alkiza still depend exclusively on farming; although a larger portion of the residents keep a bond with the land, maintaining orchards and vegetable gardens, keeping a few animals and planting trees (Adok 1998).

In order to understand rural identity in the Basque Country today several things must be taken into account. On the one hand, evolutionary views of human history have conceived of peasant life as being associated with discursive images which presuppose opposition, e.g. unkempt appearance; body odour; sociocultural backwardness; primitivism; and others elicited by the notion that peasants are tied to land and animals (Maget 1971). On the other hand, there have been movements such as the Romanticism of the late nineteenth century or the New Age of the late twentieth, which have produced positive images of the countryside, its residents and their culture. These movements, however, are notorious for their intellectual, spiritual or ecological approach to the countryside. However, its proponents are almost never involved directly in farming or cattle raising. Furthermore, the Basque nationalist movement has projected images which are paradigmatic in this regard. Basque nationalism developed, as positive images of traditional Basque culture multiplied. Thus, nationalists liked to praise farming and cattle-raising families, who were said to have kept and transmitted Basque culture through generations (Azcona 1984).

Basque ethnographers of the early twentieth century were also involved in the creation of positive images of the countryside, which the budding nationalist movement idealised. In this sense, Basque nationalism was an urban ideology which used the peasants and their rural life as an element for political action (Heiberg 1989). Today, however, when nationalism has a wide base in the rural, Basque-speaking areas, its leaders seem to have relegated farmhouses and farmers to the background. Rather, the Guggenheim Museum in Bilbao is the choice representative of current

Basque culture for Basque nationalism (Zulaika 1995; MacClancy 1997). Without abandoning the idealised vision of the Basque peasant, nationalism now looks to the cities for images more prestigious than those the countryside can offer.

In this chapter I argue that thinking about how rural Basques experience their identity at present requires us to consider several referents. For instance, when peasants in Alkiza speak the Basque language (Euskara), they mark a conceptual difference between, on the one hand, *baserria, baserritarra,* and *baserrikoa*; and, on the other, *kalea, kalekoa,* and *kaletarra.* The words in the first group express nuances of the concept of countryside; those in the second to the city and the urban lifestyle. Thus, *baserria* means farm; *baserritarra,* farmer, and *baserrikoa,* someone from a farming family who does not make a living from agriculture. *Kalea* means city (literally, street); *kaletarra,* a city-dweller; and *kalekoa,* from the city (Fernández de Larrinoa 1991).

The sociocultural referents that residents in Alkiza use to express local identity are varied, but always the result of the tension with which they have internalised the semantic fields contained in the terms *baserria/baserritarra/baserrikoa,* on the one hand, and *kalea/kaletarra/kalekoa,* on the other. This tension comes from the fact that both sets of words create corresponding sets of social images whose main function is to stigmatise, disparage, and culturally disqualify the other.

To a city-dweller, *baserria/baserritarra/baserrikoa* refers to the rustic, the *Homo sylvestris,* while *kalea/kaletarra/kalekoa* represents progress and civilisation. To a peasant, however, *kalea/kaletarra/kalekoa* refers to a dark, menacing and undesirable environment. The interpretative transcendence of this contrast can be better understood in the context of what Mexican anthropologist Roger Bartra has written about culture and civilisation in Europe: the myth of the savage is essential to the concept of Western culture, and is the source of the West's idea of civilisation (Bartra 1996).

In Alkiza *baserria/baserritarra/baserrikoa* and *kalea/kaletarra/kalekoa* are specific variants of the myth of the savage, in the sense that both find their own identity precisely at the point where they converge. *Baserria/baserritarra/baserrikoa* is where *kalea/kaletarra/kalekoa* discovers the images with which to construct a 'self', and vice versa. The cultural stereotypes that each kind spreads about the other are illustrative: the person who is employed in farming and lives away from the urban centre is poorly educated, backward, ignorant and somehow defective. To reinforce the grotesque aspect of this image, Basque peasants are often portrayed in a situation where they have to communicate in Spanish, a language they do not speak fluently.

Similar characters continue to be displayed today, although now they are allowed to speak Basque. The public television Basque channel ETB1 (*Euskal Telebista1*) presents shows in which interviews and imitations encourage the model we describe. The question arises: how can Basque people be ridiculed when speaking their own language? Well, beginning in the 1980s, the modernisation process marked a distinction between *Euskara Batua,* the recently constructed Standard Basque, and time-honoured dialects of *Euskara*. Batua has come to represent the city-dweller, the press, textbooks and literature, the speech of radio and television broadcasters, and local graduates. Scenes from TV shows often depict situations in which the differences between the city and country dwellers, or between the global Basque and the local Basque, are very marked. Astride this first difference are other contrasts, such as culture, prudence, and refinement versus ignorance, indiscretion, bullying, and poor taste.

The cultural product that best illustrates the cultural vision described above is the play *Kutsidazu bidea, Isabel* ('Show me the way, Isabel'), successfully staged in Euskara in several peasant towns and villages in 2003. That year, the programme for the local festivities of Alkiza included the staging of the play on the central plaza. The adaptation of a story originally written in Basque, it tells of a young, Spanish-speaking man from San Sebastián, who does not speak Euskara very well so takes a month-long course in it in Alkiza. To make sure that the students learn the language, the course includes a period of immersion during which they lodge in the homes of local families, which naturally are peasant families. According to its blurb, the story describes with humour and irony the confusing social situations and cultural mix-ups that people face when they do not share the same symbolic codes or communication instruments. The book is well known among Basque language students, since it is recommended in the programme of the Euskara schools for adults. The theatre version is also well known in rural areas, where the high turnout is rather remarkable, since farmers are not usually theatre-goers. Plays are not a common entertainment in small rural towns in the county of Tolosa. As a rule, the Department of Culture of Guipúzcoa is in charge of programming cultural activities in the rural areas of the province; these consist of an itinerant programme of concerts, conferences, slideshows, films, and sometimes, theatre. Even though all small villages in Tolosa have a Cultural Centre where these activities take place, the attendance of local residents is usually low.

In fact, those in charge of organising the festivities in Alkiza were unsure of the appropriateness of a play in the programme. They decided to include it for three main reasons: the popular reception of it in other nearby villages; the direct concern of its subject matter to Alkiza itself; and the cast included a much-liked actor, who appears regularly as an imitator on TV shows, and lives in a neighbouring municipality. The poster to announce the play showed the household group next to the student. The locals wear old, worn-out clothes and hold outdated farming equipment, with an old farmhouse in the background. The way they are posing suggests they are mentally defective. The whole play revolves around the idea that the student finds himself living among lunatics. The family photo on the poster is grotesque. The gags in the play are exaggerated to the utmost in order to get the audience laughing.

The portrait of the peasant in this play is quite different from the one offered by the descriptions of peasant families at the end of the nineteenth century and the beginning of the twentieth. In the photographs of Eulalia de Abaitua Allende-Salazar

(1994, 1998) or those that Jesús Ramos (1999) included in his book of vintage postcards, for example, there is an evident effort to make the subjects look clean, elegant, and dignified, regardless of what the actual living conditions of these peasant men and women were. This is not surprising, since we know that the Basque ethnographers of the time propagated an idyllic image of the life and the people of the mountain villages. Earlier Basque ethnographers idealised the Basque peasant family as the embodiment of Christian values and social stability (Estornés Zubizarreta 1983), threatened at the time, in their view, by the growing influence of socialism and other revolutionary ideologies, as well as by industrial migration, which pushed people from the rural villages into the marginal living conditions of the industrial urban centres (Martínez Martín 1996). Thus, the images of *Homo sylvestris* with which *kalea/kaletarra/kalekoa* perceive *baserria/baserritarra/baserrikoa* are of two kinds: those of the Rousseaunian 'noble savage'; and those of the savage that must be conquered and tamed. Or, to borrow a terminology (Carrasco 1996), we could say there is the 'friendly peasant' and the 'defiant peasant'.[1]

Therefore, there are popular images which tend to validate social scenarios in which those of peasant origin have to see themselves as carriers of a negative cultural identity. During my fieldwork I have collected a large number of anecdotes that depict current local versions of the *Homo sylvestris* with which people of Alkiza feel uncomfortable but have internalised in the course of their socialisation process (Fernández de Larrinoa 2007). And there is another side to the same coin, since *baserria/baserritarra/baserrikoa* look at *kalea/kaletarra/kalekoa* according to their own parameters and to the images they have created of the city and its inhabitants, whose changing cultural referents I explain below.

As the urban industrial workshops became established in the late nineteenth and early twentieth centuries, the city gradually displaced the woods and mountains as the place from which the images that reinforce the peasant's self, its difference, and its positive identity were generated. Ethnographic research from the early twentieth century, such as that of Barandiarán and others, shows that legends and myths, along with geographical features, rock formations, and buildings are full of caves, mountain ledges, bridges, and groves inhabited by the Goddess Mari, the Basajaun, and a collection of other fantastic creatures whose menacing presence haunt the country dweller (Barandiarán 1997). These are characters whose features combine human, animal, and vegetable attributes, and in which it is easy to recognise the specific version of the *Homo sylvestris* that the Basque peasant created before the industrial revolution. However, the Basque peasant of the late twentieth and early twenty-first centuries no longer refers to the mountains and the woods as the main source of danger to their lifestyle. Danger today comes from the cities and the people who inhabit them, the *kalea/kaletarra/kalekoa* group.

City dwellers, given their particular perceptions of the rustics, strive to impose the cultural supremacy of the city over the countryside. Similarly, Basque peasants have constructed an imagery with which to demonstrate their sociocultural superiority over city dwellers. Within this set there are two types of narratives, descriptions, and explanations which the peasants use to develop corresponding images of the city and its inhabitants. The first type centres on the idea that cities are filthy, dangerous places where people live under a constant threat. When I began to visit the area in the late 1970s, peasants from Tolosa county used to refer of Tolosa city (the industrial, commercial, and administrative centre of the region) with terms such as *zulo zikina* and *zulo iluna* ('dirty hole' and 'dark hole').

To peasants, the *kaletarrak* are dangerous people. When they visit or come to live in the countryside, they ignore the rules and behave as if everything that is within their reach belonged to them. In springtime they take walks and cut through the pastures, spoiling the hay. In the summer they forget to close the gates that keep the cattle in the fields, and walk their dogs off the leash where the cattle are grazing. In the autumn they come in groups to gather chestnuts, pecans, apples, and other fruit, and walk into private orchards as if they were their own. They even pick beans from people's gardens. In wintertime they break into shepherds' cabins if the weather turns bad, or just to eat their lunch sheltered from the cold. There are many anecdotes of instances in which *baserritarrak* express the anguish that takes hold of them when *kaletarrak* come into their environment. When this happens, the intruder is referred to as *kalekumea*. (The term *kalekumea* comes from *kalea*, street, and the suffix *–kumea*, used to refer to animals' offspring and vermin.) Significantly, in the 1980s *kalekumea* had taken the place that wolves, bears, and mythological characters had in the folktales recorded by academics in the late nineteenth and early twentieth centuries.

There is a second meaning attached to *kalekumea*: *gu baino gutxiagokoa*, or 'that which is lesser than us', which gives rise to many local stories. *Kalekumea* also represents a lesser ability – as compared to that of the country dweller – to deal directly with the demands of life, especially when they imply a physical effort. People who farm for a living see city dwellers as having very limited means to survive in a world without money as an element of commercial exchange. Farmers often express the opinion that people from the cities would slowly die out if there was an industrial crisis since, they reason, they have no land and no idea how to work it. Without wages or state welfare, they would not be able to get food.

The dying of the traditional?

When I entered the village in 1982, I encountered a sociocultural reality in Alkiza that did not fit into the framework suggested by the classical ethnographies of the area (Douglass 1969, 1975; Aranzadi 1974; Caro Baroja 1974; Ott 1981). While these concentrated on a Basque society of subsistence farming, the inhabitants of Alkiza were in 1982 confronting other elements coming from outside. I was to learn that throughout the 1970s and 1980s peasant identity was troublesome in Alkiza, since tradition and modernisation confronted each other. By tradition here I mean the body of knowledge about peasant Basque society created by folklore and ethnography researchers (Fernández de Larrinoa 1997). Cultural traditions were losing social weight in Alkiza while agriculture was becoming mechanised, and people emigrating. The local system of social organisation was changing as *exotiká* died out (Stewart 1994). By modernisation I mean the influence of industrial development in the county of Tolosa, where the family-owned paper factories, sawmills, and small mechanic workshops employed many workers from the area's farms, and from other parts of Spain. During the 1980s, out of thirty-five people of working-age in Alkiza, fifteen worked in industry in Tolosa. At much the same time, in Alkiza farming machines substituted the traditional wood and wrought-iron equipment and ploughing teams. Raising cattle, particularly dairy farming, became an intensive industry in several farms. Also, importantly, this period witnessed the culmination of an economic process in which national tendencies of industrialisation, mechanisation, and modernisation were key referents with which peasants internalised images of themselves.

Perhaps it was not surprising then that the ethnographic data I was collecting in Alkiza tended not to fit the organisational and festive-ritual model that anthropologists and folklorists had drawn up to explain the details of traditional rural Basque society. The three pillars which, according to the scholars, held up Basque peasant culture were tumbling in Alkiza. First, the system of inheritance and the transmission of the family agricultural exploitation no longer followed the traditional form of *mayorazgo* (where the sole heir is the eldest son), at least not in the way that the anthropologists had described up to that point. Second, the system of reciprocity and mutual assistance among farmhouses was no longer based exclusively on a criterion of ritual neighbourhood as previous works of anthropology had reported. Third, my research into the folklore, composition and ritual-aesthetic usage of the spoken word among Alkizians uncovered an unexpected cultural situation. The cultural forms which had characterised local life in the past were changing content during my fieldwork. They continued to be practised, but their referents had changed. In the following pages I will briefly describe some of the sociocultural peculiarities that arose throughout the investigation with regard to these three themes.

Inheritance

In the 1970s Alkiza's heirs begged off the duty of running the family house in order to take salaried work in the small industrial workshops established in the valley's municipal seat. The job of running the house would then fall to another son until he in turn went to work in the valley, a keenly pursued goal. In this way the intergenerational transmission of the house and its associated complex of livestock and agriculture changed its referents in Alkiza. Until then the rule had been that the house went to the son best suited to work in the field; now the emerging practice was that the house went to the son least suited to finding work in the workshops in the valley. The norm of sole heir remained, but changed in referent.

Reciprocity

Ritual reciprocity between Basque farming houses, expressed in relationships of neighbourhood, have been well documented by previous ethnographers (Douglass 1969; Ott 1981). In this exchange system, each farmhouse in the village lends to one or more assigned farmhouses a certain type of help, or specific services, either to do with economic activities (e.g. the preparation of the fields, the harvest, haymaking, the slaughter of domestic animals, and the manufacture of products), or with religious-ritual activities (arranging the wake in the event of a death in the domestic group, or some other activity connected with the Church). Ritual neighbourhood is mutual help between homes for tasks that are beyond the abilities of a single domestic group. What is significant in this case is that domestic groups do not improvise where to seek the needed loans and services: the corresponding home or homes are already assigned.

In the county of Tolosa, the Basque word *auzoa* refers to the ritual neighbourhood house, and *auzokoa* to its dwellers. When asked about this custom, my informants had no difficulty identifying the relationships of *auzokoa* among households in the village, but noted that they were not always in operation, i.e. there were domestic groups who sought help from others living in houses where there had been no prior relationship of *auzoa*. The people I interviewed indicated that for an ever increasing number of matters domestic groups were not responding to the relationship of *auzoa*, partly because the tasks that required cooperation between neighbours were no longer carried out, partly because the acquisition of modern machinery meant that domestic groups no longer needed help for some tasks, and sometimes because the household which operated as *auzoa* had been abandoned and remained empty.

The word

Following previous investigators of oral culture in Euskara my original interest centred on compiling, directly from the mouths of Alkiza's inhabitants, samples of mythology, legends, sayings, songs, and verses. To this end I interviewed several villagers, who gave me interesting versions of local couplets, songs, and legends. Several matters caught my attention: as I compiled oral material, I began to see that these oral pieces no longer belonged to the sphere of local social relationships but to the memory of past times. This was demonstrated by the way in which I had to access the information: not a single person under the age of forty was able to reproduce the stories, songs, legends, or verses in the style which the Basque folklorists had published in their compilations. In fact, I found few in Alkiza who were learned in mytho-historical narratives, lyrical or epic songs, or in the improvisation of verse. Among these, fewer still were willing to perform in public; furthermore, not once in the duration of my fieldwork did I note a readiness on anyone's part to listen with a view to learning the pieces well enough to be able to continue the tradition.

Unexpectedly, my research on traditional singing in Alkiza was, however, to find myself in a contradictory situation. Oral culture in Euskara was revitalised in the

1980s thanks, to a great extent, to the launching of Basque public television and radio, as well as to the integration of Euskara into public education, both as a subject and as spoken language. There were books published and audio and videotapes made about rural Basque culture, which were shown on television, played on the radio, and sold to the public. Some of the folklore genres that the budding Basque cultural industry promoted were *kantu zaharrak* (old ballads and romances), *bertso zaharrak* (old verses), and *bertso berriak* (new verses). However, my research into the genres of folklore in Alkiza led me to the following conclusion:

> Today there are few genuine sociocultural contexts in which to interpret the oral compositions of the Basque folklore artists of the past; even when there is such a context, the people involved would not feel it was appropriate to revive or recreate the compositions of their elders, since they consider them 'things of the past', *démodé*; even *bertsolaritza*, the oral genre with more social resonance in the Basque Country, is a marginal activity in Alkiza. (from my fieldnotes)

Village cultural decadence and the lively format for the day: storytelling

During my stay in Alkiza I noticed that, both there and in neighbouring villages, there was a vigorous form of verbal activity which contrasted with the decline of cultural features described above: *kontuak esatea* (storytelling), an activity I interpret following the way Jean Duvignaud has proposed, as simple talk, chatting, social intercourse which happens outside work, politics, and religion. He argues that there are times and places where people gather to talk and share everyday stories or emotions. People talk in cafes, restaurants, bars, plazas, public laundries, hallways, waiting rooms, and train and bus stations. This talk serves to build stories that take freely from the elements and themes with which a culture defines itself. Since these elements are nothing other than the everyday values, myths, and symbols of a society, Duvignaud argues that simple talk is a social activity based on the verbal manipulation of everyday life's images and representations. Thus, the gathered people compose and propagate stories made of a yarn that arbitrarily combines elements from their current system of social classification (Duvignaud 1980).

In Alkiza adults engaged happily in storytelling when they were idle. It took place in bars, plazas, grocery stores, in *herriko ostatua* (the village coffee shop), after Saturday or Sunday Mass, after a local festivity, during mealtimes at the farmhouse, and in the Monday and Saturday markets in Tolosa. Finally, people told stories during the dead time between finishing one task and starting another, or when meeting a neighbour while walking to or from the fields. During these occasions people may talk about any local event. Within this context of informal talk, villagers told stories whose characters belonged to the everyday world of the narrators. The stories were told during trivial social encounters as a verbal entertainment. Through them, those gathered spoke of their cultural identity and social status both in the local sphere and in society at large. This is what cultural interpretation analysis, like that of Clifford Geertz, has defined as 'saying something of something', that is, a form of meta-language (Geertz 1973). Significantly, I collected many stories that exemplified the conflict between two referents and the resulting strained, dual identity of many peasants. In Tolosa, during the 1980s, it was common to hear people from peasant families tell stories which described working at the farm as a heavy burden identified with celibacy and slavery, while working in factories and living in the city was considered liberating; it fostered family life and allowed access to new goods and services (Fernández de Larrinoa 2007; also Fernandez 1989).

Furthermore, villagers made *kontuak esatea* a sociocultural activity through which they could negotiate the contradictions of their changing identity, between the inherited identity of loyalty to one's elders, in which the farmhouse played the role of sociocultural matrix, and the liberatory appeal of working for wages in the factories. In this sense, the farmers of Alkiza were acting like their counterparts in other places in the Basque Country. For example, in his study of peasants in north-eastern Guipúzcoa, who at the time combined farm work with jobs in the paper industry, Joxe Miguel Apaolaza writes:

> For the *baserritarra,* or peasant, the factory is a place where the only meanings played out are those of urban life: financial and sociopolitical demands, strikes. The peasant's behaviour at the factory is peculiar and full of specific features that hint at the powerful contradictions within.
>
> They think their time at the factory is transitory – even though some of them have been working there for over twenty years – that they are there only as long as it is necessary, as long as it takes for the farmhouse to become once again profitable ...
>
> The *baserritarras* have always refused to become part of urban society. The reason for this self-exclusion is not comfort, or the inability to move in both spaces, rural and urban society, but rather, the firm belief that rural society is superior ... This behaviour does not extend to the younger generations. (Apaolaza 1981: 53–4)[2]

Towards today

Today Alkizians do not express sociocultural approval or rejection by referring to the pros or cons of industrial work. Rather, notions such as 'social well-being', 'agricultural-nutritional quality', or 'rural development' provide the discursive images used to talk publicly about living in the contemporary countryside (Ray 1997). Thus in this section I discuss how, in the current socio-economic context, the villagers endorse or rebuff the category of 'peasant', and what are the present sociocultural mechanisms they use to express features of local identity.

'Rural development', as a concept, is part of the institutional and administrative discourse of the European Union, a transnational institution which has approved guidelines for social, economic and cultural intervention in the agricultural spaces of its associated nations. Among the EU's objectives is to ameliorate the economic and political marginalisation of rural and farming communities in the mountain regions, to address the problems of demographic decline and environmental degradation, and to resist the cultural homogenisation that urban models promote. Thus, the EU promotes measures and subsidies which stimulate the diversification of rural economic activities. Of course, this process of rural development is one taking place within a movement of economic Europeanisation (European Commission 1999; 2002; 2003; 2004).

Recently researchers have noted how the issue of cultural resources has begun to loom large in rural development plans. In order to revitalise the declining economy of farming regions, public administrations are promoting certain cultural resources: e.g. traditional festivities, local crafts and culinary traditions, typical farming landscapes, local products, and markets (Faure 2000). In a growing number of places this has encouraged the social activation of local cultural elements as economic goods or merchandise (Throsby 2001). This has resulted in a process of production and consumption of cultural symbols where the emphasis is (a) on promoting cultural tourism in the countryside and providing the infrastructure required for such activities; and (b) on the marketing of farming products as distinctive to the region. Hence the coinage of the new expression 'rural cultural heritage' (Ruiz Urrestarazu 2001; Fernández de Larrinoa 2011).

At the same time, the EU has classified certain spaces as 'disadvantaged mountain areas', making it possible for local development promoters to advocate investment in rural spaces, and favouring the economic activation of rural identity symbols. Following EU guidelines, the Strategic Rural Basque Plan 1997–2000 proposes four areas of development: (a) professional training in new farming, cattle raising, and forestry technologies; (b) leisure and tourism; (c) nature conservation; and (d) preservation of collective memory. The Basque government thus promotes a notion of 'rural Basque space' in which the definition of space has more to do with lifestyle than with primary productive activities (Departamento de Agricultura y Pesca 1997).

Josetxu Martínez Montoya has argued that there is an important sociocultural change process taking place in the Basque Country. He refers to three particular processes guiding this restructuring: rural spaces become urbanised; rural territories turn to tourism; and the rural economy turns to tertiary activities. The effects include the increasingly blurry distinction between rural and urban spaces, and the shifting of villagers' identity markers from rural ones to urban-rural. Rural space thus becomes a locus in which to represent emerging sociocultural identities that reappraise the values of 'local' and 'hometown' (Martínez Montoya 1996; 1999; 2002; ch. 5). For example, in Alkiza, the village once upheld an image of rural farming. Today, thanks to new patterns of settlement there, its image is changing in accordance with an urban understanding of rural space.

In the past, city dwellers associated Basque peasants with positive, laudatory images and negative, *Homo sylvestris* ones. The memories of these images are still strong, and today lie alongside newer public images of the Basque farmhouse, which have changed referents but are still nevertheless contradictory. Here I look at these images and the contradictions they produce. But first I need to outline the changes in the social architecture of the village.

Three innovations in housing use: the 1970s and 1980s

During the 1970s and 1980s, there was a pattern of cultural authenticity among the speakers and students of Euskara, linked to the idea of its pre-Indo-European origin and the rural habitat of its current speakers. This pattern had two main variants. In the colloquial variant, the dialect of Euskara spoken in the mountain villages was considered more authentic than other forms. Some considered *Batua* as inferior as they thought it 'artificial': a laboratory product assembled by scholars without taking into account people's everyday speech. Similarly, they put down *kaleko Euskara* (city-dweller Basque), to them a degenerative form polluted by Spanish, the dominant language in the cities.[3] Alkiza, among other small mountain villages where Euskara was spoken, responded to this image of cultural authenticity.

The intellectual variant was stimulated by the aesthetic theories of sculptor Jorge de Oteiza (1908–2003), who had had a strong influence in the local artistic circles of the time. He argued for a concept of Basque cognitive authenticity based on the pre-Indo-European nature of Euskara. According to him, its antiquity gave its speaker a *sui generis* system through which to interpret reality. From this base, he strove to demonstrate the existence of a particular Basque aesthetic vision, essential for the interpretation and production of a genuinely Basque art (Oteiza 1963). During the late 1960s he also played a key role in stimulating a movement, known today as the Basque Art School, which aimed to rehabilitate Basque identity through artistic experimentation. Among the various Basque aesthetic ideas elaborated by the School, the ecological-linguistic proposal was one of the more important. Also, a significant number of artists established their workshops in rural settings, and often remodelled old farmhouses for this purpose.

It was within this context that several families arrived in Alkiza during the 1970s and 1980s. Two young Spanish-speaking couples settled in houses outside of the village. They came from the city, and were employed in the valley. They spent their leisure time caring for small vegetable gardens and fruit orchards for their own consumption. Their children attended the local school where Euskara was the medium of communication and therefore became friendly with local children, monolingual Euskara speakers. This also encouraged a feeling of belonging, and made it possible for the children to grow up in an Euskara-speaking atmosphere of *euskaldun*. The two couples themselves made an effort to learn some Euskara, which they used in the family to model a positive attitude towards the language for their children. A third young couple also left a nearby big town to build a house with a small garden and orchard in Alkiza. This couple spoke Euskara, and one of them worked in the service industry in the village. They too sent their children to the local school. Another settler of this period was a painter of the Basque heritage movement, who moved with his family to an abandoned house in Alkiza, which he then renovated to serve as the family home and his art studio. Euskara-speaking emigrants from a city, they also sent their children to the local school and kept an orchard. Thus, this small group of ex-urban families aspired to become part of a new ecologic-cultural context through their identification with horticulture, the local school, and the language. They constituted a new social category within the village.

Another first during this period was the establishment of home-based workshops. When, in the 1970s, a young man – who was not to inherit the farm and had an industrial job in the valley – married, the new couple did not move into an urban flat but bought land from the family's farm and built a house there. Even more unusually, in the 1980s he quit his job and set up a small industrial workshop in his house. The workshop was still active in 2011 and, now assisted by his son and daughter, he works sharpening metal pieces sent by companies of the region. Similarly, the husband in a family which had settled in Alkiza in the 1970s, decided in the 1990s to quit his job in the valley and also started a small industrial workshop in his family home. With the help of his son, he maintained it until his retirement in the late 2000s.

A third innovation in residential pattern was the following. The owners of a compound located on the town's plaza decided to build a new house next to the old farmhouse. The house followed urban parameters with regards to materials, style, and distribution. The heir, his family, and his father moved in, two years after it was finished, while his unmarried uncle and sister stayed in the farmhouse. Here, father and son decided to live together with the son's family in a chalet-type house which, although near the farmhouse, possesses all the comforts of urban houses in the valley. The heir worked in a small industrial workshop in Tolosa county, while his father was a full-time farmer. This case did not follow the traditional trend where the children who marry, but will not continue working in the farm, must leave the farmhouse. Notably, it introduced a way of local living new to Alkiza. What is interesting is that the seekers for cultural authenticity and the constructors of home-based workshops have not had any imitators since, while the builder of a second home next to his old one has.

Flat, villa, double-family houses

By the 1990s the traditional farmhouse was becoming badly outdated: some, whose owners had moved on, stood empty; childless singletons inhabited others; yet others were occupied by adult offspring who had rejected their inheritance and worked outside the home but still periodically assisted their elders with farming tasks. Since this time, Alkiza has instead become home to three new residential concepts: flats, villas, and double-family houses.

Blocks of flats had become common in parts of Tolosa county since the industrial development of its towns from the 1960s on. They were occupied by non-Basque labour migrants and by local peasants who did not have or refused the right of primogeniture, and who on or after marriage left the paternal home. In traditional

Alkizian farmsteads, when a son or daughter other than the heir marries they must leave. Their options are: if he/she has married the heir to a different farmhouse, then the couple may keep the social status of *baserritarra* (peasants). They may also buy or rent a flat in a housing block in the valley, thus acquiring a dual public identity: no longer *baserritarrak,* they are socially identified as *baserrikoak,* i.e. born and raised on a farm, which carries some of the images associated with the term *baserritarra.* From the peasants' point of view, however, '*kalean bizi da*', 'they are living in the city'. And yet, according to local peasant opinion, *baserria* and *kalea* are opposing models. Until the 2000s, in Alkiza, there were only three flat-style buildings. Of traditional size and design, made of stone and wood, with a sloping roof, they are adjacent and face the plaza. In the village, then, living in a flat was rare, while in the towns nearby it had already become an extended practice.

A new-style villa is very different. Unlike flats (usually associated with waged workers), villas are spacious homes, normally built in a privileged part of town or near town, and confer on their inhabitants a higher social status. Just as blocks of flats have created working-class neighbourhoods, so the concentration of villas has produced exclusive residential neighbourhoods. In the past, living in a villa was restricted to families from the ruling class whose wealth grew with the economy and the industrialisation of the country. Today, however, the trend of living in villas has become generalised in the Basque Country.

As the purchasing power of the urban middle class grew during the 1970s and 1980s, people acquired second homes or flats on the Basque coast or nearby. Acquiring a chalet or vacation flat was for many their initiation into conspicuous leisure consumption. The development of villas in rural towns and mountain villages in the Tolosa area is thus due to various elements, including pressure in the real estate market; excellent land communications infrastructure; an urban imaginary which connects rural living to quality of life and social distinction; and the development of digital technology, which permits tele-cottaging.[4] A consequence of all this is the change, since the late 1990s, in the architecture and the landscape design of many rural towns in Guipúzcoa. Rural municipalities enabled this change (by granting building licences, and recategorising rural land as urban) in order to finance the renovation of municipal services. Similarly, through the sale of land, locals have generated the money to renovate their homes or modernise their farming facilities. It is in this general context that a housing development consisting of five double townhouses and one detached two-family unit were built during the years 2004 and 2005 in the neighbourhood of the central plaza in Alkiza, and sold immediately to young people.

The construction of *etxeak* (single or double-family homes) was a new use of landscape which had arrived in Alkiza in the 1990s (Figures 6.1 and 6.2). About eleven new houses were built in the municipality between 1991 and 1999: three in the plaza, two nearby, the rest further away. Two were built by a real estate entrepreneur from Tolosa, originally for his own family's use but both, to the chagrin of the

Figure 6.1 The village of Alkiza, 1945.

town hall, were sold to young families from San Sebastián within a short time. Also, two old buildings, located near the plaza, were bought, restored, and are now homes for couples with children. The rest of the houses were not built by a profit-seeking intermediary but by locals. These were villagers who would not inherit or had rejected their inheritance; they built on the family's farmland, so living near their aged parents, who were still tending the farm. Some features of these houses, such as size and style, as well as the fact that their inhabitants were employed in activities other than farming, make farmers identify them as *kaletxeak*, 'city housing'. But people from out of town who do not share the farmhouse culture usually describe the houses as chalets, or villas. The houses stand on an ambiguous space in the local map: the proximity of the family farmhouse, the fact that the inhabitants participate regularly in farming work, that they keep vegetable gardens, fruit orchards or crops for cattle feed in the same land make them not, in the strict sense of the word, *kaletxeak* or chalets. It is interesting that neighbours use the term *etxea*, house, to refer to one of these buildings. However, they always use *baserria* to refer to the farmhouse, and chalet or villa to refer to the houses built by real estate agents or construction companies to make a profit.

This small wave of construction gave the town a feeling of renovation which became stronger as the number of apartment buildings around the town's plaza grew in the 1990s.[5] During the 2000s, this urban growth continued, particularly around

Figure 6.2 Alkiza, 2006.

the plaza.[6] One cause was the rise of 'officially protected housing' promoted by the Basque government in line with an EU objective for rural development: to stop the gradual emigration from villages by giving locals incentives to remain in their hometowns. To that end, the Basque government, together with the rural municipalities, designed an intervention plan whose goal was to create affordable housing for locals. Alkiza participated successfully in this scheme: in 1998, two new buildings with a total of eight flats were finished; seven years later, sixteen flats in four recently completed buildings were allocated to young locals.

Contemporary social relations

The village today is thus made up of the following: (a) locals living either in *herriko pisuak*, municipal flats around the plaza, or *etxeak*, two-storey, single-family houses on land near the original family farmhouse; (b) outsiders, some of whom have either renovated abandoned farmhouses, or built a detached house within near the village; others have bought a flat, while yet others have bought a single or a two-family villa in the town from a real estate agent; and (c) the *baserritarrak*, the farmers who live in farmhouses set far apart from each other. The confluence of these three residential styles in present day Alkiza has led to an unprecedented social and cultural experience for its inhabitants. The question is, what kind of relations are there between the people who live in the farmhouses and those who live in flats or villas?

For those born in Alkiza and nearby villages, there are certain social practices still in use which communicate a sense of exclusion or belonging, for example the communal meals of *cuadrillas*, a group of co-evals who spend social time together. In Alkiza, the *cuadrilla* is a group of people of the same age and gender whose relationship is based on the acquaintance and socialisation of its members in their school years, when they all attended the village school. The *cuadrilla* is a surviving fragment of the traditional society whose decline in the 1970s and 1980s I described earlier. During my fieldwork, the *cuadrillas* of Alkiza met on Saturday nights, after the family dinner and after mass, at the *ostatu*, the local coffee shop. The girls gathered outside, the boys inside. When all the *cuadrillas* were complete, their members organised themselves in the available cars and headed for the bars in Tolosa. The *cuadrillas* also met on Sunday afternoons, again at the *ostatu*, then in Tolosa. Once the members of a *cuadrilla* marry, their relation to the group is reduced to the periodical dinners and luncheons for the village's yearly festivities.

By belonging to a *cuadrilla*, a person becomes part of a network linking him or her to other local youths they would otherwise not meet. Taking part in *cuadrilla* relations (which is nothing more than exercising the right to participate in collective activities by ascribing to a group of the same age and gender) reinforces links that the members associate with the village, since it is the setting of shared school days, through childhood up to the end of adolescence. Thus, in the 1970s and 1980s incoming adults, who by definition did not belong to a local *cuadrilla*, had a hard time taking part in local social life and so had to devise their own network of relations to link themselves to their neighbours. Since the school came to represent the idea of 'collective local life' in the late 1980s and early 1990s,[7] their children were able to integrate, first, as members of *eskolako umeak*, the village's school children, and then in turn as *herriko gazteak*, the village's young people, finally becoming members of *cuadrillas*.

The case of the adults has been different. The couples that settled in Alkiza during the 1970s and 1980s have shared with their children the referent of school as the mechanism of inclusion in local social life. But the degree of connection of the children and the parents to the village life is notably different. Those who settled in Alkiza as adults have, as a rule, only formed superficial and discontinuous links to local social organisations. This superficiality is a consequence of the rigidity of peasant social structures, which are unable to accommodate *kanpotarrak*, outsiders, in local life. Several *kanpotarrak* families arrived during the 1970s and 1980s looking to find some kind of cultural authenticity. Justified by the conceptual difference between *baserria* and *kaletarra* and the images each notion casts on the countryside, the peasants of Alkiza were not particularly receptive to the newcomers.

For outsiders, the process of adaptation was long and had mixed results. For example: (a) during the 1980s, a family made several complaints to the authorities because a neighbouring farmer harassed them insistently; (b) a wife interviewed in the late 1990s explained how difficult it had been for them to join in local life; and it was not until her children started at the local school that they made a few acquaintances. However, as happened with their children, couples found in the local school a way of linking with other families in the village, mostly through active participation in *gusasoen elkartea,* the parents' organisation of the school. This is an administrative body created by the public administration to foster the participation of society in the running of public schools and their activities. In Alkiza, the *gusasoen elkartea* had not really worked until young couples from outside the village joined in during the 1980s, as farmers had had little interest in school or in the formal education of their children. The school in Alkiza, as an institution, reveals much about the degree of people's social inclusion or exclusion in the socialisation and social gathering networks of the village. There is a specific collective event related to school which emphasises degrees of inclusion and exclusion: the community dinner organised by the *gurasoen elkartea* on the eve of San Juan, 23 June, on the town's plaza.

The San Juan festivities are well known in Tolosa and other parts of the Basque Country and southern Europe. In Alkiza, the tradition is to light a bonfire using firewood and old household utensils and other things on the evening of 23 June. Until recently, the norm was that each family lit their own bonfire on their property. The festivity was an intimate, private one, involving the *baserria,* the smallest unit of the landscape which has a specific social meaning among farmers and peasants of the area. When the *gurasoen elkartea* broke into local life, its members considered that the San Juan festivities were an ideal opportunity for a social gathering. Since 1993, the *gurasoen elkartea* lights a great bonfire on the town's plaza on the eve of San Juan. The celebration includes an outdoors dinner financed, cooked and served by the organisation's more active members (Figure 6.3). After the meal, the bonfire is lit; as the flames subside and turn into embers, young and old alike jump over the fire. The *gurasoen elkartea* invites the whole community to attend the dinner and bonfire by issuing formal, written invitations, and thus gives the celebration a communal character that was lacking before. Attendance is nevertheless low, since not everyone in Alkiza celebrates the festivity in the same way, and most of those who live in old farmhouses continue to light their own bonfire. When I attended the celebrations during 2001, 2002, and 2003, I could confirm that the participants in the *gurasoen elkartea* bonfire were for the most part the local people who lived in *herriko pisuak* and *etxeak,* although people from outside Alkiza, who live in the apartments by the plaza, also attended. Even though this is Alkiza's only community-oriented celebration, its organisers have failed to attract either the farmers and peasants or the outsiders who send their children to private schools away from the village. Thus the celebration has become representative of people in a specific social segment who, by participating with their children, create a space in which to express social neighbourly links: mainly young people born in farmhouses who have settled with their spouses in flats, adapted rural buildings or new houses;[8] and outsider couples who identify with the idea of cultural authenticity in the terms described earlier.

Figure 6.3 The festivity of San Juan, Alkiza, 2006.

For the last decades San Juan has been an invented festivity linked to school life in Alkiza. Those who take part display their links to their neighbours and the degree to which they are part of a socially constructed space. However, in contrast with the role it played in the 1980s and before, in the late 1990s the school did not act as a space of cultural and social integration for newcomers. Rather, it became an institution immersed in controversy, and the source of social division among residents. It happened that some people started questioning whether a rural school really possessed the educational requirements to prepare children to continue their education in an urban centre and among urban teenagers. In addition, in the early 2000s, a violent incident between young children led two local families to withdraw their children from the school. As a result, members of the *gurasoen elkartea* can see that withdrawing their children from this very small school is a threat to its very existence. They also believe that taking children out of school is a disloyalty to the community spirit which should surround the local school.

Several families that moved into villas and chalets in recent times have chosen to send their children to private schools in urban centres. A rift thus became noticeable between the people who live in *baserriak* and *etxeak* compared to those who buy villas or chalets. The latter have not developed social links with the rest of the neighbours, and some of them have sent their children to be educated in the city, while locals use the municipal school. Several inhabitants of villas and chalets leave the village early in the morning for the daily commute, and return in the evening, and have so become the owners of Alkiza's first dormitory houses. These results are very different from what the local authorities had in mind when they granted permission to build the houses: they wanted to promote the settlement of young couples in hopes that this would mean more children attending the local school, and so reducing the chance of its closure.

Although in 2011 most parents support the local school, in 2005 it was no longer a local referent representing the future of the village; rather, it was a problematic institution that created unease and started arguments among neighbours. To a great extent, the unprecedented growth of real estate in Alkiza in the 2000s displaced the school in favour of the construction industry as the symbolic referent that represents the idea of growing collective life in the village. Many said: 'Houses are being built, and the village grows; therefore, there is life in the village'.

Towards a conclusion?

According to a population survey, there were 362 people living in Alkiza in 2011. This number reflects a considerable increase from previous years.[9] It also indicates a change in the dominant demographic tendency of the second half of the twentieth century, when Alkiza had an increasingly older population. This shift in the patterns of rural residence is the result of specific changes in attitude towards rural space, which has recently acquired new meanings, and through which a notion of rural life is spreading that is rapidly separating itself from the economic activities of the primary sector. The population increase in Alkiza is the result of two combining processes, one internal, the other external: (a) young people have the opportunity of settling in their home village at an affordable price without having to be part of the farmhouse domestic group; and (b) some young urban couples feel that living in a villa in the countryside is a sign of quality of life and social distinction. That is, living surrounded by such landscape as Alkiza offers, villa buyers get to experience the 'getaway' excitement every day, and not, as other people, only on weekends or holidays.

Both these processes however, have a common source. The reason why flats, houses and villas coincided as housing options in the village of Alkiza in 2005 was the high cost of housing in Basque cities. Alkiza is now a place where real estate speculation has started its ascent. Local people have stopped considering their land as valuable in terms of vegetable or cattle farming; rather, they ask what price it might fetch them in the rising market of house construction. In Alkiza there is distinction between *baserria/baserritarra/baserrikoa* and *kalea/kaletarra/kalekoa* both conceptual and spatial, at least until very recently. In the 2000s they share spaces, and this has resulted in a reformulation of the distinction. In present day Alkiza, farmhouses, flats, villas, houses, heirs, non-heirs, men, and women share spaces, times, and forms of living together which they did not before. The decrease in active farmhouses is counterbalanced by a significant increase in building flats, chalet-style single-family houses, and villa developments. Among the people living in Alkiza, the number of *baserrikoa* (someone who comes from a farming family but no longer works in a farm) is rising, as is that of *kaletarra* (someone from the city who holds a city job).

Real estate speculation has stimulated the construction of flats for locals and of villas for outsiders. It has also enabled the possibility of Alkiza becoming a dormitory town, and has shifted the locals' understanding of their property to that of a tradable good which can give their home economy a quick and significant lift. Forgotten is the fact that these lands were in the recent past spaces invested with familiar uses and meanings with intimate symbolic and emotional values; that they were associated with a specific body of knowledge, to tools and equipment, to the memories and social referents which were to be faithfully transmitted to the next generation within the domestic group, or to another farming family. At the same time, there are those who see in the proliferation of new buildings a process of re-valuation of the village. Still others see the opportunity to make a quick profit. Those who came to Alkiza looking for cultural authenticity watch with concern the deterioration of the rural landscape and architecture which were the product of the cultural history of the local peasants and farmers. As population rates were dramatically declining in the village, most locals and newcomers pointed to the school as a community referent, and the local authorities granted construction permits and recategorised rural lands as urban in an effort to keep the population up and thus the local school open.

To conclude, in Alkiza there is an ongoing shift from traditional, farming-oriented community boundaries to modern, urban-oriented ones. There have been attempts by several social segments to publicly construct a new collective representation of the 'village', as the example of the San Juan's eve festivity suggests. However, such attempts have not succeeded as makers of the village imaginary. Today, many Alkizians are uninterested in constructing open local symbols with which to portray and give sense to both changed and changing life in households as well as in the village. Instead they feel at ease consuming images of the passed-away *baserritarra*. And this is why the play *Kutsidazu bidea, Ixabel* was enjoyed so very much in Alkiza and nearby peasant communities: laughing as a celebration of what we no longer are. Still with us, though no longer us.

Notes

1 María Soledad Carrasco Urgoiti used these terms to define a similar distinction in the images of Muslims that appear in the traditional Christian-Moorish festivities of Spain (Carrasco 1996).

2 Author's translation from the original Spanish text:

> *La fábrica para el baserritarra es el lugar donde exclusivamente se muestran para ellos todos los significados de la vida urbana: luchas por reivindicaciones económicas y socio-políticas, huelgas. Su comportamiento en ésta es muy peculiar, con muchos rasgos específicos que muestran la existencia de unas contradicciones muy fuertes.*
>
> *Por un lado piensan que su paso por la fábrica, aunque algunos llevan más de veinte años, es una situación transitoria, que ha de durar únicamente el tiempo necesario, hasta que sea posible que el caserío vuelva a ser rentable como lo era ya hace muchos años.*
>
> *[...]*

Los baserritarras en todo momento se han negado a formar parte de la sociedad urbana. El motivo o la razón de esta automarginación no es la comodidad, el poder nadar entre dos aguas: la sociedad rural por un lado y la urbana por el otro, sino la firme convicción de que la sociedad rural es mejor … Este comportamiento no es extensible a los más jóvenes.

3 This is why many Euskara students preferred rural towns as the setting in which to practise the spoken language. It also explains the Basque language lessons organised by a Euskaltegi in Alkiza during the summer. As we saw before, such lessons served as narrative thread for the play *Kutsidazu bidea, Isabel* (Sagastizabal 1994).

4 Buying a villa reflects the combination of two mutually reinforcing factors: the first is figurative, and refers to the propagation among the urban population of a rural imaginary which defines countryside housing in terms of life quality; the second is utilitarian, and relates to the fact that the high price of the city flat makes the villa an attractive option. Rural towns are well connected and just a short ride away from Tolosa. San Sebastián is just 28 km apart from Tolosa, and is connected both by highway and by rail. This has allowed the emergence of social behaviours related to the acquisition of countryside home which are new to Tolosa county, such as commuting and telecommuting.

5 Two brothers from another village restored a run-down building and now live each in a flat with their wives and children. In 1996 a developer transformed an abandoned building on the plaza into four modern flats: three were acquired by outsiders, the fourth by a young man from the village and his wife, who have lived there since and now have children. Two years later two more buildings, each with four flats, were finished. These flats were promoted by the local authorities so that young people from Alkiza could settle there with their families. Also, two old buildings, located near the plaza, were bought, restored, and are now homes for couples with children.

6 In 2005, sixteen 'officially protected' flats were finished, and have already been bought by young local people; a traditional farmhouse was transformed by its owners into a two-family house; another two-family house went up near the ruins of an recently demolished farmhouse; five terraced houses were completed; a developer started work on a separate two-family unit building.

7 Elsewhere I have mentioned the emergence of social practices which substitute that of *mayorazgo*, now in decline, and which symbolise the idea of continuity of the group in the rural setting. For example, in 1987, the *eskola txikiak* (small schools) group formed in Guipúzcoa to help keep the schools in the small villages open and resist the concentration in larger towns, a tendency fostered by public policy. Thus, I wrote: 'however, new social practices indicate that, apart from the house, it is still possible to symbolise the existence of a rural community. This symbolic practice centres now in the efforts to maintain the local school. The rural world at the end of the century is struggling to keep its schools open. If the absence of heirs is a dramatic example of the emptiness of the homes and the economic disappearance of the farming/herding family enterprise, the closing of the schools dramatizes the death of the village itself' (Fernández de Larrinoa 1997: 389).

8 And also those who live in farmhouses near the plaza and have remodelled their farmhouses in the 1990s, following the standards of urban housing.

9 Alkiza had 658 people in 1854; in 1960 it was down to 401; in 1981 there were 272; in 1991 only 242; in 1996 the population went up to 260; in 2002, to 266; in 2005, 326; and in 2011 it was 362.

References

Abaitua Allende-Salazar, Eulalia de 1994 *La familia* (Bilbao: Museo arqueológico, etnográfico e histórico vasco).

——1998 *Miradas del pasado* (Bilbao: Museo arqueológico, etnográfico e histórico vasco).

Adok 1998 'Prospección social para la planificación socio-económica y búsqueda de mejoras y alternativas en Alkiza (posible creación de un programa de desarrollo rural integrado en Alkiza. Tolosaldea, zona 5b' (Brochure).

Apaolaza, Joxe Miquel 1981 'El baserritarra en la fábrica', *Ethnica*, 17. 51–62.

Aranzadi, Telesforo de 1974 *Etnología vasca* (San Sebastián: Auñamendi).

Aranburu Ugartemendia, Peillo Joxe 2001 *Alkiza, auzo eta hiribilduaren azterketa historikoa 1348–1950)* (Astigarraga: Artes Gráficas Michelena).

Azcona, Jesús 1984 *Etnia y nacionalismo vasco: una aproximación desde la antropología* (Barcelona: Anthropos).

Barandiarán José Miguel de 1977 *Mitología del pueblo vasco* (Lasarte: Etor-Ostoa).

Bartra, Roger 1996 *El salvaje en el espejo* (Barcelona: Destino).

——1974 *De la vida rural vasca* (San Sebastián: Txertoa).

Carrasco, Mª Soledad 1996 *El moro retador y el moro amigo (estudios sobre fiestas y comedias de moros y cristianos)* (Granada: Universidad de Granada).

Cloke, Paul and John Little (eds) 1997 *Contested Countryside Cultures* (London: Routledge).

Clunies-Ross, Tracey and Nicholas Hilyard 1992 *The Politics of Industrialized Agriculture* (London: Earthscan).

Departamento de Agricultura y Pesca 1997 *Plan de Actuación para el desarrollo del medio rural vasco 1997–2000: marco general para una política a favor del espacio rural vasco* (Vitoria: Gobierno Vasco).

Douglass, William 1969 *Death in Murelaga: Funerary Ritual in a Spanish Basque Village* (Seattle: University of Washington Press).

——1975 *Echalar and Murelaga: Opportunity and Rural Depopulation in two Spanish Basque Villages* (New York: St. Martin's Press).

Duvignaud, Jean 1980 *El juego del juego* (Mexico: Fondo de Cultura Económica).

Estornés Zubizarreta, Idoya 1983 *La sociedad de estudios vascos* (San Sebastián: Sociedad de Estudios Vascos).

European Commission 1999 *Europe's Agenda 2000* (Brussels).

——2002 *Community Policies and Mountain Areas* (Brussels).

——2003 *Rural Development in the European Union* (Luxembourg).

——2004 *New Perspectives for EU Rural Development* (Luxembourg).

Faure, Muriel 2000 *Du produit agricole à le objet culturel: les processus de patrimonialisation des productions fromagères dans les Alpes du Nord* (PhD Thesis, Lyon: Université Lumiere Lyon II, Faculté de Sociologie et d'Anthropologie).

Fernandez, James 1989 'La esclavitud de las vacas: la antropología como vocación entre campos en crisis', *Actas do II Coloquio de Antropoloxía* (Santiago de Compostela: Xuño).

Fernández de Larrinoa, Kepa 1991 *Hitzak, denbora eta espazioa* (San Sebastián: Elkar).

——1997 'Estructuras emergentes', *Zainak*, 14 (San Sebastián: Sociedad de Estudios Vascos), 375–89.

——2007 *Dones del lugar* (Pamplona: Pamiela).

——2011 *Manifiesto por una antropología razonada: el papel del antropólogo en el estado neoliberal (crítica cultural del desarrollo local y el patrimonio cultural europeos)* (Pamplona: Lamiñarra).

Franklin, Samuel H. 1969 *The European Peasantry: The Final Phase* (London: Methuen).

Geertz, Clifford 1973 *The Interpretation of Culture* (New York: Basic Books).

Goering, Peter, Helena Norberg-Hodge, and John Page 1993 *From the Ground Up* (London: Zed).

Heiberg, Marianne 1989 *The Making of the Basque Nation* (Oxford: Oxford University Press).

Kearney, Michael 1996 *Reconceptualizing the Peasantry: Anthropology in Global Perspective* (Boulder, CO: Westview Press).

MacClancy, Jeremy 1997 'Negotiating 'Basque art' in J. MacClancy (ed.) *Contesting Art: Art, Politics and Identity in the Modern World* (Oxford: Berg), 183–214.

Maget, Marcel 1971 'Los campesinos' in J. Dumazedier *et al.* (eds) *Ocio y sociedad de clases* (Barcelona: Fontanella), 73–92.

Martínez Martín, Mª Ascensión 1996 *Guipúzcoa en la vanguardia del reformismo social: beneficencia, ahorro y previsión (1876–1936)* (San Sebastián: Fundación Kutxa).

Martínez Montoya, Josetxu 1996 *Pueblos, ritos y montañas: prácticas vecinales y religiosas en el tiempo y en el espacio de la comunidad rural (valle de Arana)* (Bilbao: Desclée de Brouwer).

——1999 'Estudios de antropología sobre el medio rural', *Inguruak*, 25, 67–90.

——2002 *La identidad reconstruida: espacios y sociabilidades emergentes en la ruralidad alavesa* (Vitoria: Servicio Central de Publicaciones del Gobierno Vasco).

Oteiza, Jorge 1963 *Quousque tandem* (Auñamendi: San Sebastián).

Ott, Sandra 1981 *The Circle of Mountains: A Basque Shepherding Community* (Oxford: Oxford University Press).

Ramos, Jesús 1999 *Imágenes de la vida tradicional vasca a través de la antigua tarjeta postal* (Pamplona: Ortzadar).

Ray, Christopher 1997 'Towards a theory of the dialectic of local rural development within the European Union', *Sociologia Ruralis*, 37, 345–62.

Ruiz Urrestarazu, Eugenio 2001 'Patrimonio rural y políticas europeas', *Lurralde*, 24, 305–14.

Sagastizabal, Joxean 1994 *Kutsidazu bidea, Isabel* (Alberdania: San Sebastián).

Stewart, Charles 1994 *Demons and the Devil: Moral Imagination in Modern Greek Culture* (Princeton, NJ: Princeton University Press).

Throsby, David 2001 *Economics and Culture* (Cambridge: Cambridge University Press).

Zulaika, Joseba 1995 *Crónica de una seducción* (Madrid: Nerea).

7

The recuperation of Galician pottery: craft professions, cultural policies, and identity

Elena Freire Paz

This chapter reflects on why certain simple and even rudimentary objects have continued to be used in the twenty-first century in the most technologically developed Western societies, and on how they are valued for having a rustic beauty despite not having any evident utility from a narrowly pragmatic point of view. The focus is on the evolution of a concrete activity – Galician pottery – within a broader array of crafts which all share, to a greater or lesser degree, the symbolic connotations that people in contemporary societies grant to objects that mark the past.

There are two distinct but complementary reasons for doing research on traditional pottery. First, because making pottery was a widely practised occupation in Galicia until recently, it is possible to gather a substantial amount of ethnographic information about this activity in relation to the still recent past. During the first half of the twentieth century, the pieces made from clay formed part of the everyday experience of the population, the majority of which was situated in rural areas, reliant on scarce resources and partly on subsistence production. Owing to its affordability and high quality, Galician-made pottery served the needs of people in the less powerful classes, i.e. the great majority.

Second, pottery has been subject to a noticeable process of 'recovery' in recent years. This has been encouraged by various levels of government, which have provided funding for a recovery programme in Galicia. This revitalisation of craft professions has been promoted through a shared policy developed by both the Galician autonomous government and the EU, through a gradual application of cultural policies that aim to strengthen local identities within the globalising process which implicates all levels of government.

The full spectrum of activities within contemporary societies has become incorporated into the dynamics of the globalisation process due to world economic forces (Sassen 2007). Therefore, it seems worthwhile to demonstrate the persistent presence of a set of objects from the world of craft production that began in the distant past and persists into the present, despite these globalising forces.

In the late 1990s, various Galician institutions began a gradual campaign to recuperate traditional trades. Their strategy was to select a series of activities which had formed a part of Galicia's distinctive material reality until recent times: in about the late 1960s. The first of these activities from previous time periods that happened to be chosen was pottery, a trade that had possessed a strong historical presence throughout the Galician territory. In addition, unlike other crafts that had disappeared completely (such as the production of linen), people continued to work in some specific locations in Galicia, though in a very residual way and mainly for the tourist market, in the 1970s and 1980s (see Seseña, Vossen, and Köpke 1973).

In fact, information existed about the presence of numerous workshops in the four Galician provinces during the first half of the twentieth century, meticulously detailed in reference works such as that of Luciano García Alén, *La alfarería de Galicia* (1983). That is, there were already a few minimal sources that could function as authoritative references and provide justification and scientific support for any actions taken later on.

The transformation of Galician pottery: inventing tradition

From its beginning, the revitalisation of Galician pottery made necessary the delimitation of certain concepts. The question of geographical boundaries did not seem to be under discussion: Galician ceramics were those produced in Galicia, though this did not refer to only one design – for the objects made with clay are very heterogeneous through the Autonomous Community's territory. Instead, the difficulties in recovering traditional Galician pottery centred on the definition of 'traditional', an ideological concept with social and political implications. In Spain 'tradition' forms part of a programme of conservative thought, which tends to select facts or cultural objects, to legitimise models of social and institutional organisation along the lines of an interpretation directed by the very same frameworks.

In this case, the political and ideological framework is determined by a politico-economic project that starts in European institutions, and which is projected on to distinct territories in different ways: the trend is towards the reduction or destruction of the system of primary production, the provision of subsidies for this decline, and the generation of local, alternative economic projects oriented to the tertiary sector, especially to the utilisation of resources for tourism. In this case, traditional pottery signifies both a product based on certain surviving traces of a more or less remote past, and also a parallel project aimed at inculcating certain values and beliefs associated with this past and, in consequence, a sociocultural construction that rests on an idea of group identity.

The passage from a model of traditional pottery to that of the recovered pottery resulted in a series of changes: physical ones in terms of the material peculiarities of the pieces and the conditions of their production; functional ones with respect to their utility and manner of existence in society at large; and structural ones in the sense of the ideological modifications (systems of beliefs, values, etc.) imprinted on the sociocultural schemes on which they are projected.

In the ethnographic description of the process of recovery we can find both these changes and a specific definition of 'traditional Galician pottery'. This denomination includes nowadays any piece produced in the workshops that have an official certificate of guarantee and originality sent by the corresponding *Consellería* [Ministry] of the *Xunta de Galicia*. Nevertheless, a process of 'recovery' has taken place in the maintenance of this handcrafted traditional activity, i.e. in a way, a mechanism of identity creation. An image was created which gave form to a homogeneous and unique past, which did not correspond either with the historical reality of the pottery trade nor with that of any other crafts: that reality was always multifaceted, adapting to different situations and contexts and, therefore, in all cases heterogeneous and variable depending on the infinite needs that could be met by pieces made with clay. To create the 'traditional' prototype, a temporal limit was established in connection with the near disappearance of the trade, which took place at the end of the 1960s. Profound social, economic, and cultural changes occurred in Galicia during this period. At the same time, regional and European institutional structures led to the creation of a brand of Galician pottery, via diverse mechanisms of authentication of the pieces, which included the consideration that these material objects contained immaterial traces of Galician identity.

To specify the material changes that occurred in the objects I am referring to, in general we can say that previously and today the potters elaborated their pieces with clay loam. In technical terms, this loam is the result of the decomposition of a feldspar rock, whose colouration goes from white (if in pure condition) to multiple ranges and tonalities between grey and yellow, even including an intense red, depending on the impurities it contains. The fundamental characteristic of the clay is its plasticity, determined by its capacity for hydration, which allows it to take on water without dissolving or decomposing. During this phase of wetting, the clay can be moulded. Then begins the process of calcination or drying, during which the moulded item contracts into a stable, given form.

Potters produce their pieces by mixing two classes of clay. One is a slightly plastic mud, with minimal porosity, very soft to the touch and tending towards a dark range of colours, mainly in grey, an intense blue or brown, or rarely a deep black (called *carbón*, coal). The major downside of this type is that it does not *liga* (acquire a sufficiently mouldable consistency to enable manipulation, as it is kneaded and turned) and is therefore extremely difficult to work with. The upside is that it is strongly resistant to heat, so is very useful for making objects that will have to withstand strong temperatures, e.g. cooking vessels. The most prominent characteristic of the second type of clay is its great plasticity, making it tough to the touch; its colour is lighter and ranges from yellow to ochre. These types, when mixed, complement one other because each has qualities the other lacks. A large part of the professional knowledge of the potters stems from their ability to gauge the appropriate proportions of each to create a mixture, adapted to specific cases and pieces, according to the specific qualities which they want them to have.

These types of clay are found in nature normally under about a half metre layer of soil, though that depends on the characteristics of the area. Once through this top layer, the first vein of clay appears (usually 25–50 cm thick). This clay is too sandy to use. But a seam of useful clay lies immediately below (about 30–40 cm thick); its top cap, which is of better quality, is 'the flower of the clay'. Until the 1960s, the clay was extracted manually, by digging a circular or rectangular hole, normally about 3 m wide by 1.5–3 m deep. Once this first hole had been made and the veins of clay located, the craftspeople would make a series of underground horizontal galleries, through which they would look for the different seams of clay. These days, potters use clay from the same places as before but the procedure is completely mechanised; also, for some pieces, contemporary potters use ovenproof clays proceeding from the ceramic industry, which their forebears did not use.

Moulding comes next, usually on a wheel, formerly powered by the potter, but today is motorised. This is a phase of the work where a craftsperson can demonstrate his skill, since it relies implicitly both on technical knowledge, and on artistic considerations, whose application make the potter a 'creator'. As one commentator claims, 'A piece moulded on a wheel expresses as many aspects of its maker's personality as their calligraphy' (Hamilton 1989: 80).

After decoration, the piece is finished and the potter, wielding a wire or auxiliary tool used in the shaping process, separates it from the wheel with a clean and rapid cut. Drying comes next: here it is crucial to take advantage of the most favourable climatological conditions, without directly exposing the pieces to the sun. This is because a significant amount of water was added to manipulate the clay; once the piece is moulded, it cannot properly harden until this water has been removed. The expelling water phase must be progressive and slow to avoid possible fractures or fissures, which would ruin the pottery. Traditionally, drying time took four to six days in summer, eight to twenty in winter. Nowadays, these times can be altered, if articles are needed urgently need, thanks to the use of modern heating systems.

The last phase of the production process is firing the pots, during which the clay is totally hardened and the forms are definitively fixed. This was traditionally done in wood-fuelled ovens specifically constructed for the task by the potters themselves. Given that objective parameters did not then exist, this was a further phase when master potters could demonstrate their empirical knowledge, to determine the temperature and the necessary time to fire the items correctly. Generally, the maximum temperature reached inside the chamber did not have to be higher than 1,000°C: from this point on the pieces would begin to fuse. Firing lasted between six and seven hours, with gradual differences in temperature which the most experienced potters were able to monitor based on the changes in the colouration of the clay. According to my informants, in the initial phase they went from a dark grey (owing to the impregnation of smoke) to white. The most intense phase then began, with the constant addition of more fuel to ensure that the oven reached a maximum

Figure 7.1 Pieces made before 1960, and a modern reproduction of an original shape (the breastmilk pump piece).

temperature, for at least two hours, during which the pieces turned reddish. From then on, the pace of firing decreased slowly, until the oven's heat was finally extinguished and the pots left to rest. This phase of production has been the one most subject to innovation: today potters use electric hermetic ovens with external temperature controls. Also, in order to apply the modern glazes, the firing has to proceed through two interrupted temporal sequences; something completely new compared to the ceramics made up until the 1960s.

Until the recent revitalisation, Galician pottery could be classified functionally: pieces related to food, its production, its conservation and, especially, its preparation and consumption; pieces connected with physiological needs; some pieces had a playful character; and others formed part of a household's furnishings (Figure 7.1). This array of items covered the daily housekeeping needs of rural Galician families, and they would be acquired by direct purchase from the potters themselves at markets and local fairs.

Today, in contrast, buyers of clay pieces assign them a basically decorative function. Only clay roasting and cake pans are still used for their original domestic purpose, though these have come to be used almost solely to roast meat and fish. This shift towards the pottery's ornamental uses has gone hand in hand with physical changes. First, the objects are smaller in size and volume; second, glazes and waterproofing are now used. These additions were very limited in the past, to keep down the final cost of the pots; today they have become generalised, given their new, ornamental use, and to help keep them clean.

Also in contrast to the past, different workshops are today producing different pieces. I investigate three paradigmatic cases: Buño, Bonxe, and Gundivós. Buño is a coastal locality of the province of A Coruña with the largest concentration of contemporary pottery in Galicia; so much so that the visual projection of the village centres on the craft and, since 2009, there is even a dedicated ethnographic museum. Buño potters have chosen to use a great quantity of decorative resources on pieces made in the traditional format, based on chromatic variety and on the superposed applications of clay in compositions that are mainly phytomorphic and geometric.

In Bonxe, a potters' village situated near the city of Lugo, only one workshop is kept active. Here pieces of traditional origin, which would have rarely been decorated, now bear a dominant geometric motif: the paintbrushed application of liquid white clay lines, in a series of hemispheres ('half-moons'). A maximum of three dots are painted inside each of these arcs. Of course, the pieces are also polished in their entirety thanks to the use of glaze. What is significant is that the father and daughter who run the workshop justify these motifs by saying they have their origin in Roman ceramics,[1] and that the half-moons represent the silhouette of the *canaveira*, a traditional tool used when turning the clay on the wheel. Their discourse is grounded on the implicit idea that, proud of their trade, they decorate the pieces with an element that is a representative element of their craft and therefore, today, comes to be a prolongation of its extension.

Gundivós is a small village located in the very south of the province of Lugo, with an area of influence that extends to the province of Ourense. There are currently four active potters in this centre which has recently come to occupy a favoured place in the production of traditional Galician pottery because of a clearly differential feature: the finished black jet appearance of the pottery. This characteristic feature of Gundivós production is actually a recent innovation, starting in the late 1990s. Historically, only a few pieces were made this way in the village (*xarros, escurrecubas* and *xarros, escurrecubas*), and then only because they were containers used in the production and transport of wine, and therefore had to be impermeable. Potters waterproofed pieces by the application of pitch, not glaze. Pitch, or pine resin, is a solid granulated substance applied to the interior of the already baked pieces; their fusion is provoked by warming them again, directly over a fire, which also burns the piece on the exterior (Figure 7.2).

The material and functional changes in pottery production have been determined by institutional interventionism, which has gone from zero to a process of absolute direction; so much so that there would not have been any recovery of the pottery craft without this institutional presence. At the same time, the social value and the usefulness granted to the objects come from an ideological project that underlies the policies of the different public institutions intended to provide alternative economies

Figure 7.2 Pieces of traditional pottery made in the twenty-first century in Galicia.

and jobs for rural areas to replace the unviable primary-based economy. Of course, the limited economic scope of this measure, insufficient itself to replace the totality of the previous economic system, can be considered in some sense as the institutional Trojan horse, which comes accompanied by a series of parallel interventions of an ideological character.[2]

In this way the institutions are creating an ideological base related to an idea of tradition, already controversial, and with a certain conception of cultural, not national identity. In the Galician case, the recognition of a difference, based on culture, did not suppose a confrontational position towards the idea of the Spanish nation, when it emerged dispossessed of political connotations, unlike what could happen in other zones like, for example, the Basque Country.[3] Beside lacking this disadvantage, there is no doubt that it had certain economic advantages: the provision on the part of the European Union of a series of economic measures, fundamentally based on subsidies and on the distribution of European funds directed to the most disadvantaged regions, meant that recipient institutions (town halls, provincial governments, and the Xunta de Galicia) needed to design projects in which to invest these funds in rural space and in the tertiary sector. It explains the convergence between the cultural, the economic, and the political-ideological; it is a matter of trying to preserve a cultural manifestation of rural Galicia when the economic and social conditions for it no longer exist or are dismantled.

This ideological base gives rise to the re-creation or adjustment on the part of the interested potters and of the society in which they live. In the case of the craftspeople, as I have already pointed out, this recreation leads to the construction of a discourse about their activity, adapted to the new circumstances and setting out from the fact that such a public discourse did not exist previously. It is the institutions that grant a public dimension to the potters' activity, having placed the activity in social contexts which it had never before occupied and having granted it a relevance which it had never had. In the traditional world, the public exhibition of the potters was limited to their presence in markets as sellers of their objects. In this situation, it was not necessary to create any type of speech either for the production of the objects or for their sale: the commercial exchange was limited to the pieces, not to a parallel ideological content.[4] It is with the institutional intervention that the public presence of the potters is demanded, as carriers of a knowledge that is not only technical but also existential, experiential, and representative of a cultural model; we can say that they turn into the catalysts of the cultural transmission and of the immaterial heritage that the clay pieces carry.[5] The new buyers need someone to explain to them what or who a traditional potter is, for which these craftspeople need a life history linked with pottery.[6] Hence they create this speech concerning some working conditions that do not correspond with current reality. The fact that part of society has adopted a series of new values associated with the potter's craft and its past is demonstrated in the corpus of traditional pieces that the institutions create through founding 'collections' – a species of museum catalogue about the variety of clay objects. Of course, in the process, some pieces, which were in great demand and with a significant presence in Galician society fifty years ago, have been obviated in this process of recovery. The reason for this omission is that it is difficult to raise a clay urinal to the category of a cultural artefact beyond the showcases of an ethnographic museum, where the value of the artefact is determined, mostly, by its antiquity. Thus, traditional pieces such as the *canecos*, the urinals, the oil-lamps, etc., which are evocative of a past of privations and for which it is difficult to create new meanings, tend to disappear from the catalogues and the workshops of current production.

Economic reasons for change

Some researchers in cultural anthropology and related fields study the conditions that allow for the maintenance of craft and other traditional activities. This body of research usually looks at the cultural circumstances in countries that, within a capitalist socio-economic framework, are termed developing nations. These countries can be found mainly in Latin America, Africa, and Asia: places long associated in the Western imagination with the exoticisation of popular culture. In contrast to that work, I here deal specifically with the maintenance or endurance of a series of craft professions in Galicia, a society integrated politically and economically into the

EU.[7] This is an area that while being part of Europe is also situated geographically and historically on the periphery of the Spanish State to which it belongs, and of the whole EU.

This peripherality was confirmed when the EU established comparative rankings of all regions of its Member States and designated a series of regions as worthy of attention from its Regional Funds. These are designed to be redistributive, and are therefore only disbursed to regions of lesser development and specific economic problems, according to the EU's priorities ('objectives').[8] After Spain's entry into the EU in 1986, Galicia was designated to receive funds under more than one of the Objectives, both as an area with a lower level of development as measured by per capita Gross Domestic Product of less than 75 per cent of the EU average (of the Member States of the period), and also for being an area of rural decline. Connected with these designations was the idea of budgetary investments, presumed to be necessary (at least on paper) to achieve a level of economic balance for each territory vis-à-vis the other countries and regions which at that moment belonged to the Union.

The political and economic situation was complicated for Galicia in the 1990s shortly after Spain had joined the EU. It was disadvantaged compared to other regions that had already made the necessary changes to be more competitive in the European and world markets. Moreover, it had to confront the profound changes that had occurred since 1984 as a result of the CAP. As Edelmiro López explains:

> With the perspective that can be gained as a result of the passage of time, we can affirm that Galician agriculture was integrated into the European Community at a time that was not advantageous ... This European context, along with some of the conditions the Spanish government accepted in the Founding Treaty and the concrete way in which later reforms were applied, together created a frankly unfavourable context. (López 2000: 169)

In this context, the agricultural and fisheries sectors declined dramatically in Galicia with great numbers of people who had worked in the primary sector having to look for economic alternatives. For instance, the number of agriculturalists declined from 525,000 in 1976, to 247,000 in 1996, and then, even more dramatically, to 97,000 in 2007; i.e. a drop of almost 45 per cent in those first two decades, accelerating to 61 per cent in the following decade (Instituto Galego de Estatística 2008).[9]

This dramatic decline of the agricultural and fisheries sectors in Galicia and similar parts of Europe meant that governments became interested in retraining people to take up new kinds of jobs, in some cases jobs that would allow them to exploit products and other characteristics associated with their local areas and that might fit into the tourism sector. This situation derived from a double interaction. On the one hand, this change resulted from the decline of one sector (the primary) and the emergence of another, almost totally new, one in these rural areas (cultural tourism). Some traditional communities reacted by using this new sector to strengthen their local cultures. This is the reaction Claudia Toselli observed when she argued that 'cultural tourism can play a stimulating role when it revalorises, affirms and recuperates cultural elements which characterise and identify each community in the face of a globalised world' (Toselli 2006: 175).

The process of rural areas converting into receptors of tourism is motivated by a desire to gradually accommodate rural economic structures to this new reality. Here, the role of governmental policy is not limited only to providing economic resources for these new activities, including crafts and the traditional world in general. Indeed, as Llorenç Prats affirms, 'no heritage activity of any type is neutral or innocent, whether or not the respective managers of heritage are conscious of this or not' (Prats 1998: 68).

Looking for a way to promote culture: identity as heritage

This political and economic turning point in the 1980s was clearly connected to the definition of cultural heritage, developed by UNESCO in 1982 during the World Conference on Cultural Policies, in Mexico City. Part of this definition:

> The cultural heritage of a people includes the works of its artists, architects, musicians, writers and scientists and also the work of anonymous artists, expressions of the people's spirituality, and the body of values which give meaning to life. It includes both tangible and intangible works through which the creativity of that people finds expression: languages, rites, beliefs, historic places and monuments, literature, works of art, archives and libraries. (UNESCO 1982)

With this declaration, there was an explicit recognition for the first time at the world institutional level of what, until then, had formed a de facto part of people's cultures.[10] According to whatever canonical definitions are most current, we no longer think about culture as little more than an adaptive response of a specific human group to the environment in which it developed. If we take a structuralist view, culture can be understood like a system; i.e. an ensemble of elements interrelated via a series of rules for coexistence and interaction (Lévi-Strauss 1984; Jaaware 2001). It is obvious that change can occur within a cultural system as a result of the disappearance of some elements, the incorporation of new ones, or the semantic transformation of those already present. This relates, therefore, to a system at once protean and dynamic, which has an 'energeia' in the sense that Humboldt (1990) attributed to languages. In this state of things, a complementary notion to that of culture is that of the heritage pertaining to cultures which act, from a traditionalist viewpoint, like a brake on social change. Under this conception, what belongs to the realm of 'heritage' tends to be conserved, and constitutes a social construction based on the official recognition afforded to this realm from the various pertinent areas of governmental policy.

The most relevant aspect of the UNESCO declaration cited above is that, under the umbrella notion of 'the cultural heritage' of various peoples, we need to include not only those things traditionally considered to be relevant to what one might term 'official culture', but also any significant element (material and immaterial) of the culture of human communities as well. This therefore makes virtually everything susceptible to being made into 'heritage' and, in particular, into a form of ethnological heritage. Indeed, in reference to the concept of the 'ethnological', Juan Agudo Torrico has argued that:

> [ethnological] does not refer, therefore, to particularly differentiating specific ethnographic components which are more or less unique but to valuing each cultural component in relation to its significance for the way of life, values, self-perception, etc., of the collective which has generated and used said heritage; in this way, it therefore turns into a witness to collective memory. (Agudo Torrico 1996: 222)

In effect, a confluence has occurred between the cultural standards which are used to mark out most cultural groups at an international level and the interests of governmental institutions at the local level, as well as those of the Autonomous Community of Galicia, the Spanish State and the EU. These have been converted into the main catalysing forces behind various actions which have placed a value on heritage under the rubric of government 'cultural policies'.

In this sense, pottery's chances of being given priority over other crafts by the political institutions came from a variety of circumstances. In the first place, there was the possibility of rekindling a dying tradition without any excessive rupture, without losing much in terms of the original forms of the objects, their symbolic values, or their uses. In practice, as we have seen, important modifications were being introduced. But this was not because potters had forgotten older designs and techniques; rather, because they adapted to new cultural and economic circumstances.

A new social consideration: what is a potter today?

These modifications were particularly evident in terms of the production process, which was gradually mechanised, making the artisans' work much easier and allowing a new generation of potters (many of whom had not previously been directly linked with the profession) to take it up and make a future of it. Another influential factor was the new conservationist and didactic interest in the craft professions evinced within different levels of government, particularly at the provincial level and, in the public education sector, where agreements were reached, to develop a two-fold programme. One part was oriented straightforwardly towards educating the public and spreading the word about the profession as a career. The other was geared towards training and technical skills, and the delivery of courses to train new craftspeople. This second option was taken up by the public with relative success as offering job opportunities, even if involving temporary or complementary work in rural areas where there were not many employment options. Therefore, for the young people who signed up, these training courses were their first contact with pottery as a traditional craft occupation.[11]

Thus there was a break with the traditional way of transmitting craft knowledge, above all due to government intervention, since the entire process of recovering pottery skills was made into a planned, fostered, and managed project. The traditional system of apprenticeship involves the master potter and various apprentices working together in his workshop until the latter eventually become independent. Here, that system was replaced by a formalised relationship, as a regulated system of apprenticeship of a professional and technical nature was set up. Another change was that the traditional system of transmitting knowledge as part of a direct family inheritance of a craft was similarly replaced by strictly professional relationships in which the instructors rarely had any kin relationship with their students.

As a result, a training period of one hundred hours (the typical length of the courses) now gives participants an artisan's certificate (the *carta de artesano*). With this, apprentices can open an independent craft workshop after the completion of their training. Clearly, the reduction in the length of the training period, in relation to the traditional system, is not only quantitative but an issue of quality as well. In previous decades, apprenticeship to a master potter was neither prescriptively delimited, nor were there any obligatory curricula or any regulated and formal training system; rather, it lasted the entire life of the artisan who combined domestic work with an activity which contributed to the income of the household unit. In addition, there were no professional distinctions made between the roles of master craftspeople (*maestros*), journey people (*oficiales*), and apprentices (*aprendices*). It was only the specific activity itself that distinguished, in practice, the degree of skill evident in the work executed by some potters versus others. With the present system, in contrast, a limited period of time spent in an apprenticeship grants the individual and the work produced by him or her the sacralised character that emerges from the formula 'master craftsperson (or artisan)'. This provides institutionalised recognition to the person who has mastered her or his profession, regardless of the actual level of craft skill obtained in the process.

At the same time, government intervention is also evident on the other side of the apprenticeship-training process. Government offices appoint instructors on the basis of these individuals' affirmation of their level of skill, despite the government having no mechanism to affirm that these teachers have the sufficient technical skills in a craft to teach it. Therefore, this form of craft recovery did not involve a decision or initiative from the people who were associated with craft occupations in the past, but rather a new economic opportunity offered by the Autonomous Community government. After an initial period of this policy, official recognition was belatedly given to the importance of individuals who had both the technical knowledge and represented the practical history of craft production. These individuals, who had a long association with craft production, came to be seen as forming part of the collective memory of Galician identity. On the basis of the interest shown by the government, the artisans acquired a consciousness of the importance which the new society was placing on their role and on them, and not only on the objects which they produced. This meant that they themselves were converted into symbols of identity.[12]

It is not surprising that this situation has resulted in a cultural reinvention of the potters, a group that had very little social prestige historically. This reinvention has a somewhat epic tone with respect to how the changing role of the profession is framed, not only in terms of the real-life experience of individual potters but as a reframing of potters as qualified representatives of a particular aspect of memory and the historical past. It is common for the life history of potters to be presented as central to the craft. This mythologises craft production in a way more connected to present government policies than to past practices in craft production. In the past, the halo of collective images about Galician identity, today associated with pieces of pottery and the artisans who make them, did not exist. Rather, pottery was connected to an ordinary material reality and potters were seen as being part of a useful profession that dealt with the necessities of daily life. At the same time, it is understandable that some artisans conceive of their own life histories as being almost heroically tied to the longed-for recovery of a dying way of life. This remains true, despite the fact that this craft had long since lost its primary social utility, and only became a recoverable economic opportunity when various levels of government decided to promote it as a window onto Galician culture. An obvious support for the argument is that not all of the artisans who had knowledge of the profession and had practised it for many years, decided to take it up again during the revitalisation process. Despite the relative success of this revitalisation, it is clear that the current market for pottery products will not support a large growth in the number of people working in this profession, since it is no longer related to creating pieces for people's everyday needs for tableware and other items. Rather, potting now occupies a symbolic space which is concretised through the use of craft pieces as decorative rather than practical objects. Among the large quantity of potters who practised their profession until the 1960s, it was normally those who were closer to people in government who returned to this craft activity and, in virtually every case, each person has produced a very reduced number of pieces. There are only one or two potters working in most of the productive centres aside from locations such as Buño, where pottery has managed to open up an important space of its own as a specialised form of production.

Clay pieces as cultural symbols: new meanings for old objects

Another important component in the successful recreation of the craft of pottery as a heritage activity involves the interval of time related to the relative inactivity in pottery production between the 1970s and 1990s. This two-decade lull was fundamental in allowing for a renewed semantic emphasis to be placed on both the objects produced with clay and the artisans who produced these objects. This was a necessary phase that allowed for the distancing and objectification necessary to change the symbolism associated with the pieces from one that held largely pejorative and negative content (e.g. as being unnecessary in a modern society) to a new and more positive content. This was true for both the potters and for those who used the pieces.

In the past the potters belonged to a sector of the peasantry that either did not own land or owned very little, and for whom agriculture and livestock raising were complementary rather than main economic activities. This was in a society in which the ownership of property was a criterion for prestige and formed the basis of the social hierarchy. Those who bought and used pieces of Galician pottery prior to the 1960s were from both rural areas and from Galician cities and towns, but they were always from a lower social class. In each case, they purchased clay pieces out of necessity or because they could not afford other types of more expensive dishes, such as the fine china and porcelain which only the wealthy used on an everyday basis and which some of the middle class would bring out on special occasions. In the post-1960s period, clay was replaced by other industrially produced materials (above all, plastic, glass, and cheap metals) and it thereby lost the negative connotations it had acquired when connected with a situation of necessity. This gradual change meant that clay came to have a symbolic patina of prestige based, above all, on its value as an object that represents Galician identity in a society that is bit by bit becoming more urban and industrial, with a tendency to forget its origins, and so in turn initiating a process of mythologisation. Below I discuss some of the values that are projected via the craft of pottery as a result of its association with government policy planning that sometimes uses certain symbols in a manner similar to commercial marketing.

The question of collective identity is probably the symbolic axis which best gathers together and summarises the values attributed to the craft of making things with clay. In one sense, this relates to a strong reaction to the external forces of globalisation which tend to sever local or community identities. This involves a reaffirmation of a particular identity; in this case, a Galician identity which can offer something to people in the face of some degree of cultural homogenisation prevalent on a global scale. As Ulrich Beck noted, 'paradoxically, a return to nationalism is a common response to globalisation' (2004: 17; my translation). This symbolic process involves an emphasis being placed on certain features, such as ruralism, that are considered to identify 'traditional cultures'. Alongside this more general association of Galicia with ruralism are other characteristics that are associated in popular culture and by various authors to specifically 'Galician' culture: these include the idea of Galicians having a 'melancholic' character, being sentimental, nostalgic for their place of origin, and devoted to a culture of hard work and effort (Freire Paz 2004). In the context of the revival of pottery, these types of characteristics became portrayed as intrinsic aspects of the work associated with this craft activity. This helped convert the craft into a representation, often partially idealised, of the past and of a collective Galician identity. Pottery is now seen as a local resource that can additionally attract buyers for other products, specifically food items, which are being marketed successfully, partly due to their connection with people's individual memories and search for personal origins. Pottery containers can be used to echo the idea of being a member of a collectivity that shares the same markers of identity. The promotional efforts of public institutions are, in large part, responsible for the generation of this collective image which is nothing save the expansion of specific traditional catchphrases or clichés that have been taken on by Galicians themselves and promoted through generalisations about common, shared cultural features associated with being 'Galician'.

It is not a total accident that the use of this ideology, which tends to create a collective consciousness, coincides with a specific political process in contemporary Spain that involves the move to a concept of a multicultural, multilingual, and plurinational state. This fits with the contemporary recognition of historical nationalities and the creation of a system of Autonomous Communities which are moving towards more and more self-governance. This process was born politically at the end of the 1970s and the beginning of the 1980s and was later strengthened with the 1986 entry of Spain into the EU, which entailed accommodating to European policies. These included the concept of forming part of a 'Euroregion' that, for example, was given a concrete shape in the candidature of Portuguese-Galician Immaterial Heritage for UNESCO status. This example includes a territory that belongs administratively to the Spanish State (the Galician Autonomous Community) and another to the Portuguese State (the north of Portugal), united by the supranational fact that they possess some common cultural bases which create a link between them within Europe and distinguish them from the other territorial areas within their respective States. In short, this refers to a process whereby signs of identity are created as a result of political factors and can come from an international as much as a local level. The homogenising characteristic of globalisation can thereby have an impact alongside the reinforcement of local identities so that, paradoxically, distinct cultures seem to grow more similar the more we differentiate ourselves.

In addition, one of the characteristics of pieces made of clay, as with other crafts, is that they are timeless, in the sense that they can virtually carry specific meanings from the past into the immediate present. Naturally, the most disagreeable aspects of the past are idealised, avoided, and substituted for in this cultural process. Therefore, the image of the collective work practised by rural Galicians when there was little industrial development and the help of others was needed to complete certain tasks in a short time becomes summarised, above all, in the ludic and festive aspect of social gatherings, which in the Galician case are especially related to specific foods (Castro 2001; Roseman 2004). The majority of pottery pieces are associated with various foodstuffs, having been used to prepare or serve food on. In the past, pottery was also used in common by members of a family or broader community, and so may reinforce an image of the Galician collective to counter the context of today's society in which individual consumption has primacy. Another image generated by pottery pieces, and especially those used for the transportation or storage of liquids, is an association with eroticism and moments when rural people escaped ordinary social constraints. Certain pieces are related to activities that took place outside domestic spaces, such as fetching water from community streams, or performing collective tasks, for instance harvesting grapes or slaughtering pigs (Castro 2003). These activities commonly involved a festive atmosphere, especially when carried out by youth, and were often connected to establishing relationships which went beyond the limits of what was strictly related to the work at hand.

The idea of authenticity is also associated with the objects made by potters from clay in contrast to those made through industrial production methods. The differences are obvious and are based on the limited scale of production possible with craftwork as opposed to mass production, in the use of manual and craft techniques as opposed to industrial machinery, and in the singularity and originality of each piece. The very fact that artisans sell their pieces or their art at the same time that they narrate or exhibit the parts of their life histories linked to the practice of their profession and/or to the history of craft production means that the pieces are being set up as authentically safeguarding the vicarious experience of the tourists who buy them. It is clear that the government attitude, as previously mentioned, is directed in large measure to certifying and guaranteeing the authenticity of these pieces and, therefore, the experience associated with them.[13] What is being sought is a guarantee of authenticity, as though this were an indispensable characteristic that places a special value on a craft. Craftwork is, by definition, a changing activity with respect to the use of particular models, forms, decorations, and materials and tools because it adapts to a number of specific requirements. However, even in the case of a process of recovery, modifications are made with respect to the traditional models (Figures 7.3 and 7.4). This allows one to speak about the possibility of a rupture, given that it has not been possible to totally maintain a solidarity with the past in terms of the clay itself, the tools used to do the work, the forms or size of pieces, the baking process, the physical qualities of the piece (their weight, colour, resistance to the firing, porosity), the types of decoration, or naturally (and this is the first to disappear) the uses and functions for which the pieces were originally made. In reality, what guarantees authenticity are not the pieces themselves but the immaterial values associated with them and the experience of those who purchase pottery, who may not need to recover a fully 'authentic' piece or its elements in order to decide on its value.

There are also other, related values, assimilated by or easily attributed to clay, which emerge as a result of parallel circumstances. In today's world, people's lifestyles and food choices as well as other areas of life have been heavily impacted by their concerns over the environment. As part of these concerns, a distinction is made between the overall system of production and exploitation of the world in which we

Figure 7.3 Diachronic evolution of a breastmilk pump piece (*pezoeira*).

Figure 7.4 Souvenirs sold as traditional pottery.

live against the traditional systems, considered by many to have been more rational, sustainable, and respectful of the environment. In this dialectical framework, the products made from clay and, in general, all crafts are connected with an economic model promoting the ideal of sustainable development.

The preoccupation with health – one of the obsessions of the modern world, along with the search for natural and organic products – also has a clear connection with the world of clay craft. Clay is, obviously, an organic and natural material that is recyclable in all phases of production. At the same time, the food industry uses clay dishes (even if they are industrially produced versions) to package certain products that it wishes to sell or label as organic, especially ones produced through artisanal methods. This relates to a reciprocal relationship in which the container and the content interact and share symbolic values that come from the notion of the 'natural earth'. Natural products are produced from the earth and, in a purposeful play on words, clay is made from the earth.[14] In addition, in a mythical allusion with religious origins, clay is associated with a confluence of earth, water, and fire and therefore a return to its origins. In this case, it is not so much the work of the institutions that spreads this semantic baggage, but more the interaction of the craft with the market, a market that had previously rendered pottery largely irrelevant in face of new products though it has now adopted this recovered craft to promote new connotations.

With the governmental creation, or re-creation, of pottery as craft, new connotations for pieces made out of clay have been conferred in a programmed and institutionalised way. It would be illusionary to think that this profession would have been able to recover and maintain itself without government support. This relates not just to the economic aid that was available in the first phases of the process of recovery but also to the ideological use of the clay pieces as part of the cultural policies enacted by the various governments in order to create new signs of Galician identity. There are two aspects to consider here: in the first place, pottery came to signify a way to identify and differentiate Galicians from others. These signs generated internal social cohesion under the rubric of a craft. And second, this semantic process reflected meanings that were associated with the past and the present, what was nostalgically yearned for and what yet might still come to pass (Fernandez 1991).

The politics of tradition and the recovery of Galician pottery

The recovery of crafts fits well with the application of the notion of a 'politics of tradition', with four fundamental effects (Cruces 1998: 84). The first of these is *traditionalisation*. This is understood to be a process that involves States not only supporting heritage conservation, but also fixing on and creating hierarchies that place some forms of culture over others. One can say that, in this way, while supporting the recovery of pottery, government institutions have also privileged this activity over others which, objectively, could present the same values and importance from the point of view of the conservation of traditional culture. On the other hand, within the full gamut of pottery, a priority has been placed on recuperating those physical pieces which, although they are accompanied in many cases through oral transmission by artisans' discourses about their own past circumstances, do not pay real attention to actual social processes. The focus of these accounts is therefore historical, like a recalling or a demonstration of the conditions associated with pottery in the past, but not like an account of actual dynamics that would recount their social roles and specific relationships.

At the same time, there is a *legitimation* effect that is mutually constituted between the public institutions and the groups or individuals who manufacture and sell objects that become 'heritage' items (Cruces 1998: 85). When governments grant a symbolic status of prominence and legitimacy to certain things, this recognition of human groups and their activities will become seen in an official and institutionalised way that could not be achieved through open competition through capitalist economic processes. The artisans working with clay enjoy a social prestige derived directly from their link with government institutions and their methods of promotion and adoption, in what one can think of as a type of guardianship. Of course, from the standpoint of the free market, this situation grants strength or a guarantee of survival despite the inherent weakness of particular economic sectors. Moreover, government institutions have proceeded to protect the work of pottery and of the artisans in a way that is both personalised and individualised. This involves the promotion of key or representative figures in each productive zone. As such, it also can be seen to become a form of control over the potters' discourse. This discourse, under government sponsorship, becomes directed towards a formal, externally oriented presentation of the special features of potters' work and indeed implies a historical reality for a role that is actually conferred by formal institutions.

The third effect of the politics of tradition is the *demarcation or establishment of conceptual limits* (Cruces 1998: 85). Government institutions contribute to the projection of the symbolic meaning of pieces of clay via the mechanisms of advertising and other forms of promotion. This process generates a web of conceptual meanings that intermingle with the meanings already existing in society in relation to pottery, as we saw in the case of the rescue of the values of the rural, the natural, and the ecological. This process of generating social meanings plays out, above all, in the conceptualisation of cultural or group identity, vis-à-vis the outside, to 'be something in the face of differences' (García 1998: 13) within the context of globalisation (García Canclini 1989). It involves the unavoidable comparison of 'us versus them' and can be used to reinforce specific values of Galician culture to the detriment of others, with the intention of creating an image based on shared characteristics that are projected as held in common. Clearly, a decision was made to opt for a recovery of traditional pottery versus other crafts or traditional occupations. Even within this rubric, specific representative types or forms of brands have been differentially generated in association with specific areas such as Buño, Niñodaguia, or Bonxe, while other areas and pottery practices have been ignored.

The fourth point is that we are talking about *objectification* (Cruces 1998: 86) – a mechanism that institutions employ to formalise the symbolic content of a specific culture or a certain aspect of heritage. This consists of a political or policy intervention that involves simplifying the contents of a society's actual heritage, by reductionism and the extraction of a limited number of common denominators. This leads to an abstraction of values in order to generate a decipherable code of significations for the members of the society that is being identified, a code that is meant to conform to a model of ideal references. In José Luis García's words: '[T]he expression "cultural heritage" draws people's attention, up to a certain point arbitrarily, to some aspects of (that which considered to be) cultural' (García 1998: 9). In this sense, the system removes the concrete in order to prioritise the global and that which is held in common, thereby suppressing the individual peculiarities that lead to the elaboration of the various versions that could be used for a collective past. Contemporary pottery in Galicia, as it has been presented, has based its semiotic efficacy on the celebration of positive values that Galicians recognise as their own. These values simultaneously minimise past social conflicts and help downplay conflicting ideologies that are present in contemporary Galicia.

Conclusion

If we generalise from this particular example, the process of recovering the craft of pottery allows us to observe the mechanics involved in government institutions' redefining traditional Galician culture, based on an adaptation to global models. This relates to a prototypical process: an ideal is formed by combining various general principles with a series of more local values. It is these more concrete values – in this case those that intersect with the practice of pottery in Galicia – that make the universal model representing the global world less automatic. The connection with local, concrete values puts this universal model into practice, giving it a pragmatic character and granting it a functional role which, ultimately, allows the local population to identify with it.

The value system offered by the global model, which is abstract and generic, lacks a true link with tradition; however, society accepts this imperfection on the altar of authenticity, avoiding the negative aspects of what was objective historical reality in order to permit elements of the past to function as present day symbols of identity. In this way, people are practising a principle of socially cooperating with the discourse proposed by government institutions. As part of this discourse, that which is defined as pertaining to the idea of traditional culture alludes to a system of symbolic values that are embedded in an ideological construction, which is in turn justified through a reference to the past and is of a meta-referential character (i.e. it ultimately refers to itself). The past is constructed as an ideal model from the perspective of the present day, given that the idea of traditional culture is created in the present and gives a coherence and continuity to that which likely did not exist. This occurs on the basis of a discontinuous memory that is purposefully created in the present through an idealised copying of the past, incorporating elements of that past but placing them within a new system.

It can therefore be argued that government intervention into the recovery of craft traditions involves a double construction: first, the elaboration of the objects being manually produced; and second, the play of symbols. The memories that are generated by the objects which are displayed by potters and viewed by others become part of a ritual process, and the objects become a type of fetish in which our dispersed memories are deposited, unifying our identities through common, abstract values. Following Martin Heidegger's (1994) idea of the importance of the foundational myths of distinct peoples, it is possible to argue that pottery is part of a common history that explains Galicia's contingent present.

Notes

1 It must not be overlooked that the reference to the Roman world or to that of the '*mouros*' is not historically precise but rather of a mythical or atemporal character. Conversely, it is also obvious that there can exist an appropriation of the values associated with the Roman culture given that the city of Lugo had its origin (though with a previous pre-existence) in a military camp in the epoch of Augusto under Paulo Fabio Máximo's delegation, and abundant vestiges of this epoch exist throughout the whole city and its environment.

2 A telling example of this insufficiency to replace the total economic system is the fact that, in the whole province of Lugo, only six persons produce pieces of traditional pottery, and only three of them are dedicated exclusively to this work; the others combine it with other economic activities.

3 A certain line of Galician regionalist thought of the nineteenth century, as represented by Alfredo Brañas – Catholic and traditionalist regionalism – is adopted, in some senses for the political party that governs the *Xunta de Galicia* between 1990 and 2005, placed politically in the spectrum of the Spanish right, inheritor of certain ideological and personal contents of the pro-Franco period. At the same time, this same ideological trend, foreign to political revitalisations, had a presence in the pro-Galician and anti-Franco sector from the 1950s onward, through figures such as Ramón Piñeiro.

4 Certainly, traditional cultural products exist that are based on the social figure of these craftspeople, as similar cases. Nevertheless, they tend to be limited to reproducing certain social stereotypes and not to projecting a new image. Therefore, for example, there are sayings that vulgarise this figure and his trade such as '*Non te cases cos oleiros, que os hai na miña terra; / os oleiros de barro, de barro fainos calquera*' ('Don't marry the potters, there are some in my area; / the potters of clay, anyone can make [things] with clay'), together with others that emphasise the managing of cash money as '*Casa conmigo, Rosiña / mira que son cacharreiro / durmirás en boa cama / e sempre terás diñeiro*' ('Marry me Rosiña / look I'm a maker of crockery / you will sleep in a good bed / and always have money'), or '*Non te burles do oleiro / que da terra fai diñeir*' ('Don't make fun of the potter / from land one makes money').

5 The already existent commercial circuits are neither periodic nor local (fairs and traditional markets); today buyers acquire the objects in the craftspeople's own workshops, conceived of through the networks programmed and supported by different institutions as museistic workshops, or exhibitions-fairs.
6 Young people who mainly come from urban Galicia, disconnected from the system of traditional production, approach these pieces with a conscious attitude that makes them think they are buying a part of their identity or from their past. The foreign tourists who buy are moved by another type of motivation which has a cultural base but is more linked to the idea of originality, in their search of differentiation, exclusivity, and uniqueness, but not of identity.
7 Encarnación Aguilar argues that the idea of promoting rural development on the basis of strengthening existing cultural values and the natural attributes of different regions are the 'results from our [Spain's] integration into the CAP' (Aguilar Criado 2002).
8 In 1991, the European Union established the LEADER (an acronym from the French name *Liaisons entre Actions de Développement de l'Économie Rurale*) to disburse some of the redestributed funds. The first LEADER lasted until 1994 and LEADER II until 2001, being replaced by the programme LEADER Plus.
9 These figures refer to changes that had a major economic impact over a short period, affecting not just economic production but also social organisation in Galicia.
10 Since 1982 UNESCO increasingly recognised the immaterial facets of heritage, in 2003 defining these as 'the practices, representations, expressions, knowledge, skills – as well as the instruments, objects, artefacts and cultural spaces associated therewith – that communities, groups and, in some cases, individuals recognized as part of their cultural heritage' (UNESCO 2003).
11 Only some of them would go on to develop this employment possibility as a full-time professional occupation (Roseman 2003).
12 From a semiotic point of view, it is significant that the government's advertising posters during this period concentrated iconographically on two elements: certain objects were chosen to illustrate the typical pottery of each region or community; also, the hands of older potters were included with a clear reference to the past.
13 In 1992 the Galician Parliament passed the *Lei de Artesanía de Galicia* (Law of Galician Crafts) prescribing that 'the Ministry in charge will dictate the precise rules for accrediting the quality of craft products and will create distinctions and will confer certificates of quality' (Xunta de Galicia 1992). As a consequence, an identifying logo was conferred by the Ministry of Industry (*Consellería de Industria*); it is now used alongside potters' individualised stamps.
14 Earth and clay are actually different materials, as much for their composition as for their physical qualities, uses, and look. Another paradox is that the glazes used traditionally are toxic and have had to be substituted for others.

References

Agudo Torrico, Juan 1996 'Patrimonio etnológico e identidades. Los nuevos contenidos ideológicos del trabajo etnográfico en Andalucía', in E. Aguilar Criado (ed.) *De la construcción de la historia a la práctica de la antropología en España. Actas del VII Congreso de Antropología Social* (Zaragoza: FAAEE), 219–34.

Aguilar Criado, Encarnación 2002 'Cultura y desarrollo rural desde la perspectiva de la globalización' in *Actas del IX Congreso de Antropología Social* (Barcelona: FAAEE. CD Rom edition).

Beck, Ulrich 2004 *¿Qué es la globalización? Falacias del globalismo, respuestas a la globalización* (Barcelona: Paidós Ibérica).

Castro, Javier 2001 *Ayunos y yantares: usos y costumbres en la historia de la alimentación* (Madrid: Nívola).

——2003 'Viño e historia: aspectos simbólico-culturais', *I Congreso de Patrimonio Etnográfico Galego: in memorian Xaquín Lourenzo Fernández 'Xocas'* (Ourense: Deputación Provincial), 213–20.

Cruces, Francisco 1998 'Problemas en torno a la restitución del patrimonio. Una visión desde la antropología', *Política y Sociedad*, 27, 77–87.

Fernandez, James W. 1991 *Beyond Metaphor: The Theory of Tropes In Anthropology* (Stanford: Stanford University Press).

Freire Paz, Elena 2004 *La recuperación de la alfarería tradicional en la provincia de Lugo: procesos socioeconómicos y culturales* (Santiago de Compostela: Universidade de Santiago de Compostela).

García Alén, Luciano 2008 *La alfarería de Galicia* (A Coruña: Fundación Pedro Barrié de la Maza).

García Canclini, Néstor 1989 *Las culturas populares en el capitalismo* (México: Editorial Nueva Imagen).

García García, José Luis 1998 'De la cultura como patrimonio al patrimonio cultural' in *Política y Sociedad*, 27, 9–20.

Hamilton, David 1989 *Alfarería y cerámica* (Barcelona: Ediciones Ceac).

Heidegger, Martin 1994 *Construir, habitar, pensar* (Barcelona: Ediciones del Serbal).

Humboldt, W. 1990 *Sobre la diversidad de la estructura del lenguaje humano y su influencia sobre el desarrollo espiritual de la humanidad*, trans. A. Agud (Barcelona: Anthropos).

Instituto Galego de Estadística 2008 *Datos de poboación*. Published at http://www.ige.eu/web/index.jsp?paxina=001&idioma=gl. Accessed 19 November 2014.

Jaaware, Aniket 2001 *Simplifications. An Introduction to Structuralism and Post-Structuralism* (New Delhi: Orient Longman).

Lévi-Strauss, Claude 1984 *Anthropologie structurale* (París: Plon).

López Iglesias, Edelmiro 2000 'O sector agrario galego ás portas do século XXI', *Revista Galega de Economía*, 9:1, 167–96.

Prats, Llorenç 1998 'El concepto de patrimonio cultural' in *Política y Sociedad*, 27, 63–76.

Roseman, Sharon 2003 'Poniendo la artesanía gallega y el turismo rural gallego en el mapa global: políticas administrativas y propuestas locales', in C. Bueno and E. Aguilar (eds), *Las expresiones locales de la globalización: México y España* (México: Centro de Investigación y Estudios Superiores en Antropología Social y Editorial Miguel Ángel Porrúa), 381–404.

Roseman, Sharon 2004 'Bioregulation and *comida caseira* in rural Galicia, Spain', *Identities: Global Studies in Culture and Power*, 11:1, 9–37.

Sassen, Saskia 2007 *Una sociología de la globalización* (Buenos Aires: Katz Editores).

Seseña, Natacha, Rüdiger Vossen, and Wulf Köpke 1973 '¿Desaparece la alfarería española?' *Diario Informaciones* (Madrid, 24 November).

Toselli, Claudia 2006 'Algunas reflexiones sobre el turismo cultural', *Pasos: Revista de Turismo y Patrimonio Cultural*, 4: 2, 175–82.

UNESCO 1982 'Mexico city declaration on cultural policies', *World Conference on Cultural Policies*, Mexico DF, 26 July–6 August. Published at http://portal.unesco.org/culture/en/files/12762/11295421661mexico_en.pdf/mexico_en.pdf. Accessed 19 November 2014.
——2003 *Convention for the Safeguarding of the Intangible Cultural Heritage*, Paris, 17 October, www.unesco.org/culture/ich/index.php?lg=es&pg=00006. Accessed 19 November 2014.
Xunta de Galicia 1992 *Lei 1/1992*, DOG March 11, Lei de Artesanía de Galicia.

8

Fear and loving in the west of Ireland: the blows of County Clare

Jeremy MacClancy

> One of Ireland's premier tourism counties, Clare is amazing. It has an abundance of visual riches from the famous river Shannon ... to its rugged Atlantic coastline with its towering cliffs and golden 'blue flag' beaches.

So states one local tourist website. Another speaks of Clare as 'an ideal destination for those in search of the outdoors', a 'beautiful area' with 'charming villages'. According to a third, 'West Clare is an area of unspoiled beauty', 'one of Ireland's best kept secrets', while a fourth claims 'its unspoiled natural beauty is highly prized and its dramatic coastline entices many visitors. County Clare has a living Gaelic tradition, which can be heard and seen in its music and arts.' Individual towns are treated similarly: Doolin becomes 'a place of breathtaking beauty surrounded by the spectacular bare limestone landscape of the Burren'.[1]

Geologists and historians tell a different tale. The soil is poor, boggy, where water cannot easily drain because of the dense underlying clay. The karst limestone formations of the Burren in the north-west of the county are no better: Oliver Cromwell, on his Irish campaign, famously complained the area had 'not enough trees to hang a man, not enough earth to bury him'. The climate is rainy and, towards the coast, wind-bound. Bordered on three sides by water (Galway Bay, the Atlantic, the River Shannon), it was a relatively isolated county, which maintained much of its traditional Gaelic way of life well into the eighteenth century. Historically, it was also a disadvantaged county. Most travellers to Ireland avoided the area altogether. Those few who did make the journey were usually pleased by the landscape, but more often appalled by the extreme poverty of its people. From the seventeenth century on, visitors spoke of ragged locals leading mean lives in miserable hovels 'no better than pigsties'. One German passing through the area before the Great Famine stated that he 'passed not a single village, nor a single hut fit for human habitation ... nowhere else do we find human beings gnawing, from year's end to year's end at the same root, berry, or weed.' One visitor, arriving a few years after the Famine, wondered where in the world he was:

> The features, manners and costume of the majority of the country people ... added to the language they spoke, and (to an Englishman) curious stock of goats, mules, and

asses in which they dealt, made me almost start to think that, instead of being in some far-off primitive land, I was in reality within a twenty-fours' ride of home and among citizens of the same nation!

The tradition of emigration boosted by the Famine and the switch in land ownership from landlord to tenant did lead to a gradual rise in living standards from the late nineteenth century on. Even so, Clare never came to be considered an agriculturally rich county.[2]

Irish writers based in Dublin perceived yet further dimensions of the area. In the late nineteenth century, Clare's *gaeltachts* (Gaelic-speaking areas), its traditional ways and backward economy helped make it a prime site for the high-priests of the Celtic Renaissance. Lady Augusta Gregory, nationalist and folklorist, held court for Yeats and others in her Clare house, Coole Castle, and the poet spent time doing a little fieldwork in the area, which he thought an ideal zone for collecting folk beliefs (Foster 1997: 195). After visiting the Aran Islands off Clare, Yeats urged the young writer J. M. Synge to 'live there as if you were one of the people themselves; express a life that has never found expression'. Between1898–1901, Synge visited five times, gathering material there he later used in his plays. In his account of these stays, Synge acts the amateur ethnographer translating the ways of these insular characters for an educated, urban audience. He sees the locals in patently primitivist terms: unsullied by a brutalising 'civilisation', these elemental types live in concord with their storm-swept, wave-washed homeland. They are both wild and refined, resigned and passionate, makers of a 'rude but beautiful' poetry (Synge 1907; Robinson 1992).[3] To Synge, they are exemplars of what we urbanites have lost.

Anthropologists came remarkably early to Clare, and provided a more prosaic form of ethnography. Members of the Ethnological Section of the British Association visited Aran in 1857, followed by a longer sojourn by the Cambridge anthropologist A. C. Haddon in 1892 (Haddon and Brown 1893; Robinson 1992: xv). Between 1932 and 1934, a pair of Harvard anthropologists, Conrad Arensberg and Solon Kimball, based themselves in a mid-Clare village and carried out what is usually regarded as the first exercise in intensive fieldwork among a West European people. Clare, they thought, had 'something of the old tradition still alive'. Their now-classic monograph, *Family and Community in Ireland*, is considered a model study in a high functionalist mode, with its detailed analysis of the structure, process, and relations of smallholder families, begrudgingly adapting to the present because firmly anchored in the past (Arensberg and Kimball 1940; 1968: 37; Byrne, Edmondson, and Varley 2001).Writing in the wake of the Depression, with its vicious exposure of the dangers within laissez-faire capitalism, Arensberg and Kimball portrayed these small farmers as predominantly subsistence producers, only marginally inserted in a cash economy.

Robert Cresswell, another American anthropologist, who went to a north Burren parish in the mid-1960s, found 'general destructuration' to be the rule then: the declining autonomy of local producers, ever increasing use of money in circuits of production, a widening gap between large and small farmers, and an end to belief in the power of fairies and their Celtic kin (Cresswell 1969). These factors, combined with the depopulation caused by the Famine, emigration and low rates of reproduction were leading to the demise of kinship as a base of social organisation. If Cresswell perceived the 'disintegration' of traditional society, his successor, Hugh Brody, who lived in an unnamed west Clare village in the late 1960s, took an even bleaker view.[4] According to him, communities had broken down and traditional mores devalued. People no longer believed the customary way of life could continue, and had now lost faith in its worth anyway. Where Arensberg and Kimball underscored harmony, Brody saw contradiction and tension, which became ever more evident as the local culture fragmented. Despondent, demoralised, robbed of a residual dignity, locals led increasingly lonely lives, in the isolation of their own homes (Brody 1973).[5] Suicides were not rare and 'mental breakdowns' were becoming an almost routine part of local life.

Perhaps this is the point at which I must declare my own special interest. My father, a doctor, was born and raised in Ennis, the county town of Clare. His father was County Surgeon at the County Infirmary from 1908 to 1950. A man very well aware of his own dignity, he and other Catholics of his class saw themselves as rising to fill the hierarchical positions left vacant by the decline or departure of the Protestant Ascendancy. This solid sense of social rank, where the middle class looked down on the less well-off, and townspeople thought themselves superior to rude rural folk, was, however, strongly tempered by a common commitment to an ideology of egalitarianism.[6] My grandfather and his ilk might have been well aware of their own position in the pecking order, but they still knew that they were expected to engage with others, at least in selected contexts. To give one example, on a golf links, the well-to-do might play a round with a butcher and a small shopkeeper, but would later drink among their own in the clubhouse. An open friendliness to all, based on recognition of a common humanity, was expected; those who set themselves apart or broadcast their own achievements were strongly derided as 'too full of themselves'. A hard-nosed commercialism was anathema, and embodied in the much-denigrated figure of the '*gombeen*', entrepreneurs on the make. Relations were meant to be affective, not nakedly instrumental, for one's own petty gain.

What I perceived, as a child on repeated holiday trips in the late 1950s and early 1960s, as good-natured people coasting in a peaceful timelessness is now spoken of as adaptation, willing or not, to economic stagnation and the heavy hand of a traditionalist church. With little to aspire to for most, time was not valued. Talk, however, was and a man with a 'gift for the gab' and a sense of humour much appreciated. In sum, Clare in those days appeared to me an insular, quiet county of few opportunities and friendly people united by a common desire to make the most of what company offered: conversation, music, and Gaelic sports. No wonder so many suffered mental illness!

Tourist promoters, historians, writers, anthropologists: all produced their own vision of Clare; all worked from their own interests. The promoters have only the most roseate of views, while the historians tend to stress disadvantage, the writers to romanticise the locals, and the anthropologists to tribalise them. My point is simple: there is no unitary or definitive image, whether external or internal, of the county. Thus when a new kind of person started to come to Clare in the early 1970s there was no simple, dominant vision of the area. Rather, these 'blow-ins' or 'blows', as locals termed them, perceived the complex, slowly shifting reality of the county in their own way, according to their own interests and to the welcomes they received. In this chapter, I wish to investigate who these immigrants were, what images of Clare they had, how they fared, how the locals perceived them, and how have they all got on, or failed to.

A note on method: a London friend of mine had been a Clare blow-in herself for many years. She gave me the name of a friend, a blow long-resident in the county. In Easter 2003 I stayed with him during my compressed fieldwork there. He introduced me to a large number of blows, whom I duly spoke with. I sent a draft of this chapter to all those for whom I had addresses. I am grateful for their comments, some of which I have heeded. During my fieldwork, my cousin (my FBS), Malcolm MacClancy, a Dublin graduate born and bred in Clare, acted as my research assistant, interviewing locals about their attitudes to the blow-ins. His value was underlined when my host told a neighbouring farmer about his guest and what I was doing. The farmer replied, 'Just as well your man is talking to the blow-ins. For he wouldn't get a word of truth out of us'.[7]

The blows

The longest-resident blows, and many others, divide the arrival of incomers into three waves: the first, who were known as 'hippies', came in the late 1960s and early 1970s; the second, who were pejoratively classed as 'crusties', arrived in the 1980s; the third started in the 1990s and are often termed 'suburbanites' by the longer-established blows.

The first arrivals state today that they had become disenchanted with their urban way of life, whether in Britain, continental Europe, or America. Greatly influenced by the counterculture that had then begun to emerge, these early blows rejected many of the middle-class conventions in which most of them had been raised. For instance, John (all names used are pseudonyms, unless stated otherwise) said that in the early 1970s he had been very keen to leave his native USA because he was strongly opposed to the Vietnam War and because his country was then 'boiling' with new ideas and youth discontent. The blows wanted to lead a different kind of life, though many were initially unclear what exactly they might be.

Many first travelled around Ireland, living in a caravan, staying in different places for periods of time. They came to Clare later, and often only by chance. Four examples:

(a) in 1969 Jane, a young English woman then in her late teens, went with her boyfriend to live in the Wicklow Mountains, south of Dublin. There were already 'alternatives' living in the area, but Jane and her man, who regarded themselves as hippies, saw themselves as different to these already established incomers, as most were married, artists, or otherwise dedicated to a bohemian lifestyle. Three years later she visited Clare, and found it almost empty of artist-types. The only then resident incomers were a few well-to-do English people who had bought some of the county's big houses, emptied by the Ascendancy fleeing the Civil War, and which locals had not wanted to occupy. She decided to stay.

(b) John, a recent US graduate in architecture, in 1971 came first to County Carlow, west of the Wicklow Mountains, invited by a charismatic German artist-friend, who had set up house with other compatriot artists. Their plan was to buy a house together which they would run as an art school. A local priest offered to sell them a shambolic farmhouse in northern Clare. But shortly after buying it, the Germans found the large Georgian house they had long dreamed of, and decamped. John and his new partner, a sister of one of the artists, decided to stay put, and began to renovate. He is still there.

(c) James came to Ireland in the late 1960s. He had already been 'vagabonding', as he put it, around Britain and Europe. Hitchhiking down from Belfast, he and his girlfriend were befriended by the men of a small village who let them camp in their fields for a month. A dedicated angler, he was then invited by a small landowner in the north of Ireland, to fish his lake. Come the summer, he travelled around the country, following Irish musicians who were playing in one traditional festival after another. While at a very small festival in Scariff, east Clare, James visited the nearby lake, which he thought 'enough to keep a fisherman happy for several lifetimes'. He says the idea of getting his own place was 'at the very back of my head'. But he was offered houses so cheaply so often, he returned to Britain to accumulate some money. On his return, now with a dog and a new girlfriend, he bought a small rowing boat. Over the next few months, they methodically toured its coast, pitching their tent by the shore and talking to the locals, until he found the run-down, lakeside house he was looking for. I interviewed him there.

(d) Kate dropped out of comfortable Twickenham at the height of hippiedom in the late 1960s, and moved into a nearby commune. She stressed to me how deeply idealistic she was at the time: 'I really, really did believe people would start loving each other and giving flowers to the cops.' When hippie ideals proved unworkable to her mind, she sought to debunk them and took up instead a romantic version of gypsydom: she joined a group of fellow-minded nomads who even imitated the Rom language. While apple picking in Kent, she participated in what she calls an 'arranged marriage', which fitted in with Gypsy lore. The group deliberately practised what they thought was a traditional lifestyle. The men hunted, fished, cared for the horses, and cut the wood; the women

> cooked, made bread and begged from farmers. Everyone scavenged. The group migrated to Ireland in its first year. After an initial, hard winter, they split into sub-groups, which would meet up at horse fairs, where they would form a circle of waggons. One or two married Irish travellers. For several subsequent years, Kate, her husband and their four children lived in a friend's field, or by the road in County Tipperary. They finally settled in north Clare because 'we loved the area. It's so beautiful, so close to the sea, and lots of music.' After a decade of living in a barrow caravan, they bought a house, near Gort, where they still live.

Most blows of this first-wave state they were very ignorant of Ireland, and were surprised how attractive it was when they arrived. One Dutch ex-urbanite said that before she had had dreams; when she arrived in Clare, 'the pictures in my former dreams were here, real.' Many describe their first encounter of the countryside and its people in almost Elysian terms. James states 'It was so different to anything I'd experienced in those days. There was an almost magical, timeless feel to the place, so totally entirely different to anything I'd seen before.' He remembered very clearly the small village he and his girlfriend walked into one evening on their hitchhike down from Belfast: 'There were raindrops glistening on the branches, water clearer than I had ever seen in the stream under the bridge. I felt I'd landed in paradise, like a rebirth, I'd come home.' They entered a tiny bar, where a succession of old men bought them all their drinks and competed over whose field they could stay in first. Other blows of this first wave, to whom I repeated James's account, immediately agreed and sympathised with his judgement. One, based in north Clare, remembered that on hot summer days, they would down tools and meet up at a nearby lake. He emphasised the scene was so idyllic it was almost Biblical: with babies left in the shade adults, as often nude as not, would cavort and swim in the cool water. For these early blows, rural Clare in the early 1970s really did have dimensions of paradise.

The attractions of the area cited by these incomers include the great kindness and persistent hospitality shown by so many locals, the cheapness of land and buildings, the slow way of life, and the romantic, if not patently mystical charms of the Burren. As one blow put it, Clare was so attractive because of 'the peace, the landscape'. Niall Williams, a long-established Dublin incomer on the south Clare coast who has since become an internationally successful author, put this aspect well:

> To gather myself, I turn and look down the garden and across the hedgeline at the valley. The morning is made of a quietness I had forgotten, so still and hushed it is impossible to imagine anything of significance is happening. Across the fields of Clare no time at all exists, nothing of change or moment, only a long singular season of soft weather and wet grass. (Williams 2004: 211)

Many English and German blows also saw Ireland as a very free land, compared to the restrictive societies they felt that they had been raised in. Some Germans were amazed and enchanted by the lack of bureaucracy: for example, that one could just build a new house or extend an old one without too much difficulty. They regarded the west of Ireland as almost a European outpost of the 'Third World'. One Dutch blow said she and her partner had left east Ireland because it was becoming 'more European', with better roads and more money about; they went to Clare because 'so few others were going there'. They wanted to leave behind what she called 'the West European industrialised ethos'; instead they wanted to live their version of an untouched rural idyll. Clare, precisely because it was so underdeveloped, offered them an excellent setting to put their primitivist dream into practice. To use the countercultural vocabulary of those times, these blows wanted to get 'closer to nature', to be 'in peace and harmony with it'. In other words, they wanted to live off the land, though most were profoundly ignorant of how to do that.

Most made their first priority the creation of a kitchen garden, preferably organic, maybe even biodynamic.[8] Many hunted, some with dogs, for hares, rabbits, pheasants, pigeons, wild goats, and the odd deer. Several of these early blows also fished for trout, pike, eel, and perch. James could catch seventy to eighty perch of an evening, which he would smoke in the chimney for two days, before rollmopping and then pickling them in vinegar. Some erected small windmills to generate electricity, which was used to provide lighting or grind corn for the bread they made. Many kept a few cattle, and some goats. Several English blows, living around the Gort area of north Clare, formed a goatkeepers' society, and for several years successfully sold goatmilk throughout the county as well as in Galway and Limerick. It is said that, in those days, the odd blow-in family supplemented their income by cultivating cannabis.

Most of these early blows strove to live as frugally as possible, and often succeeded. Several spontaneously stated to me how proud they had been to fulfil their goals of living in a relatively non-materialistic, if not flatly primitive manner. They stressed how much work they had had to put in, to create a viable smallholding, to reconstruct a house. Today they openly question, perhaps rhetorically, whether now, more wise, they would have embarked on the adventure had they known the labour it would involve. Though dramatically inexperienced in the beginning, these blows had taught themselves, often with local assistance, to be almost self-sufficient. They had not just had a dream; they had made it a reality. In this context it seems almost churlish to point out that most of them were only able to endure their first years in the area because the dole provided them with a very basic income.

It is important to remember that the people I talked with were the successful ones, those who had been able to stay and make a viable life in this new setting. The failures moved on, or were moved out. One blow gave me the case of Chris: a very creative, energetic man subject to bouts of depression, he heated his house with deep-freezers. Among his several projects, he wanted in particular to breed Great Danes and to start an electrical printing-press business. But his first Dane, while still immature, ate most of the press. Sometime after his wife left him, he was admitted to the county mental hospital. Another blow stated that couples who came here because of difficulties in their relationships usually found that moving to Clare was not the solution. Most broke up within a year; they either left or found new partners and stayed.

The great majority of the early blows were university graduates, upholding hippie ideals, who would admit, once I'd achieved a basic rapport, that they were assisted in buying or developing their properties by their parents.[9] Many of them saw the next wave of blows, who arrived in the 1980s, as very different: they were predominantly from England and may be classed 'Thatcher's renegade children'. They were strongly opposed to the social damage wrought by the introduction of privatisation and other Thatcherite reforms, which they felt excluded or marginalised them. A majority had lived in travellers' camps in the west of Britain, before making it over to Ireland. To many of the already resident blows, these new arrivals seemed more aggressive, harder types than their flower-power predecessors. One former hippy said that these travellers' attitudes were perceived as 'Fuck you. I'm all right'. They seemed more content to live off the dole than the land. As one early blow put it, 'They were more into take than anything else. Some stole from shops. They made the image of the blow-ins difficult for all the rest of us.' One north Clare encampment of them in particular gained a bad reputation among locals, because of the mess they made, the raves they held, and the fact several of its residents were fined for possession of cannabis. In at least one small town the bars would close weekly, on the day local blows came in to sign on and meet up with one another.

I must not paint too negative a picture here. One group of twenty to twenty-five of these 'second-wave' blows travelled in a convoy of aged vans and converted buses, enjoying month-long stays in one place after another. They wished to live as Native Americans; John remembered how pleasant was the sweat lodge they held nearby to celebrate the completion of the stonework on a blow's house.

In the mid to late 1980s, the Irish Government began to tighten up on the previously very lax system of the dole, thus forcing many blow-ins to rethink their domestic economy and maybe find alternative ways of raising an income. This turning of the financial screw stimulated many of this second wave to adapt to ways more acceptable to the locals. Some left. One might say that those who stayed became less 'crusty' and more workaday 'neo-hippy'. Perhaps the most economically successful blow-in of this period is Roderic. In the late 1970s he was a militant squatter on the south English coast and a leading housing activist there. Tired of his fellow teachers, who he thought 'grey, cynical', he moved to east Clare to help set up an alternative school, which is now the Raheen Wood Steiner National School. Several of his activist friends followed him over. In the early 1990s he started in an unplanned way to advertise locals' unwanted houses for sale, in alternative magazines, as a way 'to seed the area with interesting people'. This initial activity proved so beneficial to him, to local vendors, who would get a very good price, and to outside buyers, who were ignorant of the market, that he is now the very busy owner of a thriving auctioneers-cum-estate agency.

The third, most recent wave of blow-ins is different yet again. Perhaps the most distinctive attribute of this group is the mildness of their attitudes, compared to the rainbow visions of the original hippies and the embittered politics of the crusties. These immigrants lack the radical edge of their predecessors. They tend to combine a general wish to live in the country with a sharp-eyed appreciation of the varied benefits the new technologies offer. Thus many tele-cottage from home and commute a few days a week to part-time white-collar jobs in Limerick or Galway. As one put it to me, she and her partner wish to avoid both the stress of 'surviving on nothing' which the hippies had to bear, and the stress of maintaining a comfortable existence. 'How do you get the balance?' she asked me. As far as I can judge, these incomers tend to congregate in areas where blows have long been resident and have helped to establish a network of well-run local services, especially schooling. The exemplar of this is the area around Scariff, east Clare, which is acting as a magnet for these so-called suburbanites.[10]

Given their very different approach to and reasons for living in the west, many early blows do not hold these new arrivals in high regard. One was openly dismissive of them to me:

> The first people, the ones who survived, were pioneers. They were people who could live on nothing; they built their own homes, used their hands. The recent blow-ins are totally different. They build new houses which cost thousands. I resent them coming. For the first blow-ins, Ireland was like a frontier, like Westerners living with the Indians. The recent blow-ins expect it to be a little England. The original crowd were all alternatives: the Steiner crowd [centred around Scariff] are straighter than straight; they try alternative therapies but with modern attitudes.

The locals

When the first blows started to arrive, locals were still leaving the land. To them maintaining the family plot was a hard life which offered poor, and steadily diminishing returns. Even as late as the 1950s children might still walk to school barefoot, no matter the season. Those living in the more isolated areas would often not wish to admit they lived 'in the hills', as that was equated with poverty. So when other opportunities came up they, or more usually their qualified adult children, got out.

Thus locals were often mystified by the blows: why on earth were highly educated young foreigners coming to work the land when so many indigenes had given that up, or longed to do so? Some could not accept that these incomers genuinely wanted to take up such unrewarding, low-valued work, and therefore fantasised about their true motives. For instance, the brother-in-law of John's vendor always believed that John had bought it because he had discovered oil on the land. Some locals, perceiving the incomers' actions in local terms, could not fathom their aims. When one blow bought land in the Burren, locals said 'I was crazy buying a field of rocks. Why not buy a proper field, on which I grow something?' (Figure 8.1).

Figure 8.1 The Burren: karst limestone.

Be that as it may, many locals displayed great kindness to these newcomers in their midst. Many blows, when asked about their relations with their neighbours, will spontaneously and very happily list the unpaid labour that locals gave them to help rebuild their ramshackle houses, the tractors they were loaned, the furniture they were given, the repeated advice about farming that was freely offered, the parcels of food left out for them, the seemingly endless teas they were invited to, and so on. One said she and her partner need never have gone shopping in their first three years if they had accepted all the invitations made to them. Another cried when he recounted to me the thoughtfulness of his local postman: one day, several months after the arrival of he and his partner, the man knocked at their door with a big box of food. The blow suspects the postman knew the pair did not know many people. The following year, his French neighbour was still putting felt on his roof at the time his son was born. When, a few months later, the baby was kept in hospital because of whooping cough and poor home conditions, the postman offered to loan the blow a caravan and a radiator until he had fixed his house.

One blow claimed to me that the locals were on the whole so accepting of them because the new arrivals amused them: with their seemingly strange ways and unusual lifestyle, the incomers were good entertainment value for the locals. Several blows I interviewed took a slightly different tack: they argued that the indigenes were so accommodating because they themselves were poetical, non-logical types, traditionally tolerant of the odd within their own community. As one blow said, 'In the west of Ireland there is a madness, an eccentricity, I think, where reality and unreality, time and timelessness mix and merge freely.'[11] Another, long-resident blow-in remembered:

> When we came here first the locals accepted us in our eccentricity. I mean our immediate locals here are all completely mad in a lovely way. They'd talk to you for days non-stop about the fairies. Our neighbour said he heard lilting when he was digging a ditch and then saw the fairies coming along on horses. He threw down his hat in front of them, which meant they had to give him a horse. He got on the horse and went with them. They jumped the Shannon and then came to a huge field where the county teams of Offaly and Clare were hurling. He's no fool either. He lived in New York.

The German ethnologist Ullrich Kockel, who studied the blows in a north Clare village, has an alternative, perhaps supplementary interpretation of this apparent indigenous acceptance: 'The high degree of empathy with which the counterculture is received locally suggests that its primarily individualistic orientation is much closer the local mentality than romantic images of a "communal spirit of enterprise" that are often associated with the West' (Kockel 2002: 62). We can push this speculation further, for if locals' desire for individualism has always been tempered by the pressures of community, then incomers' behaviour might well act as a tempting demonstration of what could be. Following the lines of this argument, the actions of the incomers are seen not so much as idiosyncratic, but as exemplary.

A further possibility, which may be complementary with, not exclusionary to, the others mentioned above, is that the sustained kindnesses of locals to the incomers was invitational. Their offers of food, meals, and other gifts may be viewed as invitations to participate in a cooperative network, where assistance was not measured minutely but understood to be reciprocal over time. In this sense the local's generosity was but a manifestation of a key value underlying indigenous ways: the importance of helping one another. Of course these acts were also at the same time a claim to moral equality, grounded on a local ethics.

The denizens might have shown repeated kindnesses to the blows, but relatively few incomers went out of their way to get to know the immediate locals. Jane, something of an exception here, performed chores for her ageing neighbours: as they became more and more stiff, she would help in their gardens, put out their hay, or do their shopping. John thought the only way he would meet indigenes was to become a holder of livestock. So he bought some cattle and sought out the advice of neighbours on how to manage them. Those who got to know their neighbours best tended to be those who farmed seriously and so met with other farmers at cattle auctions and markets.

Many blows found it difficult to socialise with their neighbours because they did not go to bars or the church, and were not interested in hurling. It was easier to spend time with people with whom they had more in common: fellow blows. Some of these 'isolationists', as one blow termed them, stereotyped the locals in denigratory terms. One long-term blow-in claimed to me that, 'In the late 1960s the rural Irish were very narrow-minded, very parochial, very naive. They hadn't the tiniest idea of what was happening outside their own area. They couldn't understand why I was living in a tent. They thought it had to be poverty.'

More perceptive blows came to realise that they had entered small communities whose members were either all related to one another or had known one another since birth. Much of their conversation was about their kin, affines, and personalities peppering familial and local histories. Like native Amazonians who when meeting a stranger seek a common (if fictitious) genealogical link in order to establish a social relationship, locals would initiate conversations with a new person in their midst by engaging in a joint hunt for shared kin, in-laws or friends (Riviere 1969: 101–2). Williams, a US citizen, gives a good example of this. He married an Irish American and the two went to live in her late grandparents' house in south-west Clare. Not long after their arrival, the parish priest called round. 'Once he had inquired about our health, he moved the talk to that most important of subjects: "Who is it now are your wife's cousins?"' (Williams and Breen 1987: 124). Not surprising then that one female blow, a singleton, lamented to me, 'How could a local consider marrying me, if he didn't know my parents and the reputation of my family?'

While some blows do mention a number of very minor problems that they had with a few locals, who were ignorant of hippie ways, the only serious difficulties these incomers have had with the indigenes have almost all centred around land. In most of these cases, good-natured blows were made to play the unwitting role of middle-party in an enduring contest between two neighbours. Few of these difficulties endured more than a few months.[12]

Both incomers and denizens are very quick to point out that 'blow-in' is defined very locally. A man who moved from Dublin would be one. Some claim that even a person who came from only ten miles away might be classed as a 'blow'. There appear to be two key, underlying criteria. First, blows are not born and brought up in the rural area, however narrowly defined. In *The Spinning Heart*, a recent novel about rural Ireland, one character assesses her mother's parochialism:

> That girl whose child was taken from the crèche is a blow-in, Mam says. *Blow-in.* That phrase is used so derisively. As if to say it's a failing to not have been born and bred here, to have settled in a place outside of the place of your birth. Mam doesn't mean anything bad by it, though. It's hard to shake your prejudices, I know. (Ryan 2012: 127, orig. ital.)

Second, blows have not worked the Clare soil since childhood, nor had they taken on a genealogical tradition of working it. Williams puts this well, albeit imaginatively:

> More and more I was coming to understand, as I never had before, the full measure of difference between the city and the country person. There was a completely other sense of pride at work in the West. It was more than pride in the land, more than pride of the survivor, or the pride of freedom and independence. It was as if there was a natural and

> fiery pride in the knowledge of having been passed a special destiny of poor land and Atlantic rain. It could never be questioned, but held instead with a strong grip marked by silence, faith and perseverance. No matter what, we could never belong here the way these people did, for it struck me that they were as much a part of the landscape as any tree, rock or field. They were the West, and they knew it. And yet, from time to time – bumping along in the tractor, barrowing turf out of the bog, living day after day in the ever-falling softness of the rain – we could feel a flash of insight and empathy, knowing if only for a second something of the quality of that pride. (Williams and Breen 1987: 211)

A foreigner, no matter how long they stayed, would never be regarded as Irish. An Irish townsman, similarly, would never be seen as a local. They would be for life blow-ins, and even if their children integrated very successfully, they would always be known as 'the son/daughter of blow from X'. As another character in *The Spinning Heart* puts it, 'That lady is only a blow-in from town, a right-looking rap' (Ryan 2012: 153). Of course, an extremist form of localism is easy fodder for cosmopolitan satire. In a witty claim to rock bravado, one recent duo of incomer musicians undercut any purist criticism by brandishing their outsider status: they call themselves the Blow-ins. On their website they define the term as 'A stranger or foreigner, basically anybody whose ancestors have not lived within sight of the parish church for at least ten generations'.[13] It is all the more ironic then that, as some etymologists claim, blow-in is in fact an Australian term, originally applied to Irish immigrants.[14] Either way, to focus on the highly localised definition of 'blow-in' is perhaps to steer the discussion down an unproductive path. For, as Jane pointed out, long-term blows who had a service they could provide, whether as builder, architect, or fellow farmer, might not be seen as locals but they could still be relied upon, and that was an important criterion for the indigenes: they were participatory members of the local network.

Despite all this it is easy to argue that the key, ultimate difference to blows was not their birthplace, their upbringing, or their work patterns, but their ability to escape the scene. Once again, it is Jane who expressed this memorably: 'We were like plastic peasants.' In other words, working the land was for most locals their main, if not sole means of surviving. It was not a question of choice. They had nowhere else to go. Blows, however, had come from elsewhere and they could, if all else failed, always go back there. To this extent, it is not unfair to state that many blows, however idealist, however committed, were toying with the idea of living off the land. It was their belief in the value of rural life, not lack of other opportunity, which kept them tilling the soil. And this difference, though not usually mentioned, is one that never goes away.

Of individuals and innovators

Several of the early blows I spoke to spontaneously mentioned to me that they were loners, relatively solitary types who did not wish to be seen as members of a particular group, whether that be a goatkeepers' society or parent of a child attending a local 'alternative' school: it had too strong a collective identity for their liking. The Frenchman, mentioned earlier, to whom the postman made his kind-hearted offer, was so independently minded and so determined to do everything himself, that he refused the caravan and only accepted the radiator. James emphasised to me, 'I learn the conventional way of doing things, and then work out my own unconventional way of doing it. My way in life is: I lay down my own terms.' In the early 1970s several English blows, already resident, decided to set up a commune together in a large house by a lake. But it split up within a year.

Some might like to underline their individuality or solitary disposition, but many of the early blows still liked to hold communal Christmas dinners and, even more importantly for them, New Year and mid-summer parties, where incomer bands would play, and to which they were able to invite all the immigrants they knew. Though most long-established blows stress today that the number of incomers is now so great that they no longer know all their fellows, and that they lead far less social lives than before, they will admit that there remains a weak but perceptible sense of community among their number. Examples of this are the musical benefits held in recent years to raise money for the treatment of a blow diagnosed with cancer, or for the son of one who was knocked off his cycle. One long-resident blow described these benefits as akin to old family reunions, where he would meet people he had not seen in years: 'Somehow they hear about the event and they all come along.'

Whether as individualists or occasional participants in a broad but thin community, the blows had still to survive. From the 1980s on, it became harder and harder to live off the dole. Government inspectors might visit to see how big one's kitchen garden was, and then lop a proportional amount off one's allowance. This shrinking of many blows' core income forced them to examine their future, and whether or not it was time to start making money.

One early incomer said how fascinating it was to see what blows would turn their hand to in order to remain in the area. Almost all have set themselves up as skilled craftspeople, tradespeople, or managers of small businesses: for example, carpenters, gardeners, landscape gardeners, boatmakers, housebuilders or renovators, decorators, signwriters, cheesemakers. Some work for local fishermen. There are some lasting cooperative ventures, but most concerns are based on individuals or couples. A large number of these workers and their small companies are dedicated to the promotion of an 'alternative economy', broadly understood. Some practise as homeopaths or masseurs. Some have established small to medium-size working farms, run on biodynamic or organic principles, often selling their produce via veggie-box schemes. Several are assisted from time to time by 'woofers', volunteers sent by the Irish branch of Worldwide Opportunities on Organic Farms, who donate their labour in return for bed and board and a chance to learn organic farming principles and realities.[15] In 1996 blow-ins made Scariff the home of the Seed Savers Association, dedicated to promoting native apple varieties and assembling a national seed bank. Today it has twenty staff, running an educational facility, shop, and cafe.[16] One incomer couple bought the former workhouse in Gort and turned it into a school of homeopathy. One blow set up a company importing ergonomically designed tools. Another set up an 'alternative energy company' which successfully produced wind-driven water pumps for several years. Today, in the Ennis street market, one can find blows selling organic vegetables, potting compost, dried flowers, and home-cultivated herbs, for medicinal and culinary purposes.[17]

These industrious blows have had to be very adaptive in order to survive economically. If one venture or occupation did not work, they had to switch to another. Given their generally high standard of education, most were not resistant to the idea of undergoing formal retraining, even when middle-aged. Sue co-ran a health food store and, after doing a course in accountancy, became a distributor for health foods, acting as an intermediary between wholesalers and retailers. Her former business partner, whose formal schooling ended at sixteen, now runs two similar stores, one in Gort, the other in Ennis. Probably the best examples of just how adaptive blows can be are James, and Diana and Chris, former housing activists, friends of Roderic's:

> James: over the years, he has worked as a restorer of horse-drawn vehicles, as a professional gilly; he has repaired boats, promoted local angling tourism, and now manages his own forest. He today makes furniture, produces timber, and stages in his wood well-attended 'eco-festivals' dedicated to the propagation of eco-traditional woodland crafts, such as thatching, basketmaking, bowmaking, and green woodwork.
>
> Diana and Chris: in the twenty-five years since their arrival, they have made for sale patchwork clothes and furnishings, homespun jumpers, buttons from twigs and branches, tongue drums, wooden furniture, and sandwiches. They now have a regular stall at Ennis market where they sell home-cultivated flowering plants and salad vegetables.

One long-resident blow noted how some had by now become quite affluent while others, through the decisions they had made, remained poor. Jimmy, an Irishman, who formerly busked around Europe, became a jeweller and today owns a one-hundred acre farm. Sue does his accounts. James, though from time to time short of cash, is rich in assets as his lakeside forest could, in the hands of an ambitious developer, become a prime tourist site.

The other major factor that changed the blows' outlook was the education of their children. Several blows taught their children at home, until they were about eight or nine years old. However, as one said, 'I had had a choice. To be fair I had to do the same for my children.' Schooling, however, could become a major cause of tension between blows and locals. Many blows were shocked at how very hierarchical and traditionalist Irish state schools were. To their surprise they had very little say in the running of these schools which, to them, appeared strictly controlled by the headteacher in league with the parish priest. The great majority of the blow-in parents with whom I spoke stated that their children had had problems at the local schools they had attended. Many state that their children did not make friends with local boys and girls. As the teenage daughter of a Dutch couple complained, 'I have to be like them otherwise I'll have no friends. So I have to go to dances, listen to pop music, and talk about hurling.' One parent said his children would be asked in the playground, 'Are you a Catholic or a hippie?' He went on, 'You could tell a blow-in child at lunch because they had weird things like carrots and raisins. Anyone with brown bread in their lunch was a hippie.' Some blow-in children were bullied, many were stigmatised, local pupils deriding them as 'hippies', who mocked them as 'red-necks' in return. Even though these mutual rebukes might have been the work of a minority, they were sufficient to prevent easy play between many local and blow-in schoolchildren. One single mother said the headmaster of her son's school had aggravated matters, by refusing to accept there might be any conflict between children of either group. More than one couple removed their children from formal education completely because they were so unhappy with their local secondary schools.

Some dissatisfied blow-in parents took matters into their hands by establishing independent schools. In mid-Clare, an energetic Dublin blow, who had established a business making windows and doors and cutting flagstones, worked with local incomers to set up a 'Hedgerow' school, whose aim was to teach how to learn, rather than training pupils in rote learning. It ran successfully for five years but ultimately proved too time-consuming for many parents who acted as volunteer assistants. In Scariff, east Clare, concerned parents agreed to follow the suggestion of some very enthusiastic German blow-ins that they set up a Steiner school. Raheen Wood, as it is now known, takes children between the ages of four and thirteen and is today the largest Steiner school in Ireland, with over 125 pupils. After initial opposition, locals have started sending their children there: about one third of the intake is now native east Clare.[18]

As this example suggests, in some ways the blows have had a clearly innovative or revitalising effect on local life. Williams is clear about this, in a book that he wrote with his wife:

> It seems that if the West is to survive it will do so not because of some sudden change in the economic viability of farming, nor even because of the bestowal of local employment by foreign industries, but because of the 'blow-ins' ... Such people bring with them an appreciation of what the countryside has to offer without feeling the pessimism or sense of entrapment of some who have never left. New settlers bring new energy to the area ... The influence of these new people will eventually bring new ways of thinking about life here – about being enterprising and looking forward, about possibility and richness and a value for life that is available in these rural townlands. (Williams and Breen 1995: 154)

Besides providing educational alternatives, these incomers have also acted as potential harbingers of change in a variety of other ways, including: experimenting with drugs (usually nothing harder than cannabis); maintaining non-conventional relationships; new housebuilding styles; organic farming; and production of a much broader range of foods. John spoke of locals who had never seen peas or beetroots until he started growing them. As far as he was aware, locals rarely cultivated much more than potatoes. In architectural styles, the blow-ins have demonstrated that new houses need not be all-concrete edifices. Some homemaking incomers have reintroduced timber-framing and thatching; a few have produced almost fairy-tale like houses (Figure 1.1). John has designed a string of very striking modern houses. One blow, a self-taught carpenter, built a well-insulated timber home in the Burren. The initial reaction of some locals was sceptical: 'What are you doing that for? It'll blow away.' Several years later the house is still standing (Figure 1.2), and some locals have since had timber houses built for themselves (Figure 8.2) (see also Williams 1995: 154). By chance, none of the blow-ins I spoke with were musicians, but recent work by an anthropologist of tourism in north-west Clare suggests that incomer musicians have played a major role in the sustained revival of traditional Irish music in the county (Kaul 2004: 21).

It is illuminating that the one time a blow-in was included among the characters of an Irish radio soap opera, he played the role of agent of change. Most blows would not be so presumptuous as to compile a list of innovations and brandish it as their positive contribution to the local scene. But many of the longer-established ones are well aware of some of the effects they have had. Even though they readily acknowledge many of these changes would have come to the west of Ireland eventually, as they were beginning to happen over much of Western Europe, they do still hold up the likelihood that they were early, possible models for these changes.

The blows' innovations have been important. But what has been even more significant on the local scene is their ability to organise themselves and others, for blows have proved time and again that they are effective coordinators and activists. One local noted this difference: 'Most of the blows have that get-up and go. The local attitude to new ideas would be, "We always did it that way", or "We couldn't do that because we never did it before"'. Some of the blows' energy was directed towards revitalising local life. In the general area around Gort, for example, incomers have over the years embarked on a diversity of initiatives, such as creating or re-animating local drama groups; organising a film club (the majority of its regulars came from the local home for the mentally handicapped); setting up a community cafeteria, which for a while acted as a focus for a local LETS (local exchange trading system) scheme; and forming a Tree Society, an actively cooperative venture which involved large numbers of incomers and townspeople to plant out municipal plots.[19] In Scariff, setting up the school stimulated further activities, above all the East Clare Community Co-op, which operates community employment schemes. One of its founders states that these schemes include 'not just digging holes in the road or tidying graveyards, but painters, seedsavers, coppicers, weavers, basket-makers. Whatever energies people bring in, we help them'.[20] Other spin-offs of the Co-op are a travelling puppet theatre; The Graney, a whole-food store vaunted by local blows as one of the most dynamic and profitable in the country; and a tele-

Figure 8.2 This blow-in's house has been built around the original caravan (just visible through the leftmost window).

cottaging business, giving the otherwise unconnected access to the Net. Teachers and parents of pupils at the school also revived or revitalised seasonal celebrations: in particular, they boast of transforming the town's St Patrick's Day parade into a very popular, lively event.

Where the blows have indubitably made the greatest difference is in their environmental activism, both in halting controversial developments and in changing the awareness of locals to their surroundings.

Blows against pollution

An early campaign was one against the Irish tobacco company Carroll's, which wanted to establish fish farms in a very shallow north Clare lake. Several blows gathered scientific data about the probable deleterious effects of the proposal and protested. Planning permission was subsequently refused, though blows today admit they do not know how influential their protest was in the making of this decision.

The most significant, most memorable campaign, however, in which the blows played a noteworthy role, was that against the creation of a National Park and interpretative centre at Mullaghmore, in the heart of the Burren. First announced in 1991, the centre was supported by those who saw it as a needed opportunity for local development and the generation of jobs. Those against thought the consequent crowds of visitors would destroy the peace of the Burren and irreparably damage its fragile ecology. The debate about the centre swiftly moved from the local to the national level, and even became a key campaign issue in the country's elections. The historical course of this debate has already been detailed by others (e.g. Saunders 1996).[21] Its effective end only came in 2000 when An Bord Pleanála, the country's pre-eminent planning review board, definitively turned the development proposal down.

When asked to recall those days, activist blows are keen to emphasise the deep and (to them) surprisingly vigorous feelings which the controversy exposed. Jane said it took a brave blow-in to stand up in a town hall meeting and oppose the project. '"Who are you to tell us how things are to be done?" was a common attitude then,' she stated. Some locals did admit that during the conflict, 'there was a basic lack of courtesy'. One local priest, who praised the Burren in spiritual terms, even had to take a farmer to court for assault in a pub, because the man had abused him 'with obscene and filthy language' and labelled him 'a hippie priest': 'A gun should be taken to you, you bastard' (*Clare Champion*, 22 May 1992).

Blows also underline the stereotyping, by local supporters of the project, of those opposed to it. One remembered the placard placed above a tractor on the pathway of a demonstration:

> *Dublin 2*
> *Vegetarians*
> *Blow-ins*
> *Go Home*[22]

Blows also take pains to point out that membership of the two sides should not be stereotyped: not all farmers, they underline, were in support of the centre. As one local woman wrote to the county newspaper,

> Yet rather than meet these arguments, the supporters of the site have cast the opponents as hippies, outsiders and elitists. It won't wash. My ancient ancestors were land-grabbers and cattle rustlers in and around the Burren, as many a graveyard around the Burren will attest. (*Clare Champion*, 6 March 1992)

Some locals, when asked to discuss the conflict, stress that differences of opinion are usually dealt with in a quiet, informal manner. The common aim is to resolve tension without fuss, and to avoid open confrontation. One consequence of their ideology of egalitarianism is that, in the words of one, 'You don't put your head above the parapet.' The question, of course, is to what extent that applies to the blows. As one local put it, 'Newcomers can be movers and shakers because they are not afraid of stepping on anybody's toes. In the village people would be intermarried. Everyone would know everyone's seed, breed and generation.' In other words the blow-ins were able to stick their neck out, to publicly argue against the project precisely because they were not hobbled by a lifetime entanglement to the local community. Even though they might get on well with all their neighbours, their modulated alienation from the indigenous way of life gave them the freedom to spout unpopular views.

In some cases, the open nature of this continuing controversy led to a deep drawing of lines between neighbours, and even kinsfolk. According to one Dublin blow-in who played a major role in the protest campaign, 'The locals who opposed the project were ostracized for going against the consensus and that hurt them.' In 2003, when I did my fieldwork, several locals stressed that its effects linger. They all knew examples of former neighbours who are still not speaking to one another.

Evolution

The entry in 1973 of Ireland into the EU has had a great and continuing effect on life in the country. It was, for instance, a major cause behind the rise of the 'Celtic Tiger' in the 1990s, when the national economy boomed. This belated, relatively sudden development shifted many people's attitudes and expanded their expectations, as they sought to come to terms with, and for some to take advantage of, the new Ireland that was rapidly emerging.

The blows note manifold changes. Perhaps top of their list was the spectacular rise in the value of land and property from the late 1980s to 2008, when Ireland officially entered into recession. Next would come changing attitudes to the sale of property. In the 1970s, one could agree a price with a local vendor, go back to England to work, and then return a year later with the cash. During the Celtic Tiger years, one might agree a price, then find the local vendor had raised the price in the two weeks it took to raise the money, or had sold it to another buyer who had since appeared, making a higher offer. The housing boom also led to a changed sense of landscape: villages formerly near but beyond Ennis became part of its suburban sprawl. The continuing construction of more and more houses in even out-of-the-way villages plus the massive increase in the use of cars, which can travel fast down small country roads, meant that a sense of isolation and rural peace became ever more difficult to achieve in Clare. In the 1970s John would take his children to school in a horse and trap. As he lamented, 'That's unthinkable now. There are too many cars on the road and they go so fast!'

If the formerly stagnant economy enabled people to be so cooperative and so generous with their time, then those busy in a buoyant economy will no longer have the resources to show similar levels of kindness or concern for others. Many, both Irish and blows, argue that this is precisely what has happened. Synge was prescient on this point. In 1911 he wrote,

> One's first feeling as one comes back among these people and takes a place, so to speak, in this noisy procession of fishermen, farmers, and women, where nearly everyone is interesting and attractive, is a dread of any reform that would tend to lessen their individuality rather than any very real hope of improving their well-being. One feels, then, perhaps a little later, that it is part of the misfortune of Ireland that nearly all the characteristics which give colour and attractiveness to Irish life are bound up with a social condition that is near to penury. (Synge 2005: 145)

Blows will state that today it is almost only among the aged that one can find 'the old ways': a slow pace, a love of conversation for its own sake, an active willingness to help others, especially those in need. In this new world of harried employees and budding entrepreneurs with their eye always fixed on the long chance, the 'charm' of Ireland, which so attracted the early incomers, becomes ever harder to encounter. As one long-resident blow, now in her fifties, put it, 'A lot of the older people have some of the old magic about them. But people our age are all on the same European fast track.'

The blows no longer seem so distinctive because Clare has become so much more multicultural and because so many of their original ideas have been taken seriously, if in a diluted manner, by locals. Many cite the fact that in 2000 an Indian psychiatrist working in the Ennis mental hospital was elected to the Irish Parliament. In 2001 the winner of a regional beauty contest, Miss Lisdoonvarna, was a Brazilian. She is one of the hundreds of labour migrants who are given one-year work permits to labour in a north Clare meat-packing factory. In Ennis, African refugees now reside in the city while the majority of low-status jobs in local service industries, for example in fast-food outlets and restaurants, are occupied by East Europeans. This broadening of Clare society has met some resistance; both locals and blows will quietly claim that some of the West African and Brazilians are thieves.

Today there are many signs that locals are accepting ideas and approaches once almost exclusive to the blows. At a thriving yoga centre in the Burren, the majority of clients at their morning and evening classes are local housewives, with some farmers' wives, and even a few farmers themselves. Organic agriculture is no longer considered an eccentric practice indulged in by those who do not understand the land.

Some blows also underline the changes within themselves. One first-wave blow claimed that fifteen years ago they would help each other build their houses. Now they could not, as they all had jobs and mortgages to worry about. Another reason for a decline in any sense of community within the blows was that many had become much more integrated in their residential area. Also, most long-established blows are prepared to admit, however reluctantly or not, that though they strove to fulfil pre-modern ideals, they now cohabit a postmodern space where, for instance, local bands dedicated to Irish folk music may be completely composed of non-Irish player. (On these bands see Kaul 2004; 2009.) Further, many of the earlier blows are today acutely aware of the ironies they exemplify. Some of these back-to-nature types are now relatively very well-to-do because the land they bought for so little decades ago is today worth so much. It is as though they were unwitting opportunists, taking unknowing advantage of a brief window of opportunity in the 1970s and 1980s when advanced Western economies began to experience affluence and Ireland had yet to boom. The British former housing activist who has become a successful estate agent saved me the bother of commenting on the irony of his transformation, by raising the point himself.

In 2000 the rural geographer Keith Halfacree contended that the academic concept of 'counterurbanisation' was in danger of being applied in too restrictive a manner. Back-to-the-land migrants were being excluded because they were thought too marginal

(Halfacree 2001a; see also Halfacree 2001b). On the basis of my fieldwork, I argue that counterurbanisation in Clare, and very probably almost everywhere else in Ireland, cannot be understood without taking blow-ins and their ilk into account. Though their numbers were relatively low, they have had a pervasive effect on local life. Indeed they have now become an integral part of a broadened conception of local life. If we are to characterise contemporary Clare life, it would have to be as a sporadically dynamic, increasingly multicultural area, whose participative inhabitants include a culturally and economically significant number of blow-ins. They cannot be ignored.

The social anthropologists who worked in Clare, from the 1930s through to the 1970s, have been much criticised for their mischaracterisation of local life, especially their common lament that the area was dying (Wilson and Donnan 2006). The danger here is that contemporary ethnographers of the county who do not take the blow-ins and other incomers into account will be similarly lambasted in due course. For today, any fieldworker of Clare who fails to recognise the current diversity of its population would only be engaging in a modern version of the distorting generalisations their predecessors were justly accused of.

It can also be argued that the blow-ins are an illuminating counter-example to top-down approaches for agricultural development; for the sustained, disparate activities of independently minded individuals have led, over time, to a collective change. With hindsight, the blow-in smallholders may be viewed as integral, key motivating members of the avant-garde for environmental and organic concerns, which have today entered the mainstream. Further, they may be regarded as the model for rural resettlement Ireland, a very successful national organisation, based in Clare, which assists urban families, particularly disadvantaged ones, to establish themselves in the countryside. Indeed the EU has used it as a template for repopulating emptied landscapes elsewhere in the subcontinent.[23] In both cases the well-grounded example of the blow-ins' industriousness over the last four decades demonstrates the surprisingly wide-ranging and cumulative power of microeconomic initiatives over macroeconomic grand strategies. And, as such, they are deeply appropriate candidates for anthropological study.

The blows, in sum, are another example of the unexpected ways rural populations, attitudes, and behaviours can evolve. Because in the early 1960s, no Irish planner would have anticipated that a foreign, utopic movement spread by affluent youth from the cities would end up having a broad, reflexive effect first in one of the country's poorest counties, and then beyond. Yoga anyone?

Acknowledgements

My sincere thanks to all those who spoke to my cousin and me and to those who commented on earlier drafts: Adrian Peace, David Pepper, and my aunts, Madelaine Carter, Joan Potter, the late Ann Fruithof. I am particularly grateful to my blow-in host while I was conducting fieldwork.

Notes

1 The quotes come, respectively, from www.shannonregiontourism.ie/clare/; www.county-clare.com/; www.westclare.com/; www.infowing.ie/files/clare.htm; www.doolin-tourism.com. All accessed 7 February 2005.

2 The quotes come, respectively, from Stevens 1912 (1690); Kohl 1844; Hall 1850: 60; all cited in O'Dalaigh 1998.

3 For a fine-grained, critical analysis of the particular versions of Irish primitivism upheld by Yeats, Synge, and Gregory respectively, see Mattar 2004.

4 He revealed to me it was Quilty (Brody pers. comm. 8 June 2012).

5 Brody 1973. For critical reassessments of Arensberg and Kimball and Brody, see Gibbon 1973, Wilson 1984, Saris 2000: 20–1. There have been so many studies of Clare and nearby that the famed Irish writer Flann O'Brien declared, 'The typical West of Ireland family consists of father, mother, twelve children, and resident Dutch anthropologist' (quoted in MacHale 2002: 88). For more modern work on suicide among rural Irish males, see Laoire 2001.

6 *Michael Joe* (Cotter 1965), a local author's profoundly unromantic novel about west Clare in the 1940s, is particularly illuminating on the town/country social divide (see its pp. 148, 161–2, 180–1).

7 I am grateful to the School of Social Sciences, Oxford Brookes University, for a research grant which enabled this fieldwork, to my cousin for his invaluable research assistance, and above all to all those who gave up their time to talk with me. My host was especially hospitable, for which I thank him greatly.

8 On the attitudes of biodynamic farmers in Ireland, most of whom are blow-ins, see McMahon 2005.

9 Williams is clear about the paternal support they received, e.g. 1995: 38–9.

10 Adrian Peace, who in 2000 did a brief bout of intensive fieldwork in the middle of my own fieldwork area, states: 'My experience from living in X was that members of this third wave were much more strategic and calculating, because they had frequently visited Clare, as tourists especially, (less so) on business, and including men on fishing trips, for several years before making "the final leap". They had a much better sense of the finances they would require, the occupational changes they would have to make, and all-round adjustments in family life and career courses. I can think of several around X who bought land, built on it, and finally made the move over two or three years of gradual and strategic build-up' (A. Peace, pers. comm.) My own fieldwork material bears out these points.

He also states, 'In my experience, the final wave of blow-ins were often enough married couples comprising a local spouse who had been away for several years and a blow-in spouse, so the domestic unit bridged the divide which is key to your interpretation. Their encounter was often complex and difficult, even though they had made the calculations and strategies I referred to earlier. These difficulties could result in considerable despair for the blow-in spouse, in some cases leading to marital breakdown. My own landlady on the outskirts of X was a case in point: she assured me several times that it was only because her two (now teenage) daughters had grown up in Clare and had their formative networks there, that she didn't return to England after her husband left her. Her social network by 2000 was pretty well exclusively other blow-ins, and the high points of her year were when her sister and her children came across the water for their holidays' (A.

Peace, pers. comm.) I do not dispute Peace's findings. But I found that third-wave incomers were as likely to be pairs of blow-ins as a blow-in married to a returning local.

11 Words of Arthur Watson (real name), quoted in Kravis and Morgan 1999: 94.

12 On this point, Peace has written to me, 'Some blow-ins, at least in the final phase, ran into enormous problems with locals, especially when they became involved in joint enterprises like building and home improvement firms' (A. Peace, pers. comm.)

13 See www.theblow-ins.com. Accessed 17 June 2014.

14 See e.g. www.moonunderwater.org/2014/01/16/blow-in/. Accessed 23 June 2014.

15 See www.wwoof.ie. Accessed 17 June 2014.

16 See www.irishseedsavers.ie/about-biodiversity-conservation.php. Accessed 17 June 2014.

17 In County Sligo, north-west Ireland, an informal grouping of blow-in smallholders produced a monthly magazine dedicated to alternative-minded agricultural topics, first called *North-west Newsletter,* later *Common Ground,* between the mid-1970s and mid-1990s. At first aimed at a regional readership, it soon went nationwide (Byrne 2007: 2).

18 In one of her novels Edna O'Brien, who is herself from Scariff, presents locals as perceiving the schools in a dismissive, alien manner (O'Brien 2002: 71–2).

19 The incomers raised funds by putting on a musical evening, one local donated two lorry-loads of topsoil, another the trees, and a large number of both turned up to plant them.

The blows can also be regarded as local saviours in certain cases. One pointed out to me that when she and her family arrived in the Gort area, the local school was about to shut. The immediate entry of four of her children prevented its closure.

The Irish social scientist Ethel Crowley studied a LETS scheme in south-western Ireland (Crowley 2004). She found it played a major role in integrating incomers and that its members could be seen as a 'neo-tribe'.

20 Words of A. Watson, quoted in Kravis and Morgan 1999: 93.

21 Peace argues that the debate was so protracted and heated because at root lay opposed conceptions of the landscape, which otherwise come to the surface very rarely (Peace 2005).

22 Dublin 2 is a well-known affluent district within the city.

23 See www.ruralresettlement.com/about.html. Accessed 16 June 2014.

References

Arensberg, Conrad 1968 *The Irish Countryman. An Anthropological Study* (New York: Natural History Press. Orig. pub. 1937).

Arensberg, Conrad and Solon Kimball 1940 *Family and Community in Ireland* (Boston: Harvard University Press).

Brody, Hugh 1973 *Inishkillane. Change and Decline in the West of Ireland* (London: Allen Lane The Penguin Press).

Byrne, Anne, Ricca Edmondson, and Tony Varley 2001 'Introduction to the third edition', in C. Arensberg and S. Kimball (eds) *Family and Community in Ireland* (Ennis: Clasp Press), I-CI.

Byrne, Garreth 2007 'Blow-in settlers made an impact in Ireland', *Innate. Irish network for non-violent action training and education.* Published at www.innatenonviolence.org/. Accessed 10 June 2014.

Cotter Murray, William 1965 *Michael Joe. A Novel of Irish life* (Dingle: Brandon).
Cresswell, Robert 1969 *Une communauté rurale de l'Irlande* (Paris: Institut d'Ethnologie).
Crowley, Ethel 2004 *Local Exchange Trading Systems: Globalising Rural Communities* (Discussion Paper No. 37, Institute for international integration studies, Trinity College Dublin).
Foster, Roy 1997 *W. B. Yeats: A Life. I The Apprentice Mage* (Oxford: Oxford University Press).
Gibbon, Peter 1973 'Arensberg and Kimball revisited', *Economy and Society*, 2, 481–90.
Haddon, Alfred C. and Charles R. Brown 1893 'Ethnography of the Aran Islands, County Galway', *Proceedings of the Royal Irish Academy*, 18,768–830.
Halfacree, Keith 2001a 'Going "back-to-the-land" again: extending the scope of counterurbanisation', *Espace, Populations, Sociétés*, 1, 161–70.
——2001b 'Constructing the object: taxonomic practices, "counterurbanisation" and positioning marginal rural settlement', *International Journal of Population Geography*, 7, 395–411.
Hall, Spencer T. 1850 *Life and Death in Ireland in 1849* (Manchester: J. T. Parkes).
Kaul, Adam 2004 'The anthropologist as barman and tour-guide: reflections on fieldwork in a touristed destination', *Durham Anthropology Journal*, 12, 21–36.
——2009 *Turning the Tune. Traditional Music, Tourism, and Social Change in an Irish Village* (Oxford: Berghahn).
Kockel, Ullrich 2002 *Regional Culture and Economic Development: Explorations in European Ethnology* (Aldershot: Ashgate).
Kohl, Johann 1844 *Travels in Ireland* (Trans. from German) (London: Chapman and Hall).
Kravis, Judy and Peter Morgan 1999 *Lives Less Ordinary. Thirty-two Irish Portraits* (Dublin: Lilliput Press).
Laoire, Caitríona Ni 2001 'A matter of life and death? Men, masculinities and staying "behind" in rural Ireland', *Sociologia Ruralis*, 41, 220–36.
MacHale, Des 2002 *Irish Wit* (London: Prion).
Mattar, Sinéad Garrigan 2004 *Primitivism, Science and the Irish Revival* (Oxford: Oxford University Press).
McMahon, Naoimh 2005 'Biodynamic farmers in Ireland. Transforming society through purity, solitude and bearing witness?', *Sociologia Ruralis*, 45, 98–114.
O'Brien, Edna 2002 *In the Forest* (London: Weidenfeld and Nicolson).
O'Dalaigh, Brian (ed.) 1998 *The Strangers Gaze. Travels in County Clare 1534–1950* (Ennis: Clasp Press).
Peace, Adrian 2005 'A sense of place, a place of senses. Land and a landscape in the west of Ireland', *Journal of Anthropological Research*, 61, 495–512.
Riviere, Peter 1969 *Marriage among the Trio: A Principle of Social Organization* (Oxford: Clarendon Press).
Robinson, Tim 1992 'Place/person/book: Synge's *The Aran Islands*' in J. M. Synge (ed.) *The Aran Islands* (Harmondsworth: Penguin), vii–liii.
Ryan, Donal 2012 *The Spinning Heart* (London: Doubleday Ireland).
Saris, A. Jamie 2000 'Culture and history in the halfway house', *Journal of Historical Sociology*, 13, 10–36.
Saunders, Joe 1996 *Land, Landscape or Countryside? Irish Environmentalism and Competing Perspectives on the Burren* (Unpublished MA thesis, Dublin City University).

Stevens, John 1912 *A Journal of my Travels since the Revolution Containing a Brief Account of all the War in Ireland* (ed.) Rev. R. H. Murray (Oxford: Oxford University Press. Orig. pub. 1690).

Synge, John Millington 1907 *The Aran Islands* (Dublin: Maunsel).

——2005 *Travels in Wicklow, West Kerry and Connemara* (London: Serif. Orig. pub. 1911).

Williams, Niall 2004 *Only Say the Word* (London: Picador, 2004).

Williams, Niall and Christine Breen 1987 *O Come ye Back to Ireland. Our First Year in County Clare* (New York: Soho).

—— 1995 *The Luck of the Irish* (New York: Soho).

Wilson, Thomas W. 1984 'From Clare to the Common Market: perspectives in Irish ethnography', *Anthropological Quarterly*, 57, 1–15.

Wilson, Thomas W. and Hastings Donnan 2006 *The Anthropology of Ireland* (Oxford: Berg).

Index

Note: Italicised page numbers refer to figures